CAPITALS OF ART

CAPITALS OF ART

Rome

edited by
Stefano Zuffi

Electa

On the cover:
Colosseum, late first century AD

Translation
Richard Sadleir
David Stanton

Graphics coordinator
Dario Tagliabue

Layout
Elena Brandolini

Coordinating editor
Simona Oreglia

Editor
Gabriella Cursoli

Technical coordinators
Paolo Verri
Mario Farè

www.electaweb.it

A lifetime isn't enough. This maxim bears witness to a felicitous sense of powerlessness before the immensity of Rome. This does not mean geographical size: after all, Rome is smaller than other capitals, many of which have grown up in the last few centuries. Large areas of the historic centre can easily be reached on foot, and if visitors organize their time and itineraries carefully, they can get an adequate idea of the city's topography and proportions in just a few days, at least within the imperial walls. Rather than space, however, Rome's real dimension is time. The Eternal City suddenly opens up from the busy access avenues: a violent emotion, a firm embrace, a sentiment of history and power overwhelms the visitor. It's a sense of vertigo, an experience that changes one's life: from the car window, between one set of traffic lights and the next, one sees, emerging from the greenery of the parks, the mellow bricks of the Baths of Caracalla, then the immense Christian basilicas, then the matchless ring of the Colosseum, the expanse of the Forum, the arcaded curve of the Theatre of Marcellus, the superb ramp leading up to the Campidoglio, then, in the distance, the dome of St Peter's appears, and then, and then ... Along the banks of the Tiber, the millennia are superimposed on one another, but they meet harmoniously, with a tangible sense of historical continuity. In other places of ancient origin, the archaeological sites are isolated, circumscribed by gardens and physically separated from the life of the city: instead in Rome one is immersed in an endless continuum in which styles, eras, monuments and masterpieces coexist side by side, and this is also true of the world apart that is the Vatican.

This inexhaustible, perennially vital Rome has now managed to free itself almost completely from rhetoric, laboured interpretations, celebrations and oratorical, ministerial and urbanistic grandiloquence. It certainly doesn't need them. Indeed, right in the heart of Rome, in the shadow of the ancient monuments that send shivers of excitement down one's spine, there's still a palpable spirit of cynicism and self-mockery that isn't overly impressed by domes and obelisks, columns and fountains. That's why Rome immediately becomes familiar, enjoyable and accessible: despite the magnificence and importance of its monuments, it doesn't dominate its visitors, but invites them to participate, to immerse themselves in the dynamic flow of its uninterrupted history.

If the whole of one's life isn't enough for getting to know Rome properly, a book certainly can't claim to reveal all its marvels. It can only show its readers aspects, views, the ambience of the city: remarkable monuments, memorable sculptures, milestones of art, and also its secret corners to remind us of the enchanted loci of our encounter with the history that belongs to us. Thus we will realize that Rome may be the magic mirror of our soul, the very source of our existence.

Contents

Colosseum, late first century AD

he-Wolf to the Empire

Ancient Rome: a Thousand Years of History

Capitoline She-Wolf
early fifth century BC
Palazzo dei Conservatori

It is impossible to imagine the birth and growth of Rome without the Tiber, which has always been the generating force behind the city's urbanism. In fact, the presence of a ford near the Tiber Island meant that the salt road from the Tyrrhenian to the Adriatic intersected the road linking Etruria to Campania here. In the Bronze Age (fourteenth century BC) the first settlements were built near this ford; they were followed by a village of huts on the Palatine Hill (ninth–eighth centuries), which preceded the traditional date of the city's foundation: 21 April 753 BC. The control of this road junction proved to be of fundamental importance for the Etruscan cities and some of the "seven kings" were certainly Etruscan.

During the sixth century BC Rome was surrounded by walls and provided with an open public space, the Forum, which functioned as a centre for trade following the draining of the marshy area between the hills. This was where the centre of political power, the Regia (royal palace) and the most important sanctuaries were located. In 509 BC Tarquinius Superbus, the last of the Etruscan kings, was deposed and replaced by a republican government. The internal disorder and continuous wars led to a lull in building that only came to an end with the reconstruction after the fire caused by the Gauls (390 BC), when a larger circuit of walls was built (the so-called Servian walls) and almost all the buildings around the Forum were renovated.

With the expansion of the territory controlled by Rome, the city's appearance

Roman Forum, view of the rostra
(speaker's platform)

began to acquire its definitive character: the victory over Carthage (202 BC) turned it into the capital of the Mediterranean. This was followed by a period of urbanistic growth of unprecedented magnificence, with the construction of huge warehouses, new port facilities, vast markets, rows of arcades, splendid basilicas and buildings for entertainments. The sewer system, road network and water supply were expanded with the realization of imposing projects. Imported marble made its appearance, luxury homes and suburban villas sprang up, while the housing requirements of the rapidly growing population were met with the construction of six-storey buildings to be rented to the plebeians. The celebration of what was increasingly personal power led to the invention of the triumphal arch and the development of the individual portrait; born in the Hellenistic world, this reached its apogee by representing the appearance of a ruling class characterized by strict adherence to its ethical codes, which were flaunted with overweening pride.

After the Social War (90–88 BC), with the dictatorship of Sulla, urban development became an affair of state and monumental building finally assumed the ritual character that transformed temples, squares and colonnades into stage sets for the display of power. Initiated by Julius Caesar, the process that transformed the old city of the aristocracy into an immense metropolis that was able to perform its role of *caput mundi* became inexorable thanks to the political intuition of Augustus (30 BC–AD 14). The old Forum was rebuilt and another more imposing one was added to the one started by Caesar. Ever heedful of the symbolic importance of his actions, Augustus took up residence on the Palatine in a modest house that, however, stood between the Temple of Apollo and Romulus's hut. This was the last step needed to give substance to the mythical background of the new state.

The fire that in AD 64, under Nero, destroyed a large part of the city provided an opportunity for radical renovation, although a large part of the resources were absorbed by the Domus Aurea (Golden House). It was the Flavians who implemented a policy of returning the site of the Domus Aurea to the people of Rome with imposing public works such as the Colosseum. Under Trajan (98–117) the empire reached its maximum extent and Rome became the largest city in the world, with between 600,000 and 700,000 inhabitants. It was this emperor who built the last and most magnificent of the imperial fora and the adjacent markets. In the second and third centuries the city was expanded and embellished. The situation came to a head in the middle of the third century when the empire was overwhelmed by a series of power struggles, worsened by the economic crisis and the growing pressure of the barbarians. The hasty construction of the Aurelianic walls (271–275) terminated both symbolically and physically the period of Rome's expansion. Despite the resumption of building under Diocletian (285–305) and the very ambitious programme started by Maxentius (306–312) and completed by Constantine (306–337), the power of ancient Rome was on the wane.

Colosseum and Temple of Roma
and Venus
early first century

Viridarium, detail
30–20 BC
fresco from the Villa of Livia
at Prima Porta
Palazzo Massimo,
Museo Nazionale Romano

The Roman Forum

From the tenth to the ninth centuries BC the valley where the Forum was later built was an insalubrious marshy area serving as a cemetery for the inhabitants of the villages on the Capitoline and Palatine hills. Towards the end of the eighth century BC it ceased to be used for burials and the area was covered with beaten earth, indicating that it was now part of a single centre definable as urban. This archaeological evidence is consistent with the tradition that regards 616 BC as the beginning of the dynasty of the Tarquins, to whom are attributed important public works, including the canalizing of the Cloaca Maxima for the drainage of the valley. In this period the area was probably divided into two parts: the Comitium was intended for political activity, the Forum for commerce. After the damage caused by the sack of the city by the Gauls, new buildings and sanctuaries were constructed. With the victory over Carthage and the transformation of Rome into the capital of the Mediterranean, the Forum was also adapted to meet the new requirements for public magnificence with the construction of basilicas and the restoration of the main temples, accentuating its administrative character. Later Augustus completed the work—started by Sulla and continued by Caesar—of urbanistic systemization, using tradition as a means of winning and maintaining support. The result of the construction of Caesar's and Augustus's imperial fora was that the republican Forum became little more than a monumental backdrop intended to exalt the dynasty's splendour and prestige.
The Forum kept this function unchanged, albeit with a certain amount of transformation, right through the imperial age until AD 608, the year in which the column in honour of the emperor Phocas was erected; this was the last Roman monument. From then onwards the area was progressively filled in with earth and the monuments, except for the Christianized ones, disappeared. It is particularly significant that, in the Middle Ages, the Forum was known as the Campo Vaccino (Cattle Field). After this, until the eighteenth century, the major monuments were used as fortresses or limekilns, or were plundered for stone. It was only the vogue for exploration in the eighteenth century and the beginning of systematic excavation in the nineteenth century and still under way that once again changed the use of the area.

TABULARIUM

78 BC
Roman Forum

This imposing arched building, intended to house the state archive, was built by Sulla, who made it the monumental termination of the Forum on the side nearest to the Capitoline Hill. It was transformed into a fortress in the Middle Ages and the Palazzo Senatorio (now the seat of Rome's City Council) was built above it. On the left is the Temple of Vespasian.

ROMAN FORUM

general view

The Forum is a remarkable accumulation of almost three thousand years of history, although the remains dating from before the imperial age are difficult to identify. On the other side of the Arch of Septimius Severus is the vast area occupied by the Basilica Aemilia, which has almost entirely disappeared; beyond it is the Temple of Divus Antoninus Pius and Diva Faustina. Behind this are the arches of the Basilica of Maxentius (Basilica Nova). In the distance, the Colosseum is clearly visible. On the right, in the foreground, the colonnade of the Temple of Saturn dominates the perimeter of the Basilica Julia, which, facing the Basilica Aemilia, formed the other long side of the square. The column of Phocas soars upwards in the midst of the imperial pavement. Opposite the Temple of Antoninus and Faustina stand the three surviving columns of the Temple of Castor, flanked on the left by the round Temple of Vesta. Further along the Via Sacra (Sacred Way) of the ancients, is the Church of Santa Francesca Romana, and, to the right of this, the Arch of Titus.

CURIA JULIA (SENATE HOUSE)

interior
first century BC*–third century* AD
Roman Forum

The Curia Julia, seat of the Senate, was started by Caesar, completed by Augustus and rebuilt by Diocletian; the brick building still standing today dates from the latter's reign. It was converted into a church dedicated to St Hadrian in the seventh century (which is why it escaped the destruction that befell all the pagan buildings) and restored to its original appearance in 1930–1936. The imposing interior covered by a modern wooden roof is 21 metres high, 18 metres wide and 27 metres long. The marble floor is partly original. The seats of around 300 senators were arranged on three wide steps. In the central niche was located a statue of Victory that was the subject of a famous dispute between the pagan Symmachus and Ambrose, the future bishop of Milan, who had it removed. Although not itself of great significance, the episode assumes great symbolic importance seen in retrospect.

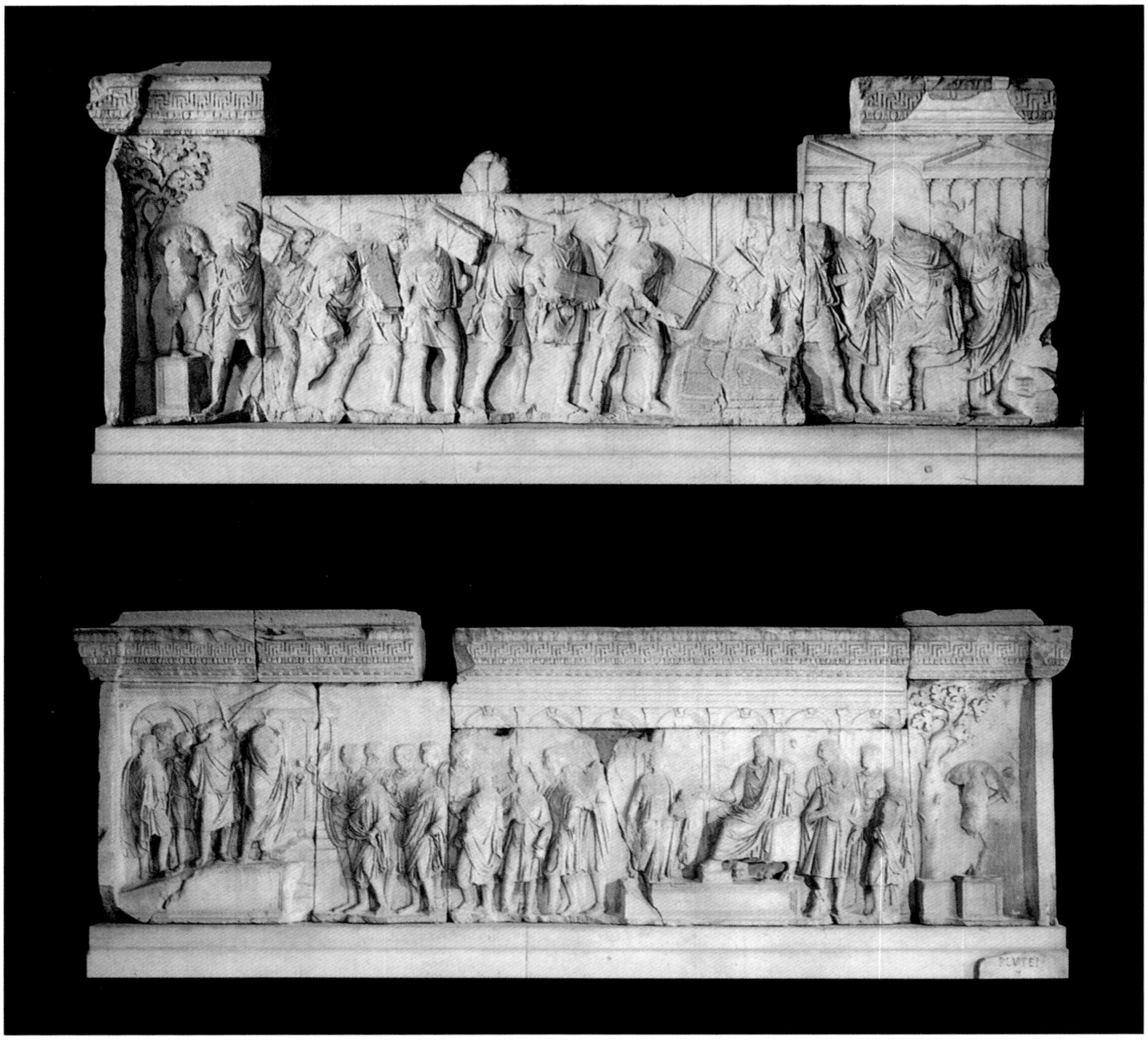

TRAJAN'S PLUTEI

above: The destruction of the registers of debts
below: The institution of the alimenta
early second century
marble
Roman Forum, Curia Julia

The Curia now houses an imposing porphyry statue portraying Trajan and the so-called Trajan's Plutei, perhaps part of the boundary wall of the Forum. With the very effective technique of the continuous relief they show two animated scenes: the amnesty of tax debts, with the burning of the registers, and the institution of the *alimenta*, a system of loans to landowners at low rates of interest, which was then distributed to poor children. The buildings visible in the background are those in the Forum dating from the early second century, from the rostra to the Temple of Divus Julius.

IMPERIAL ROSTRA

first century AD
Roman Forum

The structure in the foreground dates from the reorganization of this very ancient area carried out by Augustus, after Caesar had completely demolished the old Comitium and reconstructed all the monuments surrounding it. The hemicycle with a bank of steps in the background dates from Caesar's period, while the straight front is part of Augustus's extensions. The bronze prows of Carthaginian ships must have been attached to the front. The surface of the speaker's platform was in wood.

TEMPLE OF SATURN

fifth century BC–fourth century AD
Roman Forum

The eight granite columns, with smooth shafts and Ionic capitals supporting the architrave of the hexastyle front of the Temple of Saturn, soar majestically at the foot of the Capitoline Hill. Originally dating from the monarchic period, the sumptuous building was rebuilt several times, the last being after the disastrous fire of AD 283, but the columns have always remained upright. In front of the temple, another building housed the public treasury.

BASILICA AEMILIA

179 BC–first century AD
Roman Forum

The huge Basilica Aemilia is the only one of the four republican basilicas to have survived. Founded in 179 BC by the censors Marcus Aemilius Lepidus and Marcus Fulvius Nobilior, it was restored on various occasions and then reconstructed by Augustus and Tiberius. It seems that the building type of the basilica originated in the Hellenistic world (where it was known as the *stoa basileios*, royal portico) as a covered hall; this was divided into a nave and aisles by the columns supporting the roof and excellently illuminated by the large clerestory windows in the upper walls of the nave. In the cooler periods of the year it served as a law court, as well as for financial and political activities.

right and opposite
ARCH OF SEPTIMIUS SEVERUS

detail and view from north-east
AD 203
Roman Forum

The arch, with three intercommunicating passageways and originally surmounted by a bronze quadriga, was built in AD 203. It is 21 metres in height, 23 metres wide and 11 metres deep. The exterior, with strong chiaroscuro effects caused by the freestanding columns, is entirely faced with marble, while the core is made of travertine and brick. On the two faces of the attic there is a massive inscription with a dedication to Septimius Severus and his sons Caracalla and Geta (the part relating to the latter was erased when his brother had him assassinated and subjected to *damnatio memoriae*) celebrating the victories over the Parthians and the Adiabeni. The splendid decoration comprises victories and various divinities, a small frieze with the emperor's triumphal procession, Roman soldiers with Parthian prisoners and, most outstandingly, the four large panels representing the Parthian campaigns. The style of the reliefs is of a narrative character; schematic and effective, it evidently derives from the column of Marcus Aurelius. The arrangement in registers probably had its origins in the paintings executed to illustrate the military campaigns and displayed in the triumphs of the victorious generals. In the detail on the right, the solemn nobility of the barbarian prisoners is rendered by the vibratingly colouristic treatment, typical of the sculpture of this period.

The Basilica Julia

South of the Via Sacra is what remains of the Basilica Julia, the largest and most sumptuous building in the Forum (101 × 49 metres). Started by Julius Caesar around 54 BC and completed by Augustus, it was immediately destroyed by fire and dedicated again in 12 BC to Gaius and Lucius Caesar, the *princeps*' adopted heirs. Radically restored by Diocletian after a fire in AD 283, it probably still preserved its original appearance with the façade embellished with arches. The huge central hall (82 × 18 metres) was surrounded on all sides by a double row of piers in brick and travertine (partially reconstructed) that divided the space into five aisles. The building housed various civil courts that, according to contemporary accounts, could function simultaneously because they were separated with movable curtains lowered from above. The central nave was wider and taller than the side aisles and had large clerestory windows providing perfect lighting for the hall. The main entrance was in the centre of the south façade, at the point where a pier adorned with a Doric demi-column has been reconstructed.

VIA SACRA AND THE SOUTH-WESTERN CORNER OF THE BASILICA JULIA

first century BC*–first century* AD
Roman Forum

Flanking the entrance to the basilica stood two classical statues by Polyclitus and Timarchos documented by the inscriptions on the surviving plinths.
On the steps and floors are visible game-boards and drawings of statues engraved by the idlers of the day. The Basilica Julia was preceded on the same site by the Basilica Sempronia, built by Tiberius Sempronius Gracchus, father of the famous tribunes, in 169 BC, itself built on the site of a republican house, revealed by the excavations, which probably belonged to Scipio Africanus.

BASILICA JULIA FROM THE VIA SACRA

first century BC*–first century* AD
Roman Forum

right
COLUMN OF PHOCAS

AD *608*
Roman Forum

The column of Phocas is a commemorative monument that, according to the inscription on the plinth, was once surmounted by a gold statue of the emperor. It was dedicated in AD 608 by the exarch of Italy, Smaragdus, to the eastern emperor Phocas, who acceded to the throne in 602 after assassinating his predecessor Maurice and his five sons. The tall Corinthian column is in reality a recycled piece, dating from the second century AD; but it is of historical importance because it is the last monument to have been erected in the Forum before it began its inexorable decline.
On the right is the splendid façade of the Church of Santi Luca e Martina, a masterpiece by Pietro da Cortona that is a milestone in the history of Baroque architecture (1635–1664).

Temple of Castor

On the other side of the Vicus Tuscus—which means Street of the Etruscans and is an evident sign of the presence of a quarter inhabited by this people—stands the huge podium of the Temple of Castor, on which the three splendid surviving columns soar skyward. Dedicated in 484 BC to thank the Dioscuri, the divine twins Castor and Pollux, for their intervention in the battle of Lake Regillus against Tarquinius Superbus (499 BC), it was restored on various occasions: in 117 BC (the period when the podium was built); in 74 BC by Verres, who managed to pocket a huge sum of money by contracting out unnecessary work (this injustice was denounced by Cicero); and, lastly, by Tiberius in AD 6 (the period the columns date from).
The temple, which is peripteral with eight columns on the front and eleven on the sides, served for meetings of the senate and housed the weights and measures office.
The colossal edifice on the left, the so-called Temple of Augustus, constructed by Domitian, may have been the Athenaeum, Hadrian's famous institution for the study of Greek rhetoric and letters, in which case the niches may have contained books.

below
TEMPLE OF CASTOR FROM THE BASILICA JULIA

fifth century BC–first century AD
Roman Forum

CRUCIFIXION

seventh century
fresco
Santa Maria Antiqua

The Church of Santa Maria Antiqua is the first Christian building in the Forum (sixth century). On the walls there are early medieval frescoes, often stratified to form complex palimpsests bearing witness, next to the classical remains, to the existence of a Roman school of painting endowed with its own personality.

opposite
TEMPLE OF CASTOR

fifth century BC–first century AD
Roman Forum

The brick hall in the foreground is the so-called Temple of Augustus.

VIEW OF THE BASILICA JULIA FROM THE CAPITOLINE HILL

Roman Forum

DOMITIANIC HALL AND HORREA AGRIPPIANA

late first century BC
between the Roman Forum and the Palatine Hill

Next to the Domitianic Hall (the so-called Temple of Augustus) is a series of rooms distributed round a large courtyard: this is a complex of warehouses identified, thanks to an inscription, as the *horrea* constructed towards the end of the first century BC by Agrippa, the son-in-law and right-hand man of Augustus, which was associated with the nearby Forum Boarium and its port on the Tiber.

POOL OF JUTURNA; SHRINE OF JUTURNA

second century BC*–second century* AD
Roman Forum

To the left of the Oratory of Quaranta Martiri is the Poolof Juturna (Lacus Iuturnae) where the Dioscuri's horses are supposed to have been watered after the battle of Lake Regillus. The place where the spring was located (one of the few in the city and perhaps endowed with beneficial properties) was transformed into a basin (*lacus*) lined with marble in the second century BC. Its present appearance dates from its reconstruction during Trajan's reign.

ARCH OF TITUS

above: relief panel with the procession passing through the triumphal arch
below: relief panel with the emperor's triumphal chariot
late first century AD
Roman Forum

The arch of Titus was erected by Domitian after AD 81 in honour of his deified brother and to celebrate Rome's victory over Judaea. Entirely faced with Pentelic marble and adorned with four demi-columns on each side, the arch has a single passageway. The reliefs on the walls of the passageway are notable: on the south side is the procession as it passes through the triumphal arch, visible on the right, with porters holding aloft the seven-branched candelabrum. On the north side, Titus is riding in his chariot, driven by the goddess Roma, and is being crowned by Victory; he is preceded by the lictors and followed by personifications of the Roman people and senate. In the centre of the soffit of the archway is his apotheosis.

ALTAR WITH TURNUS AND JUTURNA

early second century AD
Roman Forum

The nymph Juturna was the sister of Turnus, the king of the Rutulians; his cult was probably introduced, together with that of the Dioscuri, by Lavinius in the archaic age.

TEMPLE OF ROMULUS

fourth century AD
Roman Forum

Traditionally believed to be a heroon (honorary monument) dedicated by Maxentius to his son Romulus, it may perhaps be identified with the Temple of Jupiter Stator, founded by Romulus at the point where the Latins, fleeing from the Sabines, stopped. The archaic open-air sanctuary, altered on a number of occasions, was finally rebuilt by Maxentius in the architectural style of late antiquity.

HORREA AGRIPPIANA

first century BC
Roman Forum

In the foreground is the courtyard of the *horrea* with the rear arches of the shops in front of the massive structure of the Domitianic Hall (the so-called Temple of Augustus). This imposing edifice is one of those that most clearly bears witness to the knowledge of architectural design and construction techniques of the Roman builders during the first century of the empire.

TEMPLE OF VESTA

late second century AD
Roman Forum

Following the fire of AD 191, Julia Domna, the wife of Septimius Severus, rebuilt the Temple of Vesta in its present form, and this was based on the structure dating from the radical rebuilding after the fire of AD 64, in Nero's reign. The modern reconstruction supplemented the few remaining marble fragments of the original temple with large quantities of travertine.
Inside burned the perpetual fire, the cult and tending of which were of great importance.

The Area Sacred to Vesta

To the east of the Temple of Castor are the heavily restored remains of the Temple of Vesta. Like all the buildings associated with pagan worship it was closed by Theodosius's decree of AD 394. Its present form dates from Septimius Severus's reign, but originally it was a simple hut, the structure of which was imitated by the later building. On the podium, the *Penus Vestae* has been identified; this was the sacred place housing the objects kept as a pledge of Rome's fate, including the palladium that, according to legend, Aeneas had brought from Troy. A number of steps lead to the House of the Vestals, the college of priestesses in charge of the sacred fire, founded by Numa Pompilius. The present edifice, built in brick, stands round a rectangular courtyard in the centre of which is a pool once surrounded by an arcade decorated with the statues of the head Vestals. Opposite is the Regia (Royal Palace), also founded by Numa Pompilius and probably the king's residence. In the republican period it became the residence of the *rex sacrorum* who, together with the *pontifex maximus* (chief priest), performed the sacral functions. The original trapezoid plan was subsequently maintained.

TEMPLE OF ANTONINUS AND FAUSTINA

AD 141
Roman Forum

The building, which is very well preserved, was erected by a decree of the senate in AD 141 on the occasion of the death and deification of Faustina, Antoninus Pius's wife, and dedicated to the emperor after his death. The temple, which is hexastyle and prostyle, stands on a high podium preceded by a modern flight of steps incorporating the remains of the altar. The impressive columns in cipollino marble, 17 metres in height, still have the grooves made to house the ropes used to hitch oxen to them in an unsuccessful attempt to pull them down, presumably in order to extract lime from them. The *cella* of the Italic type in peperino, originally faced with marble, is adorned with a very refined marble frieze typical of the cold classicism of the Antonine period. In the eighth century the temple was transformed into the Church of San Lorenzo in Miranda.

HOUSE OF THE VESTALS

first century AD
Roman Forum

Detail of the courtyard with the statues of the head Vestals, once again *in situ*.

Basilica of Maxentius

This building, one of the largest in ancient Rome, was started by Maxentius in AD 306 and was then completed by Constantine after 312, when the original entrance, on the east side (facing the Colosseum), was moved to the south side (facing the Forum), changing its orientation. The basilica was divided into a nave and two aisles by eight piers, flanked in the nave by the same number of fluted columns in cipollino marble, over 14 metres in height, which supported a cross vault, divided into three bays reaching a height of 35 metres. In the apse stood the colossal statue of Constantine, the striking remains of which are now in the Palazzo dei Conservatori. The only extant column was removed by Pope Paul V in 1613 and now stands in front of the Church of Santa Maria Maggiore. The north aisle, the only one which survived the earthquake that destroyed the building in the ninth century, still has the spectacular coffered barrel vaults (span 20.5 metres, height 24.5 metres) that so impressed Renaissance artists and inspired Bramante's design for the new St Peter's.

BASILICA OF MAXENTIUS

AD 306–312
Roman Forum

The Palatine

According to legend, Hercules and, later, Aeneas found a group of Greek immigrants on the Palatine Hill. This myth has, however, been given credibility by recent finds suggesting that Greek sailors and traders were present here before their countrymen colonized South Italy.
The discovery of Iron Age huts seems to support the tradition that the city was founded by Romulus. Already in the archaic period important religious ceremonies took place on the hill, such as the Lupercalia, associated with fertility, in which wolf-priests scourged whoever they encountered, and cults such as those of the Magna Mater, Apollo and Vesta. During the republican period many patricians settled here. After Augustus, who was born on the Palatine, decided to live here, it became the abode of the emperors and, from Tiberius's reign onwards, ever-larger and more sumptuous palaces were built. By the end of the imperial age the whole hill had become one vast building complex, and its Latin name *Palatium* came to mean the seat of power, the residence of the Caesars—in other words, "palace."
After centuries of abandonment, the hill was rediscovered in the Renaissance by the aristocrats who built their villas there. Towards the middle of the sixteenth century, at the behest of Alessandro Farnese, it was transformed into the remarkable Farnese Gardens; designed by such architects as Jacopo Barozzi, called the Vignola, and Girolamo Rainaldi, in 1625 they became one of the first botanical gardens in the world. Very little is left of this delightful place, where fascinating ruins of the imperial palace were preserved, after two centuries of excavations intended to reveal the buried remains.

DOMUS AUGUSTANA

private apartments facing the Circus Maximus with the courtyard first century AD Palatine

DOMUS AUGUSTANA, HIPPODROME OF DOMITIAN AND SEPTIMIUS SEVERUS'S EXTENSION

First–third centuries

To the east of the Domus Augustana is the sunken area of the Hippodrome, dominated by the imperial tribune, beyond which stand the ruins of the last extension to the palace, built by Septimius Severus. Also surviving are the substructures in brick terminating with the spectacular three-storeyed nymphaeum—known as the Septizodium—that was demolished by Sixtus V in 1586 for its marble.

ARCHAIC CISTERN

sixth century BC
Palatine

This cistern, the better preserved of the two surviving ones, is cut out of the rock of the hillside, lined with blocks of tufa and partially covered by a false dome. It is a precious relic of the settlements on the hill, from the monarchic period.

HOUSE OF LIVIA

smaller rooms
first century BC
Palatine

In the group of late republican houses near Romulus's hut, the house of Augustus has been identified and, within the complex, the so-called house of Livia, which contains some very important wall paintings.

HOUSE OF THE GRIFFINS

detail of the decoration
late second century–first century
Palatine

Discovered under the *lararium* of the Domus Flavia, it is the most interesting republican house preserved in Rome. It may have belonged to the orator Crassus or the consul Lutatius Catulus. Its name derives from the stucco decoration in a lunette. While the walls probably date from the first half of the second century BC, the wall-paintings were executed in the late second or early first centuries, after the fire that devastated the hill in 111 BC. The paintings are the oldest surviving ones in the Second Style, in which, for the first time, there is the illusionistic representation of the columns that appear to stand out from the wall.

DOMUS FLAVIA

courtyard with a fountain
and labyrinth
AD 81–96
Palatine

Between AD 81 and 96 a huge imperial palace was built for Domitian, incorporating a number of pre-existing buildings; the section where the state apartments were located is conventionally known as the Domus Flavia, while the Domus Augustana is the residential part. In the centre of the Domus Flavia, an immense rectangular peristyle was the hub of the public space giving access to the various rooms. The peristyle surrounded a magnificent fountain with an octagonal base, while low walls were arranged to form the motif of a labyrinth (now largely a modern restoration).

IMPERIAL PALACE AND THE CIRCUS MAXIMUS

aerial view
first century BC*–fourth century* AD
Palatine

The circus was founded, according to tradition, by Tarquinius Priscus in the place where the rape of the Sabine women took place. Originally built in wood because of the ban on the construction of permanent buildings devoted to entertainment, it was enhanced by Agrippa, while Augustus erected the imperial box and the obelisk now in Piazza del Popolo. Claudius gave it a monumental appearance, but, according to the sources, its present size of 600 × 200 metres and its capacity of between 250,000 and 385,000 spectators were only reached under Caracalla. In AD 357 Constantius II erected another obelisk, now in Piazza San Giovanni in Laterano.

VIEW OF ROME FROM THE PALATINE

From this vantage point it is possible to recognize the Curia, the Church of Santi Luca e Martina, the attic of the Arch of Septimius Severus, the upper part of Trajan's Column and the medieval Torre delle Milizie.

DOMUS SEVERIANA

Second–third centuries AD
Palatine

This is a vast extension to the Domus Augustana for which Septimius Severus was responsible. All that remains today of what must have been a splendid building are the colossal structures in bare brick, making this one of the most fascinating views of the hill from this side. Built by Domitian and restored by Maxentius, the baths were supplied with water by the Aqua Claudia, the remains of which are still visible.

VIRIDARIUM

30–20 BC
fresco from the Villa of Livia at Prima Porta
Palazzo Massimo, Museo Nazionale Romano

This is part of a splendid cycle of wall paintings from a villa, known as *ad gallinas alba* (at the white chickens), that Livia, Augustus's wife, owned on the Via Flaminia, near Prima Porta. The *viridarium* (garden) depicted on the walls of the courtyard is unique in the painting of this period: behind a low fence appears a wood with a variety of trees and shrubs, amid which birds flutter beneath a sky of different tones of blue, producing an atmospheric effect. This type of garden, containing different plants, selected and fenced, was of Persian origin and was called *paradeisos* by the Greeks. The fresh style of the paintings and their excellent condition mean that they are perhaps the most outstanding example still extant of Roman wall painting, generally known only through the works, often of a very provincial nature, found at Pompeii. They allow us to have a better understanding of its relationship with Hellenistic painting, which certainly must have provided the prototypes for this form of decoration. With a new symbolic meaning, this subject was later to become part of Christian iconography.

Arch of Constantine

With three passageways and 25 metres in height, this is the largest and best preserved of the Roman arches. Until a few years ago it was believed to be an assemblage, deferentially put together by the Senate for Constantine—who had not even celebrated a triumph after his victory over Maxentius (AD 312)—by recycling reliefs from other monuments. The recent restoration (1982–1987) has, however, shown that it is a masterly work dating from Hadrian's reign, while in the fourth century only the attic with the dedication to the emperor, reusing Trajan and Aurelianic bas-reliefs, was built, and the reliefs of historic character regarding episodes from Constantine's life were inserted. The various reliefs are an outstanding expression of the sensibility and culture of the different periods: the Trajan ones are notable for their vigorous, dramatic composition and abundant pathos; the Hadrianic ones for their classicism imbued with romantic restlessness; the Aurelianic ones (from a monument erected by Commodus) for the incipient dissolution of the plastic mass into pictorial forms; while the Constantinian reliefs are characterized by the anticlassical style, brutally expressive and crudely stereometric that was developed during the Tetrarchic period. Just to the north of the arch, recent excavations have revealed the foundations of the Meta Sudans, a monumental fountain dating from the Flavian period in the form of a cone, the enormous concrete core of which was barbarically destroyed in 1936 to make way for the Fascist parades.

ARCH OF CONSTANTINE

attic, detail of a statue
second–fourth centuries AD

The noble figure of the bound Dacian prisoner comes, like the other statues in the same position, from Trajan's Forum. The head has been restored.

VIEW OF THE ARCH OF CONSTANTINE FROM THE COLOSSEUM

second–fourth centuries AD

In front of the arch are the foundations of the Meta Sudans, dating from the first century AD.

ARCH OF CONSTANTINE

north side
second–fourth centuries AD

From bottom to top:
on the pedestals of the columns are barbarian prisoners; above the arches, river gods; higher still, the long, narrow reliefs with episodes from the life of Constantine; above these, the four Hadrianic tondos are perhaps the most outstanding sculptural works of the period, with their classicism that, unlike the rigid, official style of the Augustan period, is veined with nostalgia of a quasi-romantic nature. The scenes refer to real events, as the appearance of Hadrian's favourite, Antinous, firstly as a boy, then as a youth, seems to demonstrate. During Constantine's reign, some portraits of Hadrian were replaced with those of Constantine and Licinius.
The rectangular reliefs above, over three metres in height, probably come from a monument erected by Commodus in honour of his father Marcus Aurelius, perhaps another freestanding arch that may have been located near the column of Marcus Aurelius, which is contemporary with the panels.
The reliefs, like those on the columns, represent episodes from the campaign against the Quadi and Marcomanni. Their excellent quality and the progressive dissolution of the plastic masses into more pictorial forms, suggesting a shortly earlier period than that of the column, are in the style that culminated in the reliefs of the Arch of Septimius Severus.

opposite, below and overleaf
COLOSSEUM

late first century

Ancient Rome's most famous building is undoubtedly the Flavian amphitheatre, better known as the Colosseum, its name deriving from the colossal bronze statue portraying Nero that the latter had erected in the vestibule of his Domus Aurea (Golden House), facing the artificial lake overlooked by the villa's porticoes. When Vespasian decided to return to the citizens of Rome what Nero, the despot *par excellence*, had taken from them, he drained the lake and on its site built the huge amphitheatre, the largest ever constructed. Dedicated in AD 79, the building was inaugurated by Titus in the following year, with entertainments lasting for a hundred days when some 5,000 wild animals, which had been specially imported from Africa, were slaughtered. The work was concluded by Domitian, who was probably responsible for the complex substructures, since previously the arena had also been used, after it had been specially flooded, for naumachiae (naval battles). Converted into a fortress in the Middle Ages by the Frangipane family, the building became a source of materials until the mid-eighteenth century, when Benedict XIV installed a Via Crucis and also built a small church. After this, urgent restoration work was finally carried out; some of it was exemplary, such as that by Raffaele Stern, who shored up the unstable arches with brick buttresses. Built in *opus quadratum* (ashlar masonry) of travertine for the façade and the main load-bearing structures, and in *opus quadratum* of tufa, brick and concrete for the other parts, it has an ellipsoidal shape, with the main axis of 188 metres and the minor one of 156 metres. The façade has three storeys of arcades, each with 80 arches flanked by demi-columns (Tuscan, Ionic and Corinthian) and surmounted by an attic storey decorated with pilasters, reaching an overall height of 48.5 metres. Still visible on the attic are the sockets for the posts supporting the huge awning that covered the interior; about a thousand expert sailors were needed to spread it. Access to the *cavea* was by a series of ramps and internal ambulatories that gave onto the *vomitoria* from which the tiers of seats were reached.
The *cavea* was subdivided on the basis of the social class of the spectators: the lower tiers were in marble, but divided into three sectors, while the highest ones, reserved for the plebeians, were in wood and divided by a high wall. The arena (86 × 54 metres), separated from the *cavea* by a podium and a balustrade, was covered with a wooden floor in which trap doors allowed the wild animals to enter. Estimates of the capacity vary from 45,000 to 73,000 spectators.

FORUM OF AUGUSTUS

42–2 BC
imperial fora

The Forum of Augustus (125 × 118 metres) is relatively easy to interpret. It is possible to recognize the layout, common to all the imperial fora, with imposing porticoes on the four sides framing a temple on a podium at the north end. The monumental colonnades housed the statues of the *summi viri* (great men) of the republic, while in exedrae flanking the temple were those of the kings of Alba Longa, Aeneas, Romulus and the Julio-Claudian dynasty, following an iconographic programme which concluded with the pediment of the spectacular Temple of Mars Ultor, intended to exalt Augustus as the *Pater Patriae* (Father of the Fatherland) and present him in a quasi-divine light. All that remains of the magnificent temple are three columns.

FORUM OF CAESAR

first century BC–second century AD
imperial fora

Started by Caesar in 54 BC, it was completed by Augustus and rebuilt by Trajan (AD 113). The oldest of the imperial fora, it served as a model for the later ones, which imitated its rectangular plan, with a temple on the short side opposite the entrance. It is likely that this layout—alien to Italic urbanism and marked by an explicitly propagandistic conception, with its exaltation of Venus Genetrix, the mythical foundress of the *gens Julia*—derived from the model of the sanctuaries dedicated to the deified monarchs of the Hellenistic world. In this regard, Suetonius recalled that Caesar was arrogant enough to receive the Senate in his temple, sitting like a god in front of the statue of Venus.

DOMUS AUREA (GOLDEN HOUSE)

after AD *64*
octagonal court with an oculus in the dome

By far the largest imperial residence, the Domus Aurea occupied an immense area between the Circus Maximus, San Pietro in Vincoli, Piazza Vittorio Emanuele II and the Caelian Hill. It replaced the Domus Transitoria—the "house of passage"—that Nero built in the first part of his reign (between AD 54 and 64) as a link between the imperial property on the Palatine and the one on the Esquiline, the so-called Horti Maecenatiani (Gardens of Maecenas). The architects were Severus and Celer, while a certain Fabullus (or Famullus) supervised the pictorial decoration. Suetonius wrote: "When the palace had been completed and Nero inaugurated it, he seemed to be satisfied and said that finally he could begin to live in a residence worthy of a man." The area at present open to visitors (about 300 × 100 metres) survived because it was used as the substructure of a part of the Baths of Trajan, which were built on the Esquiline. The fortuitous discovery of the decorated rooms during the Renaissance allowed the artists of the day to see for themselves the lively antique wall decoration, animated by inexhaustible fantasy.
The term "grotesques" was invented for what were believed to be paintings in underground chambers, referred to as *grotte.* Armed with torches, numerous artists, including Raphael, went to study them.
In 1506 the *Laocoön* was found here; this statue group was destined to have a major influence on Michelangelo's sculpture.
The excavated area comprises a large porticoed courtyard with a cryptoporticus on one of the sides, a fountain in the centre and a nymphaeum with the vault covered with pumice stone and a mosaic representing *Ulysses and Polyphemus* on the east side.
The courtyard was covered with vaults when the baths were built.
The groups of rooms on the south side, now dark and damp, included the emperor's bedroom and other private rooms overlooking the lake below (this is where the Colosseum now stands).

In a number of rooms there are still traces of the original paintings—unfortunately in a bad state despite recent conservation work—characterized by rich colours and fluid brushwork. The famous room with the golden vault, giving onto a large pentagonal courtyard, is in poor condition. In the cryptoporticus there are the signatures of a number of Renaissance artists. The imposing court illustrated here is one of the most outstanding examples of Roman architecture, especially as regards the way the hemispherical dome is linked to the octagonal base

without the use of pendentives. The structure of the walls, extremely limited in size because of the very large openings onto the radial rooms, makes it a masterpiece from a constructional point of view. At midday the court, illuminated by the large oculus above, opened up onto a pleasant prospectof the lake. Because of its structure it cannot be the dining room that "revolved continuously, night and day, like the world" that Suetonius included among the numerous marvels of this outstanding complex.

ACHILLES AND THE DAUGHTERS OF KING LYCOMEDES

first century AD
room of Achilles on Scyros, central scene of the vault
Domus Aurea

Inserted in the refined illusionistic decoration, this panel certainly derives from a famous painting of the Hellenistic period, of which it preserves some elements. Its most outstanding quality is, however, the masterly freshness of the touch; better than the average level of the decorative panels, this one may be by the hand of Fabullus. Pliny mentioned that, in order to stress his special status, this painter wore his toga even when he was painting on the scaffolding and described his style as "floridus et humidus."

CRYPTOPORTICUS

first century AD
architectural composition on the wall
Domus Aurea

This is a notable example of wall painting in the Third Style, where the illusionism typical of the Second Style has been abandoned in favour of a decorative mode of a decidedly fantastic nature, characterized by inexhaustible inventiveness and lightness.

The Forum and Markets of Trajan

The last and most famous of the imperial fora, regarded by the ancients as the eighth wonder of the world, this is a huge complex (300 × 90 metres) built for Trajan by the architect Apollodorus of Damascus, who cut away the saddleback between the Capitoline and Quirinal hills. A triumphal arch gave access to a vast colonnaded square, in the centre of which stood an equestrian statue of Trajan. At the sides were two immense exedrae, while the fourth side was occupied by the Basilica Ulpia, the largest (170 × 60 metres) and most magnificent building of this type in Rome. Some of the columns dividing this remarkable building into a nave flanked by double aisles have been re-erected, although part of the site has yet to be excavated. From the basilica there was access to a small courtyard where Trajan's column stood between two vast libraries, no longer visible. The complex terminated with a temple dedicated by Hadrian to deified Trajan; one can get an idea of its size from the monolithic granite shaft and its capital lying at the foot of Trajan's column. Linked to the forum, the markets are divided into a number of levels around the exedra.

BASILICA ULPIA AND TRAJAN'S MARKETS

c. AD 110
Forum of Trajan

TRAJAN'S MARKETS

c. AD 110
Forum of Trajan

Trajan's Column

Erected between AD 107 and 113 in order to show the height of the hill before it was cut away, the column is, in fact, an outstanding monument, an all-time masterpiece, commemorating Trajan's deeds in the dramatic Dacian wars, which provided the spoils that paid for the work on the forum. Composed of large blocks of marble—3.5 metres thick—, the shaft, 30 metres in height, is completely carved with a remarkable spiral frieze in bas-relief comprising over 2,500 figures. This technical data, however, gives a very inadequate idea of the quality of the work. The unknown, but very skilled, artist, conventionally known as the Master of Trajan's Exploits, was able to orchestrate the numerous episodes into which the account is divided in order to fulfil their function as both propaganda and a historical record, but, at the same time, he tackled the theme of war in a totally new way. Thanks to a realistic and restrained style, which is detailed but wide-ranging, the exploits of the victors are rendered with a quasi-cinematographic rhythm, together with the suffering of a heroic and proud people, capable of fighting to the last for its freedom. The artist infuses the portraits of Dacian prisoners, the representations of the horrors of war and the women fleeing with their children with pathos that is the result of unprecedented involvement, managing to see, perhaps for the first time, the living individual behind the enemy's mask. Inside the column, a spiral staircase leads from the pedestal, where Trajan was buried, to the top, where his statue, which was lost in the Middle Ages, was replaced in 1587 by that of St Peter.

TRAJAN'S COLUMN

detail
AD 107–113
Forum of Trajan

Roman legionaries are loading a ship in a port on the Danube, with a walled city in the background.

TEMPLE OF VESTA

late second century BC–second century AD
Forum Boarium

The characteristic round form of the so-called Temple of Vesta —in reality, of Hercules Victor— is the oldest surviving Roman building entirely in marble. It is a fine example of a peripteral temple with 20 columns (one is missing) surrounding a *cella* that may have originally been covered with a dome.

BOCCA DELLA VERITÀ

second–third centuries AD
Santa Maria in Cosmedin

According to legend, "the mouth of Truth," representing a river god, will bite the hand of those who do not tell the truth.

TEMPLE OF FORTUNA VIRILIS

second–first centuries BC
Forum Boarium

This fine temple known as Fortuna Virilis, but in reality dedicated to Portunus (a river god who protected ports), stands by the ancient river port serving the Forum Boarium, the cattle market, and the Pons Aemilius. Founded in the fourth century BC, it was rebuilt in the second and first centuries and restored on a number of occasions. Built on a high podium with a mock peristyle of demi-columns leaning on the *cella*, this little temple is a rare example of a probably very popular style. It was transformed in a church in the ninth century and so it could be preserved. It contains frescoes dating from that period.

SACRED AREA OF LARGO ARGENTINA

third–second centuries BC

In this area there are four temples, called by letters A to D from right to left. Temple A (in the foreground), founded in 241 BC, was rebuilt in its present hexastyle and peripteral form around the end of the first century BC. The apses, however, date from the eighth century, when the Church of San Nicola was built over the ruins. Temple B is round and has been restored on a number of occasions, may date from 101 BC. Temple C is peripteral, but without the rear columns; it is the oldest (late fourth–early third centuries BC), although its present appearance dates from Domitian's restoration. Temple D, the biggest, is hexastyle with a large *cella* and deep pronaos of the Italic type, is only partially visible (early second century BC). Behind temple B, a large podium in tufa is what remains of Pompey's Curia where, in 44 BC, Julius Caesar was assassinated.

Dying Gauls

The two imposing groups in the Ludovisi Collection are today divided between the Palazzo Altemps and the Musei Capitolini. The sculptures were found in the seventeenth century when the Villa Ludovisi was being built on the site of Julius Caesar's luxurious villa, which then passed to Sallust and the name Horti Sallustiani was given to the area. The two pieces, to which should be added a third portraying a wounded woman holding a child to her breast, are of uncertain provenance. They are, however, copies, perhaps commissioned by Caesar to celebrate his victory over the Gauls, of the bronze statues ordered in 228 BC by Attalus I, king of Pergamum, and originally dedicated in that city in the square of the Temple of Athena and library above the famous theatre. These dramatic works are some of the best examples of how, in the Hellenistic period, sculptors were able to create complex groups that could be viewed from all sides (it should be remembered that the sculpture was located in the centre of a busy square). But together with the astounding technical virtuosity, still evident in the Roman copies, what is really striking in these works is their dramatic pathos, their capacity to depict the unyielding pride of the Galatians (misleadingly known as "Gauls," they were, in reality, groups of Celts who had migrated from central Europe). In the words of a historian: "Not even in the wounded who were still alive did the fury abate … nor did those who were wounded by sword or spear … abandon their rage as long as they had another moment to live." In the group of the Gaul killing himself and his wife, the confident way the sculpture is distributed in space is superb, stressing the couple's ineluctable decision to assert their right to freedom with suicide, while the dying Gaul seems to resist uselessly, but with no less pride, the inevitable approach of death. Subdued but not vanquished, the Galatians are a splendid representation of the dignity and insuppressible yearning for individual freedom that developed during the Hellenistic period.

GAUL KILLING HIMSELF AND HIS WIFE

Roman copy of the Pergamene original of 228 BC
Palazzo Altemps

SALONE DEL CAMINO

View with the Gaul Killing Himself and his Wife and Ludovisi Erinyes
Roman copies from Pergamene originals of 228 BC
Palazzo Altemps

DYING GAUL

Roman copy of a Pergamene original of 228 BC
Palazzo Altemps

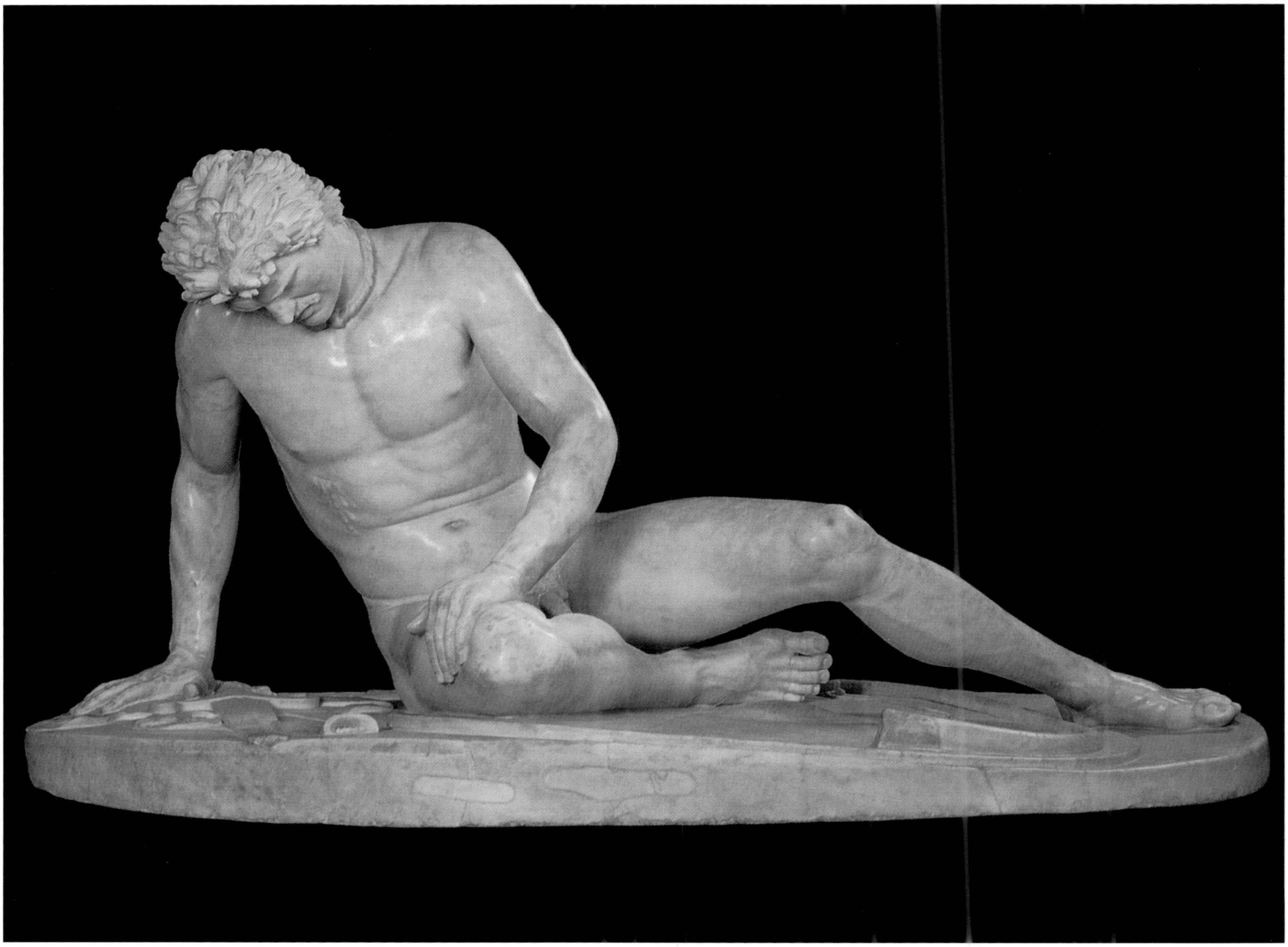

Ludovisi Throne

Not only is this one of the most famous pieces in the Roman collections, but it is also considered by many scholars to be an outstanding masterpiece of antiquity. The central relief illustrates the birth of Aphrodite as narrated by Hesiod in the *Theogony* (188–200). "No sooner had he [Cronos] cut off the genitals [of his father, Uranus] with a diamond and cast them from the land into the rough sea, they were carried away from the shore for a long time and, all around, white foam emerged from the immortal flesh. A girl took shape in this foam; she was first of all in sacred Cythera, then she went to Cyprus surrounded by the waves; thus came forth a graceful and fascinating goddess and the grass grew around her and under her beautiful feet. She is called Aphrodite (the goddess born of the foam, Cytherea with a splendid crown) by the gods and men because she was brought up in the foam; she is also called Cytherea because she stopped on Cythera, and also Cypris because she was born in Cyprus surrounded by the waves, and also Philomnedes because she emerged from the genitals."
The so-called Ludovisi Throne was found in 1887 in the grounds of the Villa Ludovisi in Rome. Usually linked with the Temple of Venus Erucina outside the Porta Collina, of the republican period, which was subsequently incorporated in the famous *horti* (gardens) of Caesar, who claimed to be a descendant of the goddess. The stylistic and iconographic characteristics, supported, so it seems, by evidence from the excavations, have induced the majority of scholars to recognize the work as an original from Magna Graecia (which would explain a number of stylistic features that are later if compared with those of the Greek art of the period), executed around the mid-fifth century BC in Locri Epizephyrii, on the Calabrian coast, and of excellent quality.
Recently the authenticity of the work—and even more so that of its companion relief, the Boston Throne (Museum of Fine Arts, Boston)—has been authoritatively questioned. It has, in fact, been suggested that it is a skilled pastiche by a nineteenth-century forger who unintentionally inserted, in a classicizing vocabulary, naturalistic elements and spatial and perspective simplifications typical of his own period and not of the one when the sculpture was supposed to have been executed.

LUDOVISI THRONE

relief on the left side
mid-fifth century BC ?
Palazzo Altemps

This may show a veiled bride-to-be woman burning incense to the goddess.

LUDOVISI THRONE

relief on the right side
mid-fifth century BC ?
Palazzo Altemps

The soft light bathing the pipe player's naked figure shapes its forms with confident but discreet naturalness.

LUDOVISI THRONE

front panel showing the Birth of Aphrodite
mid-fifth century BC ?
Palazzo Altemps

This apparently symmetrical composition is, in reality, animated by a subtle differentiation of the gestures and drapery resulting in harmony centring on the slow ascent of Aphrodite, with its hieratic symbolism, vivified by the light breath of a new world coming into being, that of love.

Palazzo Altemps and the Museo Nazionale Romano

Following the reorganization of the Museo Nazionale Romano in recent years, the section that has moved to the Palazzo Altemps is one of the most successful examples of the re-use of a historic building. The palazzo has, in fact, once again acquired the function as a museum it formerly had in the sixteenth century, when Cardinal Altemps used it for his collection of antique sculptures. Today the building houses, among other things, part of the outstanding Ludovisi Buoncompagni Collection, the result of the earliest dispersion of the Altemps Collection in 1621. The present display has been realized with criteria comparable to those adopted five centuries ago in this building for the cardinal's collection, with the aim of reviving the antiquarian taste of the sixteenth-century arrangement. Because the provenance of a large number of pieces in the Ludovisi Collection is unknown—although it is probable that many of the sculptures belonged to Cardinal Altemps—it is more than likely that some of the works have returned, several centuries later, to the place where they were originally displayed.

ARES LUDOVISI

Roman copy of a Hellenistic original of the middle of the third–second centuries BC
marble
Palazzo Altemps

It is typical of a certain current of Hellenism to portray the hero not at the height of action, but rather in the period of reflection following it, often tinged with pensive melancholy. The superb sculpture in the centre of the photograph was restored by Bernini in 1622. The seated youth visible on the left belongs to the same genre.

SALONE DELLE ERME

view with a decorative vase in the foreground
Palazzo Altemps

In this room, too, there are marbles from the Ludovisi Collection. The monumental vase in the foreground with handles in the form of rams' heads is an eighteenth-century reconstruction, carried out by using antique fragments and restoring the missing parts. The two statues, both portraying *Apollo Citharoedus*, were also heavily restored in the seventeenth century: in the one on the left the head has been restored—this has evidently been inspired by the famous *Apollo Belvedere*—as well as the arms and part of the legs.

SALA DELLE PROSPETTIVE DIPINTE

Palazzo Altemps

Together with the *Hermes Logios*, in this room there are other famous marbles from the Ludovisi Collection, including *Asclepius* (right) and the so-called *Hercules Lenbach* (left and in the photograph on the left).

HERMES LOGIOS

Roman copy of a Greek original of the mid-fifth century BC
marble
Palazzo Altemps

One of the masterpieces of the Ludovisi Collection, the statue of the Hermes Logios ("Speaking Hermes") was restored by the great Baroque sculptor Alessandro Algardi, who added the god's traditional attributes, which were then removed during later conservation. Originally, in fact, the statue portrayed Hermes Psychopompos—that is, the conductor of souls to the underworld—with a severe, engrossed aspect, in the intense style typical of Polyclitus.

ESQUILINE VENUS

first century BC
marble
Palazzo dei Conservatori

The delicate figure of the naked girl, accompanied by the attributes of the cult of Isis on the vase next to her, portrayed as she ties a hairband around her head, is one of the best examples of the eclectic art of the Augustan period. Some of the facial features and a certain sense of melancholic resignation have induced some scholars to identify the sculpture as an idealized portrait of Cleopatra, the unfortunate queen of Egypt tragically linked to the fate of Mark Antony.

SPINARIO (BOY PICKING A THORN FROM HIS FOOT)

first century BC
bronze
Palazzo dei Conservatori

This is a refined and fascinating creation of the late Hellenistic period, combining naturalism, lyrical intimism, classical references and subtle compositional harmony based on deliberate contrasts. By allowing the light to be softly reflected on the delicate adolescent body, the bronze enhances the quality of this splendid sculpture.

opposite
CAPITOLINE BRUTUS

third–second centuries BC
bronze
Palazzo dei Conservatori

This very intense head of a man is one of the great masterpieces of antique portraiture. The striking face, frequently regarded as an example of Etruscan or Italic art, may perhaps be the result of the influence of Greek art, which alone was able to give a work a sense of organicity and interior structural solidity without which the facial features, in this case more apparent than real, would drift into casuality and impressionism.
Therefore this portrait is, in a certain sense, idealized; it gives substance to a certain idea rather than reproducing the physical characteristics of a face. Seen from this point of view, this remarkable bronze is an exemplary product of the period when the Italic and Roman mentality, during the Punic Wars, was opening up towards more complex cultural horizons thanks to increasingly close contacts with the Greek world. There is, in fact, nothing that can be described as fortuitous in the resolute expression of this face.

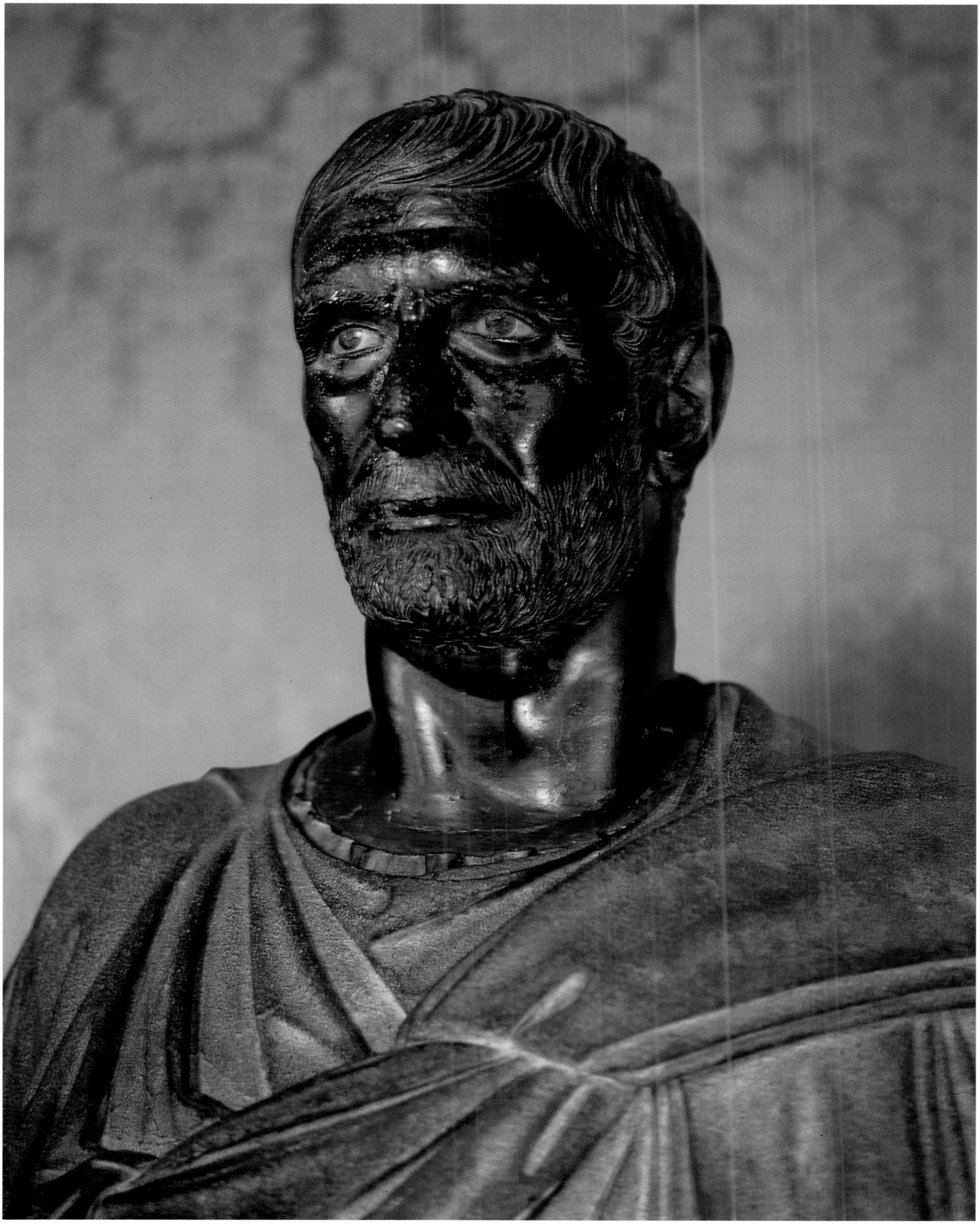

Hagesandros, Polydoros
and Athanadoros of Rhodes

LAOCOÖN

copy of the first century AD
of a Hellenistic original in bronze
of the second century BC
(160–130 BC *?)*
marble
Vatican Museums

This spectacular marble group, 242 centimetres in height, was found almost intact (only the right arm was missing, but after being found recently, it has been used to replace Giovanni Angelo Montorsoli's sixteenth-century restoration) in 1506 in one of the rooms in Nero's Golden House. Its influence on subsequent art is incalculable: the impact it had on Michelangelo is evident if the *Pietà* in St Peter's is compared with his *Ignudi* and other figures in the Sistine Chapel. The Laocoön group is probably a copy of a bronze original in the Pergamene style: the rigorously frontal conception informing it represents, however, the extreme limit of the Greek, and then Hellenistic, sculptural vision, characterized by the virtuosity of the tight rhythm, the powerful chiaroscuro effects and the pathetic accents, seemingly inspired by a very high form of rhetoric. The disintegration of the plastic form—the impelling organicity of which, as a way of controlling space, represented one of the high points of Greek art—culminates in the superb portrayal of the face, which seems almost to dissolve in the throes of the matter, as if there were no bone structure under the skin. In this sense it is, therefore, possible to assert that the Laocoön is the last work of Greek art.

APOLLO BELVEDERE

copy of the early second century
AD *of an original in bronze*
by Leochares of 350–330 BC
Luna marble
Vatican Museums

One of the most intriguing works of the antique world, it was found in the fifteenth century near San Pietro in Vincoli. It so fascinated the German scholar Johann Joachim Winckelmann that he considered it to be the work that most perfectly embodied the classical spirit. This interpretation, based on an academicizing Roman copy with a subtly nostalgic flavour, restored in accordance with classicizing canons in the seventeenth century (this restoration has now been partially removed), has also heavily influenced the way we perceive classical art. The original work, however, belonged to a stylistic period in which the typically classical equilibrium between naturalism and idealism had already begun to lose its stability, and the portrayals of the gods were also suspended in a psychologically indeterminate atmosphere, almost as if they were lost in their inner world, which shortly afterwards was disrupted by the innovations introduced by Hellenism.

ARIADNE SLEEPING

copy of the first–second centuries AD *of an original of the middle Hellenistic period of the third–second centuries* BC
marble
Vatican Museums

This imposing and solemn portrayal of the sleeping heroine is notable for the elaborate drapery and solid volumes of the powerful female figure. The impression of academic coldness may, no doubt, be ascribed to the Roman copyist.

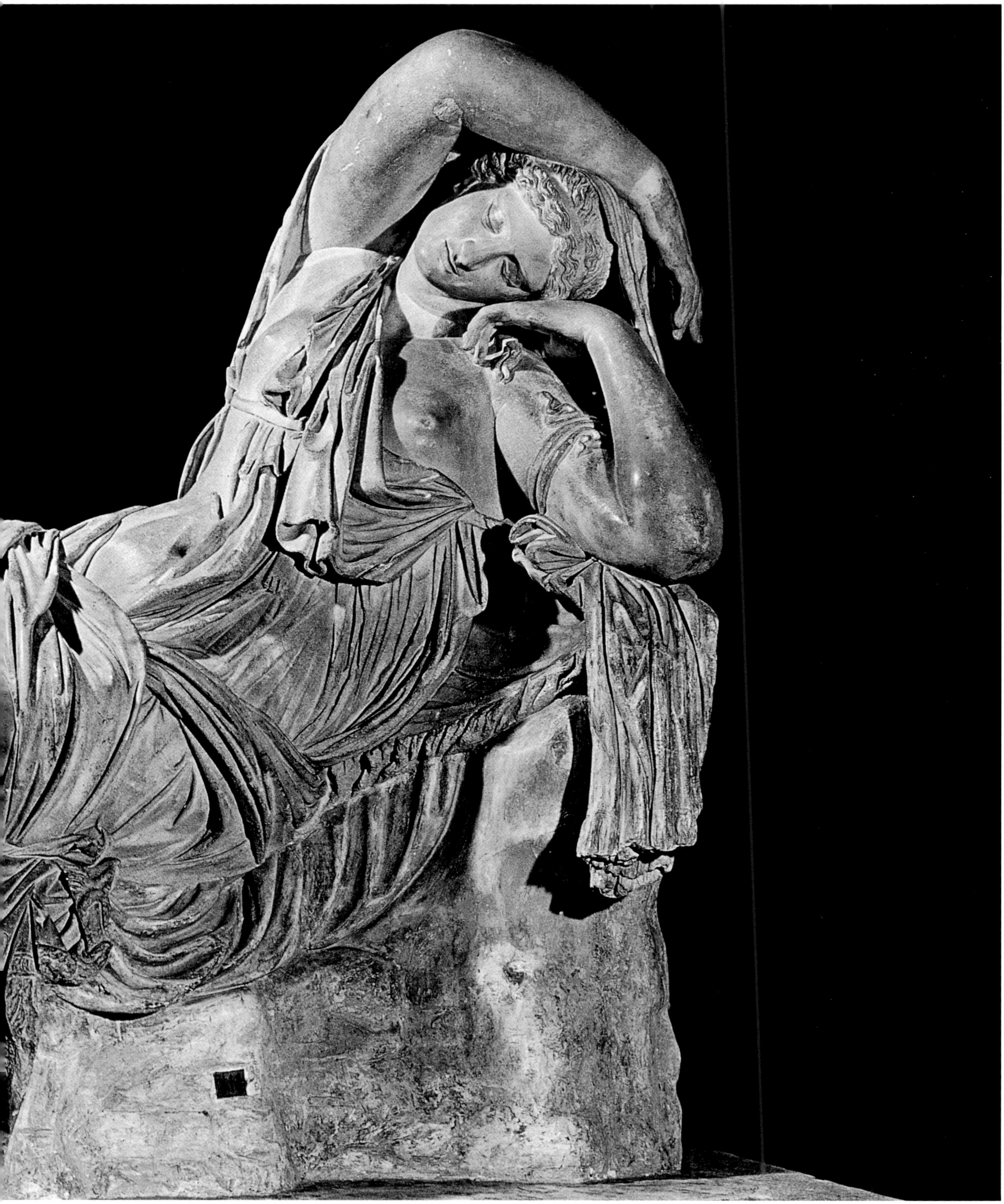

The Frescoes of the Villa della Farnesina

In the new premises of the Museo Nazionale Romano in the Palazzo Massimo the splendid wall paintings discovered in 1879 in the cryptoporticus of the Villa of the Farnesina have finally found a worthy location in a gallery built to resemble their original setting.
The outstanding cycle of paintings has been linked, unfoundedly, with Cleopatra's stay in Rome. It is more likely that the splendid complex of richly decorated terraces was built by Agrippa, for whom money was no object, on the occasion of his marriage to Augustus's daughter.
This hypothesis is borne out by the presence in the paintings of elements that may be interpreted as a precise political message, with the explicit representation of Augustus as a "novus Mercurius"and numerous stucco figures of victories on the vaults.
The cryptoporticus constituted the transverse axis of the house, linking the central block to the two wings.
The state of preservation of the frescoes, some of which date from a later period, around the middle of the first century ad, is generally excellent, another interesting aspect of this group of paintings that, together with that of the Villa of Livia at Prima Porta, is certainly one of the most important to have survived from antiquity.

CUBICULUM B, END WALL OF THE BEDROOM

fresco painting from the Villa della Farnesina
first century BC
Palazzo Massimo, Museo Nazionale Romano

These paintings are an excellent example of the Second Style, with its architectural settings, where the walls are elegantly divided with thin columns and slender candelabra supporting festoons that frame, with magnificent decorative effect, panels containing figures and landscapes. In the detail shown here, note the scene of Dionysus as a child amid the nymphs of Nysa, while other fictive pictures display an elegance of Neo-Attic origin.

CUBICULUM B, LEFT WALL OF THE ANTECHAMBER

panel with female figure seated near a herm
fresco painting from the Villa della Farnesina
first century BC
Palazzo Massimo, Museo Nazionale Romano

Possibly depicting the toilet of Venus, this delightful genre scene is a pretext for treating, with delicate tones, the theme of the female nude. On the right wall of the cubiculum is the inscription "Seleukos epoie" (Seleucus made it), perhaps a sign of the presence of Greek artists.

CUBICULUM B, END WALL OF THE BEDROOM

fresco painting from the Villa della Farnesina
first century BC
Palazzo Massimo, Museo Nazionale Romano

The Pantheon

The best preserved of the ancient Roman buildings still extant, it has survived practically intact because it was converted into a church in 609, with a dedication to the Virgin and all the martyrs (previously it was dedicated to "all the gods," namely *Pantheon* in Greek), after the emperor Phocas had donated it to Boniface IV. First built by Agrippa in 27 BC, it was completely reconstructed in AD 118–125, in its present, very original form, by Hadrian, who preserved the old inscription; Agrippa's building was rectangular. In the original design the façade was heightened and surrounded by colonnades that concealed the rotonda behind. The huge portico is adorned with 16 monolithic granite columns, 13 metres in height. The circular *cella* consists of a wall 30 metres in height and 6.2 metres thick. The dome, the largest ever built in concrete, is a true masterpiece of engineering as well as of architecture, with a diameter of 43.3 metres. The imposing interior, with its sense of immobility, forms an enveloping space that is, in effect, a sphere inserted in a cylinder (the internal diameter of the rotonda is equal to its height).
The perimetric wall is divided by seven semicircular and rectangular recesses framed by majestic pilasters and columns supporting an entablature interrupted by the apse. Part of the original decoration between the first cornice and the dome has been restored above the first recess to the right of the apse. Adorned with five concentric rings of 28 coffers of diminishing size, the dome has a central oculus, 9 metres in diameter.

PANTHEON

AD 118–125

The photograph emphasizes the frontal view of the pantheon, the portico of which, with its conventionally classical design, bears no relation to the unusual form and volume of the rotunda, which is practically an independent building. Originally this effect was much more evident, since at the top of a long flight of steps the façade dominated a rectangular square flanked by colonnades that concealed the rotunda behind. The small obelisk of Rameses II crowning the fountain (sixteenth century) was brought here by Clement XI from the site of the Iseum (Temple of Isis) in the Campus Martius.

PANTHEON

dome
AD 118–125

The splendid dome, with its oculus in the centre allowing the natural light to play over the rings of coffers of diminishing size, is one of the greatest technical and aesthetic inventions of Roman times. The atmosphere in the rotunda is one of absolute peace, due also to the absence of visible elements serving to counter the thrust of the dome. The techniques employed here were adopted not only by the Romans and in the western world as a whole, but also in Byzantine architecture and the great Ottoman masterpieces. The dome was made with a single placing of concrete, lightened by using an aggregate of tufa and pumice stone in the upper part, on wooden formwork. The building, which was subjected to despoliation, restoration and transformation, was adorned with two small bell-towers by Bernini; known as "donkey's ears," they were removed in 1883. In 1870 it became the burial place of the kings of Italy. Raphael is buried here too.

on this page
BATHS OF DIOCLETIAN

top left: left palaestra
top right: right palaestra
below: rooms to the south of the basilica
AD 298–306

These huge thermae (380 × 370 metres), the largest ever built in Rome, had a capacity of over three thousand bathers. Built by Diocletian, most of the complex is still standing and has been re-used in various ways. Arranged along the central axis were the *natatio* (swimming pool), the central basilican hall (now the Basilica of Santa Maria degli Angeli, restored by Michelangelo), the *tepidarium* (intermediary warm room) and the *caldarium* (hot hall), flanked symmetrically by various service rooms, changing rooms and palaestrae (exercise courts), in accordance with the typical design of the large baths of the imperial period.

opposite
BATHS OF CARACALLA

west palaestra
AD 212–217

The colossal ruins of the Baths of Caracalla, entirely free from later additions, are the most imposing and easy to interpret of the large thermae of the imperial period. The west palaestra still preserves part of its black and white mosaic floor.

BATHS OF CARACALLA

caldarium and adjacent rooms
AD 212–217

The huge brick piers supported the side walls of the huge circular *caldarium*; having large windows and facing south in order to benefit from the sun's heat, it was covered with a dome. In accordance with a design already in use in Nero's reign, the baths were built within a great perimeter wall measuring 337 × 328 metres, which enclosed the gardens in the centre of which stood the bath-buildings; they were supplied with water from an enormous cistern built into the hillside. The main buildings, covering an area of 220 × 114 metres and extending along the minor axis of the complex, comprised the *natatio*, the basilican hall with the *frigidarium*, *tepidarium* and *caldarium*, at the sides of which two palaestrae and other rooms are symmetrically arranged.

BATHS OF CARACALLA

west apodyterium
view from above
AD 212–217

This magnificent *apodyterium* (changing room), formerly sumptuously decorated with coloured marble, was a room where bathers could relax before proceeding to the palaestra or to the vestibule giving onto the *natatio*, the open-air swimming pool. There is an identical room in the east part of the building.

BATHS OF CARACALLA

east palaestra, view from above
AD 212–217

Like the west palaestra, this was used for open-air gymnastic exercises, and was accessible without passing through the bath halls.

BATHS OF CARACALLA

frigidarium, north side
AD 212–217

In the centre of the complex, of which it formed the hub, there is the enormous "basilica" (58 × 24 metres), originally covered with three cross-vaults and lavishly decorated, that served as the *frigidarium*. It was, in fact, an enormous hall (rather like the Basilica of Maxentius, which it inspired) in which the actual baths only occupied relatively marginal spaces, such as those to the left and the right of the central bay visible in the photograph, which was separated from the vast swimming pool by tall columns.

Tiber Island with the Pons Cestius and Pons Fabricius

Tiber Island (Insula Tiberina), located near the ford around which the first nuclei of the future city grew up, is linked to the river banks by two bridges. The Pons Fabricius, dating from 62 BC and in an excellent state of repair, is 62 metres long and 5.5 metres wide. The span of the two large segmental arches is about 25 metres. According to legend, the island was formed by the accumulation of mud on the sheaves of corn grain cast into the Tiber by the people after Tarquinius Superbus was expelled from Rome. The oldest of the cults that existed here was perhaps that of the god Tiberinus, replaced by that of Aesculapius when, as the god of healing arrived from Epidaurus on a ship that went to fetch him to ward off a pestilence, his sacred snake threw itself into the Tiber in order to take refuge on the island. The episode is commemorated by a bas-relief in travertine on the east end of the island, where a trireme with a snake coiled around the staff held by Aesculapius is sculpted (first century BC). In the eleventh century the Church of San Bartolomeo all'Isola was built over the ruins of the Temple of Aesculapius; destroyed by floods in 1557, it was later rebuilt and then restored again in the nineteenth century.

PONS AEMILIUS OR "PONTE ROTTO" (BROKEN BRIDGE)

179 BC

This fascinating ruin located just downstream from the island is the surviving arch of the "Ponte Rotto," the name given to the Pons Aemilius, built in 179 BC. The arch, dating from the sixteenth-century rebuilding in which Michelangelo also participated, stands on the original piers.

The Aurelianic Walls

As Rome grew, especially from the Augustan period onwards, it spread well beyond the republican walls, which fell into disuse because the defence of the city was guaranteed by the legions on the borders of the empire. With the crisis of the third century AD, the situation changed radically and Aurelian decided to provide Rome with a new circuit of walls as quickly and cheaply as possible. The huge undertaking, involving the construction of a total of 19 kilometres of walls, was completed in just four years (271–275), making use of all the available manpower, incorporating, as far as possible, pre-existing constructions and sacrificing innumerable buildings for their materials. The new walls, with a concrete core faced with brick, were 6 to 8 metres in height and about 3.5 metres thick. On the top there was a battlemented walkway provided with loopholes for the archers, interrupted every 100 Roman feet (about 30 metres) by a square tower projecting from the external face; these towers had a windowed room, where a pair of ballistae (catapults for hurling stones) were housed. The numerous gates were the weak point of the system. The most important ones had double arches, the others single openings, but all were flanked by semicircular towers and had an upper storey where the winch for lowering the portcullis was located. The small posterns, opening onto the secondary roads, were much simpler. In 401 Honorius, concerned by the threat of the Visigoths, adapted the walls to more sophisticated siege techniques. The walkway and towers were heightened by one storey, the old walkway was covered with a vaulted gallery open towards the city with large arches, while towards the exterior numerous loopholes allowed the archers to have considerable mobility. The military engines were located on the upper walkway, which was also battlemented, and in the towers. Notable changes were also made to the gates.

PORTA MAGGIORE AND EURYSACE'S TOMB

first century BC–first century AD

The double Praenestina and Labicana gate is now known as Porta Maggiore. This comprises the two monumental arches of the Aqua Claudia and the Anio Novus, transformed into city gates by Aurelian and incorporated by Honorius into imposing fortifications that were demolished in 1838. This exposed the curious tomb in travertine of the late republican period built by the baker Eurysaces, who had it decorated with large hollow circles resembling ovens and a bas-relief illustrating his activity.

PORTA ASINARIA

third–fifth centuries AD

This was a secondary gate without large towers and a single opening that Honorius reinforced with imposing semicircular towers incorporating the internal side of the previous square ones, and with an internal rampart.

AURELIANIC WALLS BETWEEN PORTA ARDEATINA AND PORTA APPIA

third–fifth centuries AD

PORTA OSTIENSIS

third–fifth centuries AD

Also known as Porta San Paolo (St Paul's Gate) because the apostle entered Rome through it, it is, together with the Porta Appia, the best preserved of the city's gates. The walls on both sides were removed in the twentieth century. Initially it had two openings flanked by semicircular towers: Maxentius added the curved walls enclosing the courtyard on the inside with the inner archways and faced the towers; Honorius reduced the outer archways to a single passage and heightened the towers. The building now houses the Museo della Via Ostiense, with interesting reconstructions of Ostia and the harbours of Claudius and Trajan.

PYRAMID OF CESTIUS

12 BC

To the left of the Porta Ostiensis stands the distinctive form of the pyramid of Cestius, which, like other pre-existing constructions, was incorporated in the Aurelianic walls in order to save time and money. This is the funerary monument of Gaius Cestius Epulo, bearing witness to an eclectic Egyptianizing mode that inspired other works of this kind in Rome. Originally the monument was several metres higher, but the rise in ground level has deprived it of its soaring lines.

The Roman Aqueducts

The first aqueduct in Rome was built in 312 BC by the censor Appius Claudius Caecus, who was also responsible for the Via Appia. Up to then the inhabitants had drawn water from the Tiber, from the underground water-bearing level reached with wells, urban springs or cisterns where rainwater was collected. The remarkable length of the aqueducts (up to 90 km) was partly due to the distance from the springs, but, above all, it resulted from the need to maintain a constant gradient through long curves elevated on arches or in tunnels bored through hills so that the water could easily flow. In this way, it was possible to avoid the system of siphons, which was complex, expensive and unreliable with the techniques and materials of the period. Each aqueduct was preceded by a reservoir to regulate the input of water, while along it a number of basins served to purify the water. At regular intervals in the underground sections there were manholes allowing access for maintenance work, especially the removal of the lime that would eventually have blocked the channels. The majority of the aqueducts, which came from the east, converged at Porta Maggiore, which stands at the highest point in Rome. From here the water was distributed from a tank (castellum aquae) through lead pipes. In the imperial period the flow of water to the city was 13 cubic metres per second—that is, 1,123,000,000 litres per day (this means that the amount of water available for each inhabitant was twice what it is today). During Constantine's reign the 11 aqueducts fed 11 large thermae, 856 baths, 15 nymphaea, 2 naumachiae, 3 lakes and over 1,300 fountains, as well as imperial properties and, last of all, private consumers. About 700 men were employed on maintenance work. The aqueducts functioned continuously for about 700 or 800 years, until they were destroyed by the Goths when they besieged the city in 537. Only the Aqua Virgo has never ceased to operate, and still today feeds the fountains of the Four Rivers (in Piazza Navona) and Trevi.

this page
AQUA MARCIA (COMBINED WITH THE AQUA TEPULA AND AQUA JULIA)

144–143 BC

overleaf
AQUA CLAUDIA

AD 38–52

this page
PORTA MAGGIORE WITH THE AQUA CLAUDIA

first century AD

The rusticated masonry of the arches is particularly noticeable; typical of numerous buildings of Claudius's reign, this style was revived by many architects in the sixteenth century.

opposite
TOMB OF CAECILIA METELLA

mid-first century BC
Via Appia Antica

Caecilia Metella was the wife of a certain Crassus, probably the son of the wealthy Marcus Licinius Crassus, who allied with Caesar and Pompey. The huge mausoleum (almost 30 metres in diameter and 11 metres in height) attests to the wish of the patrician families to assert themselves in the late republican period. The cylindrical drum is crowned by a splendid frieze in Pentelic marble decorated with reliefs of festoons and bucranes. From 1302 onwards it was used as a tower for the adjacent castle of the Caetani, which, dating from the eleventh century, had been built across the road; the Ghibelline battlements were added at this time. The Church of San Nicola a Capo di Bove is also part of this complex; its picturesque ruins, a rare example of the Gothic style in Rome, are visible on the right.

CIRCUS OF MAXENTIUS

309 AD
Via Appia Antica

Along the Via Appia Antica, just before the tomb of Caecilia Metella, is the imposing complex of the Villa of Maxentius (early fourth century AD), the unfortunate opponent of Constantine, who defeated him in the famous battle of the Milvian Bridge. Next to the imperial palace, yet to be excavated, is Rome's best-preserved circus, of which remain the boundary walls, the towers flanking the starting gates (*carceres*) and the central barrier (*spina*); this is where the obelisk now on the Four Rivers' Fountain in Piazza Navona was formerly located. The circus, over 500 metres in length and 90 metres in width, had a capacity of around 10,000 spectators. To the left of the starting gates, a large quadriporticus, of which the external wall remains, surrounds the mausoleum of Romulus, Maxentius's son. This tomb consists of an imposing circular drum (33 metres in diameter); in front of this stood a rectangular avantcorps that was converted into a farmhouse in the nineteenth century.

The

Mausoleum of Santa Costanza, mosaics in the barrel vault of the ambulatory, early fourth century AD

Cross and the Throne

Early Christian and Early Medieval Art

Man praying
fourth century AD
Catacombs of Ss Peter and Marcellinus

The first symptoms of the decline of the traditional Roman religion first became evident as early as the second century AD, at the time of the crisis that was later to result in Diocletian's reforms. Thus religions of Oriental origin began to spread; often they had a mystical character, especially the cult of Mithras. With the general waning of the ancient religion and the spreading of irrational and salvific cults, it was, however, Christianity that prevailed in Rome, the city that had been the scene of the martyrdom of its first witnesses, including the apostles Peter and Paul. Finally free to practise their religion (following the Edict of Milan, 313), the Christians adopted, modifying them to meet their own requirements, the forms and functions typical of pagan architecture—the basilica and, even more frequently, the centrally-planned building—together with decorative models and schemata deriving from the late Roman figurative repertoire. The pomp and splendour of the Roman Empire were replaced by scenes from the Old and New Testaments, and the glory and exaltation of the defenders of the Christian faith religion. From the paintings in the catacombs to the reliefs on sarcophagi, the events relating to the birth and spread of the new religion are recounted and celebrated in early Christian art, but the themes, techniques and styles are very similar to those of the contemporary pagan art. From the first examples of narrative cycles, such as the ones at Santa Maria Maggiore, on the sarcophagus of Junius Bassus or on the wooden door of Santa Sabina, came the very rich repertoire of themes that was elaborated

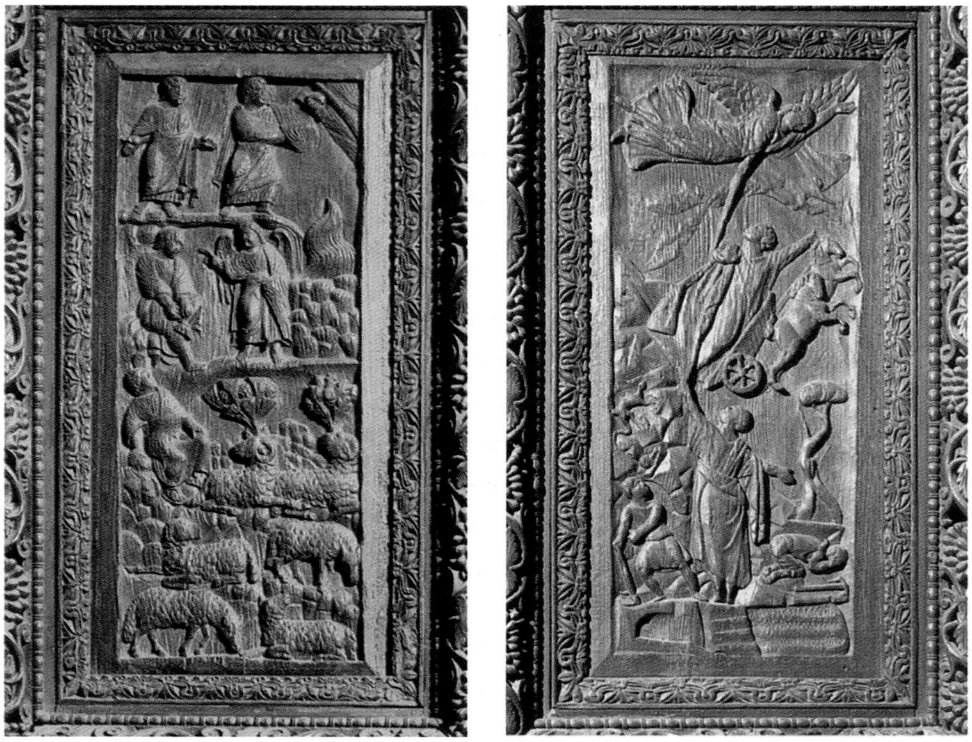

Wooden door, detail
fifth century AD
Santa Sabina

Sarcophagus of Marcus Claudianus
AD 330–335
Museo Nazionale Romano, Palazzo Massimo

by western artists over the following centuries. Under Constantine, the first Christian basilicas were constructed, including St Peter's, which was built over a pagan cemetery on the right bank of the Tiber, and St John Lateran, in a part of the city yet to be urbanized and mainly occupied by huge private estates and gardens that were completely extraneous to the monumental and religious heart of the city where the ancient gods still dwelt.

The rapid decline in imperial power over the next two centuries took place in parallel to the growth of the prestige of the pope, who acquired authority not only in the religious sphere, but also in the juridical and administrative ones as well. At the same time, the population rapidly decreased. The destruction of the old buildings and monuments, which, by and large, had survived the dramatic events of the wars against the Goths (c. 535–555), did not cease after the abrogation of the law forbidding the transformation of pagan buildings into churches. This paved the way for the despoliation of the old buildings and innumerable splendid edifices were transformed into sources of materials and even plundered of their precious sculpted marbles so they could be converted into lime. The centuries that followed are the most obscure in the city's history. The alliance with the Franks, the coronation of Charlemagne in 800 and the important developments resulting from this did not prevent the Basilica of St Peter's from being sacked by Saracen pirates in 846. In order to avoid further danger, Leo IV surrounded the basilica and the adjacent district with the walls that were named after him (Leonine Walls), almost as if he wished to physically confirm the secularization of the pope's power and interests. The fundamental weakness of papal power was, however, counterbalanced by the growth in the independence of a number of important baronial families, who transformed the ancient monuments into their fortresses against the backdrop of a city that was becoming increasingly depopulated and poor.

Elders of the Apocalypse,
detail of the mosaic on the triumphal arch
ninth century
Santa Prassede

GOLD-GLASS ROUNDEL WITH BUSTS OF SAINTS PETER AND PAUL

fourth century AD, glass and gold leaf
Biblioteca Apostolica Vaticana, Vatican

Works of art in glass were extremely common during the imperial period, and those with the decoration obtained by sandwiching designs in gold leaf between two layers of glass were in great demand. In general they portrayed the owner accompanied by an inscription with well-wishing words. This practice continued after the arrival of the new religion, but the rich Christian clients wanted the secular portraits to be replaced by images of Christ, the apostles and other sacred subjects. This example here shows a rather stereotyped image of the two apostles, represented in profile and crowded together in the limited space available.

SARCOPHAGUS SHOWING THE DENIAL OF PETER

fragment of the front
AD 330–350
white marble
Museo Pio Cristiano, Vatican

CATHEDRA PETRI (ST PETER'S THRONE)

c. 870–875
wood and ivory
St Peter's, Vatican

Practically invisible under the theatrical contrivance created by Bernini in the seventeenth century, the ancient wooden throne, formerly believed to be that of the apostle, probably belonged to the emperor Charles the Bald, and only later became the pope's throne. The precious relic consists of a wooden seat, decorated with beautifully figured ivory plaques, that was originally kept in one of the monasteries built near the old St Peter's. After various vicissitudes in 1666, it was placed in the apse of the new St Peter's by Pope Alexander VII, who wanted it to be glorified as a venerable trophy.

above
SARCOPHAGUS OF JUNIUS BASSUS

AD 359
marble
Museo del Tesoro, St Peter's, Vatican

This sarcophagus is one of the masterpieces of its day, with its elegant figures carved, almost in the round, in a classicizing style. However, the spectacular use of the architecture, which is, in reality, little more than a decorative frame, betrays the fact that it is the product of a new culture. Each compartment contains a scene and the events are disposed according to a specific scheme on two registers, with the symbolic correspondence of such episodes as Christ enthroned and his entry into Jerusalem (the prince comes to reign in the city as in the upper scene he reigns over the cosmos). The workmanship is outstanding, with a wealth of decorative detail.

left and opposite
SARCOPHAGUS WITH A PROCESSION

view of a side and detail
third century AD
Greek marble with traces of colour
Museo Nazionale Romano, Palazzo Massimo

There have been various interpretations of this fragment of a sarcophagus. It may portray the coronation of the extremely young Gordian III (238–244), hastily elected before a popular uprising imposed him by force. It may, however, simply represent the procession accompanying a young consul who has just been elected to his office. Whether he is Gordian III or a consul, the young personage portrayed with extraordinary vibrancy is an unforgettable protagonist of a period of great uncertainty and turmoil, perfectly conveyed by his expression of wide-eyed astonishment.

above
CATACOMBS OF SAINT SEBASTIAN

view of the triclia (courtyard) and piazzuola (open hollow) with the mausolea second–fourth centuries AD Basilica of San Sebastiano

Built in the fourth century AD over the cemetery *ad catacumbes* on the Via Appia where, according to tradition, Saints Peter and Paul were temporarily buried, the basilica was later dedicated to St Sebastian, who was also buried here. In 1608–1613 the architects Flaminio Ponzio and Giovanni Vasanzio rebuilt the church in Mannerist style. In 1933 the old basilica was partially reconstructed. A staircase leads down to the catacombs of St Sebastian, which, because they have always been accessible, are in poor condition, with numerous tombs, some of them decorated.

opposite
COLOSSAL HEAD OF CONSTANTINE

early fourth century AD marble Palazzo dei Conservatori

These fragments are part of a colossal statue of Constantine, originally 12 metres in height, formerly in the apse of the Basilica of Maxentius. The head is one of the most striking examples of the portraiture of the fourth century, with its brutal simplification intended to render the quasi-divine awfulness of the emperor's gaze. Many representations of Christ the Pantocrator in the apses of medieval churches derive from this iconographic concept.

this page
CATACOMBS OF ST AGNESE

second–fifth centuries AD

These catacombs are located next to the famous Basilica of Sant'Agnese fuori le Mura, built in AD 342 over the catacombs containing the grave of the saint, who was martyred in AD 251 during the persecution of Decius. The catacombs, which are devoid of paintings and other decorative elements, are divided into three main sections, the first dating from the late second and early third centuries; the second from the third and early fourth centuries; the third from the fourth and fifth centuries.

opposite
CATACOMBS OF SAINTS MARCELLINUS AND PETER

second half of third century–sixth century AD

Constructed during the third century AD, these catacombs, where various martyrs of the persecution of Diocletian were buried, contain a wide range of paintings, generally of poor quality, featuring biblical scenes, such as the ones shown here representing *Daniel in the Lions' Den* and the *Moses Striking Water from the Rock*, and also classical banqueting scenes or ones depicting athletes. In general, the figures in the paintings are sketched out hastily and adhere to stereotyped schemata.

Opus Sectile

From the fourth century onwards it became more common to decorate particularly important rooms not only with paintings or mosaics, but also with inlays of marble and coloured stone creating brilliant colour effects. There is considerable evidence that the technique originated in Egypt and that numerous panels were prepared in Alexandrian workshops and then sent to the clients, ready to be installed as required, generally on walls. The term used to describe this form of stone inlay, composed of sawn pieces of marble and other materials, is *opus sectile*. Some of the finest examples come from the Basilica of Junius Bassus, who was probably the father of the prefect of the same name who died in AD 359 after converting to Christianity and was buried in the equally famous sarcophagus.

SCENE OF A CHARIOT IN A CIRCUS

from the Basilica of Junius Bassus on the Esquiline
fourth century AD
panel in opus sectile
Museo Nazionale Romano, Palazzo Massimo

The panel represents a consul in a chariot accompanied by horsemen belonging to circus teams: it is an outstanding example of the development of the new art towards formal abstraction and two-dimensionality, both characteristics particularly suited to the technique of the *opus sectile*.

HEAD OF HELIOS/SOL INVICTUS

from the Mithraeum of Santa Prisca on the Aventine
third century AD
panel in opus sectile
Museo Nazionale Romano, Palazzo Massimo

This remarkable head, which portrays Mithras as *Sol Invictus* and seems to be animated by a romantic spirit of Hellenistic origin, comes from a building on the Aventine converted in the second century AD into a Mithraeum. This work attests to the penetration of Rome by the mystery cult of Mithras, imported by legionaries, merchants and slaves from the regions of central and western Asia.

MYTH OF HYLAS

from the Basilica of Junius Bassus on the Esquiline
fourth century AD
panel in opus sectile
Museo Nazionale Romano, Palazzo Massimo

This splendid wall panel depicting an episode from the myth of Hylas—a handsome youth, who, during the expedition of the Argonauts, went to fetch water from a pool where he drowned when some nymphs fell in love with him and pulled him in—may be a product of a workshop in Alexandria, which, during the whole of the Byzantine period, exported refined works of art throughout the empire. The presence of Egyptianizing decorative motifs associated with the cult of Isis (also widespread in imperial and late-imperial Rome) points to Alexandrian craftsmen rather than ones from Antioch, another great exporter of precious works. The present panel, in sawn marble, hard stones and glass paste, is characterized by the excellent quality of the colour, with the superb contrast of the bright red mantle against the violet and dark green of the background and the intense blue tones of the water.

SARCOPHAGUS OF HELENA

fourth century AD
porphyry
Museo Pio Clementino, Vatican

This magnificent sarcophagus in red porphyry, perhaps made by Egyptian craftsmen, comes from the mausoleum of Helena, commonly known as Tor Pignattara. It is possible that it was originally intended for Constantius Chlorus, the husband of Helena, Constantine the Great's mother. The hardness of the material, although not suitable for rendering softened outlines, delicate chiaroscuro and precise details, is perfect for the antinaturalistic schematism of the late-antique vision.

MAUSOLEUM OF SANTA COSTANZA

interior
early fourth century AD

Built around 340 AD for Constantine's daughters, Constantina and Helena,

this mausoleum was converted into a baptistery and then into a church in 1254. It is an interesting example of a centrally-planned building, formed by two concentric rings, one higher than the other. The monumental interior is characterized by the relationship in terms of structure and light between the central circular space and the ambulatory going around it. The dome in the former rises from an arcade supported by twelve pairs of columns with superb composite capitals linked to each other by long architraves, and it is excellently lit by twelve large windows. The ambulatory shrouded in silent, mystical half-light, has barrel vaults decorated with mosaics, partly inspired by the Christian iconography of the grape-harvest, but still linked to the tradition of classical art. The building's circular form is an explicit reference to the Holy Sepulchre in Jerusalem.

SANTA COSTANZA

exterior
early fourth century AD

SANTA COSTANZA

mosaics in the barrel vault
of the ambulatory
early fourth century AD

Since the mosaics in the dome and on the walls have disappeared, those on the ambulatory vault, although considerably restored, are all that remain to give us an idea of the magnificence of the original decoration, which extended to the floor, walls and dome.
A few Renaissance drawings allow us to know at least the subject of the wall mosaics: biblical scenes with human figures above a watercourse where putti and wild animals swim.
The mosaics of the vault, on a white ground, are partly purely decorative and partly reproduce ornamental heads and scenes of the grape-harvest with putti, animals and vines.
It is probable that they allude to heaven. The style is very close to that of mosaic floors—which must also have existed in Santa Costanza—of the same period.
The mosaics in the large symmetrical niches, dating from the late fourth century, or shortly after, probably resemble the huge apsidal compositions, now lost, in the first Constantinian churches.
Unfortunately, the poor workmanship and mediocre restoration make these theophanies with an imperial flavour rather unattractive.

SANTA COSTANZA

view of the ambulatory
early fourth century AD

opposite
SANT'AGNESE FUORI LE MURA

interior
fourth–fifth centuries AD

This church, built in 342 AD over St Agnese's grave, was reconstructed in the seventh century and subsequently restored on various occasions.
The imposing apsidal area is all that remains of the original building; the church is built on a basilican plan, with the nave divided from the aisles by reused Roman columns with Corinthian capitals. The elegant women's galleries, dating from the seventh century, are of Byzantine origin. The coffered ceiling was added in 1606. In the semi-dome of the apse, the splendid mosaic representing St Agnese amidst the flames between popes Symmachus and Honorius, the latter holding a model of the church, is clearly of Byzantine inspiration. This is demonstrated by the formal schematization, the flattening of the figures, which are rigidly frontal, and the abstraction of the gold ground composed of concentric rings culminating in the hand of God proffering the martyr's crown.

SANTO STEFANO ROTONDO

exterior and interior
fifth century AD

Dating from the fifth century AD and modelled on the Holy Sepulchre in Jerusalem, this was the first centrally-planned church to be built in Rome. It had two concentric ambulatories flanked by magnificent colonnades, the most external of which was ingeniously intersected by the arms of a Greek cross surrounding the central cylinder. In 1454 extensive restoration work was carried out, which, unfortunately, led to the elimination of the external ambulatory.

ST PETER AND ST COSMAS

detail
first half of the sixth century AD
apse mosaic
Santi Cosma e Damiano

This basilica was created by joining one of the libraries of the Forum of Peace (built by Vespasian from 71 to 75 AD) and the so-called Temple of Romulus. In the present building, constructed in the seventeenth century, there are important mosaics dating from the sixth–seventh centuries (during the pontificates of Felix IV and Sergius I), still partially linked, with their powerful plasticity, to the classical tradition.
Like other early medieval mosaics and frescoes, they attest to the continuing vitality of the ancient tradition that, together with the innovations from the Byzantine world, gave birth to the new Romanesque style in Rome several centuries later.

CHRIST ENTHRONED AND APOSTLES

early fifth century AD
apse mosaic
Santa Pudenziana

Santa Pudenziana was founded in the fourth century AD as "titulus Pudentis," a Roman house that had been converted into a baths building and then used as a place of worship. The church has preserved its Romanesque campanile, while the façade dates from the nineteenth century and the original basilican layout with a nave and two aisles was modified in 1588. A mosaic representing Christ enthroned flanked by the apostles survives in the apse: still adhering to the canons of perspective space and classical naturalism in the lower register, it is visionary and "medieval" in the upper one, where the apparition of the cross stands out between the symbols of the Evangelists.

SAN PAOLO FUORI LE MURA

interior and façade
fourth–nineteenth centuries

Built in the fourth century AD in a monumental style, this famous basilica, the largest in Rome after St Peter's, has been embellished over the centuries with magnificent works of art. In 1823 it was devastated by a terrible fire that only spared the area of the transept and part of the façade, which was then demolished when it was decided to rebuild it in its original form. The result was a "brightly polished utopia" that was consecrated in 1854, but the work continued until the following century. In front of the church is an imposing quadriporticus overlooked by the uninspiring façade. The interior is notable for the sheer size of the nave flanked by double aisles, divided by 80 columns in Montorfano granite, similar, despite the coldness of the reconstruction, to that of the great Roman basilicas (length 161 metres, width 65 metres; nave 30 metres in height, 25 metres in width). While the nineteenth-century decorations are of little artistic interest, what remains of the great basilica attests to its lost splendour. Beyond the triumphal arch, with its considerably restored mosaics, the soaring Gothic lines of Arnolfo di Cambio's ciborium stand out in this "antique" space. Paul's tomb (fourth century) is under the altar, while on the right is the very ornate candelabrum for the paschal candle, an elaborate work by Nicolò di Angelo and Pietro Vassalletto (twelfth century). The much restored apse mosaic dates from around 1220.

opposite
CHRIST BLESSING

ninth century
apse mosaic
Santa Prassede, Chapel of San Zenone

CHRIST IN A CLIPEUS BORNE BY FOUR ANGELS

ninth century
mosaic on the vault
Santa Prassede, Chapel of San Zenone

Santa Prassede is a very old *titulus* (a house adapted to the needs of worship) that has been restored on various occasions. The interior with a nave and two aisles preserves the layout and columns of the ninth century—although the latter were partially transformed into piers in the Middle Ages—and the most important cycles of Byzantine mosaics in Rome. On the right side is the Chapel of San Zenone, preceded by a portal made with reused materials, built by Paschal I (817–824) as a mausoleum for his mother. The cross-shaped plan, the corner columns (also spoils) and the cross-vault are in classical style. The mosaic decoration is superb, characterized by formalism of Byzantine origin; although the execution is a little heavy-handed, the dense light and thick outlines of the figures result in a concrete sense of space and volume alien to eastern art. The mosaics dating from the same period on the triumphal arch and in the apse are equally important.

on this page, anticlockwise
HOSPITALITY OF ABRAHAM

CROSSING OF THE RED SEA

THE HOLY ARK TRANSPORTED BEYOND THE JORDAN

fifth century AD
mosaics in the nave
Santa Maria Maggiore

The famous basilica, founded in the fourth century AD, was altered on various occasions from the fifth to the eighteenth centuries, when the façade was rebuilt. The interior, however, preserves the fourth-century structure almost intact.
Above the entablature are the 36 mosaic panels dating from the pontificate of Sixtus III (fifth century, in a fair state of repair with infilling dating from the sixteenth-century restoration). With their vigorous narrative tone, notable inventiveness and bright colours, they are among the last great manifestations of the artistic style of antiquity.
Dating from the same period, the mosaic on the triumphal arch, with episodes of the coming and childhood of Christ, is characterized by a more vivid and symbolic style.

SANTA MARIA IN DOMNICA

interior
seventh–ninth centuries

The name may derive from the term dominicum used to refer to the first Christian places of worship. Built in the seventh century, it was reconstructed by Paschal I two centuries later and restored in 1514 by Andrea Sansovino. The interior has a basilican layout with a nave and two aisles divided by 18 antique grey granite columns, crowned by classical Corinthian capitals. The coffered wooden ceiling dates from the sixteenth century. The triumphal arch is supported by splendid antique porphyry columns with Ionic capitals.

VIRGIN AND CHILD, ANGELS AND POPE PASCHAL I

ninth century
apse mosaic
Santa Maria in Domnica

On the imposing triumphal arch and in the semi-dome of the apse, the ninth-century mosaics are a splendid example of art of Byzantine inspiration.

CHRIST WITH POPE GREGORY IV AND SAINTS

mid-ninth century
apse mosaic
San Marco

This church, founded by Pope Mark in AD 336 and renovated on a number of occasions, was rebuilt in 1466–1469 and altered in the seventeenth and eighteenth centuries. In the apse, dating from the ninth century, there are magnificent mosaics (827–844), with the glittering light of the gold ground, representing Christ and various saints, among whom Gregory IV is identifiable by his square halo; he was patron of both the church, as is demonstrated by the model he is holding, and the mosaics. On the lower register, the lamb and twelve sheep symbolize Christ and the apostles.

CHRIST WITH SAINTS AND POPE PASCHAL I

820
apse mosaic
Santa Cecilia in Trastevere

This magnificent basilica, erected in the twelfth and thirteenth centuries on the site of a fifth-century church, has been rebuilt on various occasions, considerably altering its medieval appearance.
The interior, with a nave flanked by two aisles divided by piers incorporating the original columns, now has an airy eighteenth-century atmosphere. The semi-dome of the apse has an important mosaic dating from around 820, which, although modified, has an explicitly visionary character: the pope holding a model of the church may be recognized by the square halo that denotes living persons. He is surrounded by saints, Christian symbols and the background of quasi-abstract clouds. The lower register is of a more explicitly symbolic character: instead of the Redeemer and his saints, there is the Lamb of God flanked by two processions of lambs representing the faithful.

Glimm

Pietro Cavallini, *Life of the Virgin: Presentation*, 1293, mosaic, Santa Maria in Trastevere

ers in the Dark Ages

Around the Year 1000

For the cultural life of Rome, the beginning of the eleventh century was a moment of continuity with the previous period. During the early Middle Ages, while the city was troubled by conflicts between the leading families of the local aristocracy and between them and the Holy Roman Emperors, in the artistic output the desire to refer in a more or less conscious and programmatic manner to the late antique and early Christian forms is, in fact, evident in both architecture and decorative schemes. Following the sacking and destruction of numerous churches carried out in 1084 by the Normans under Robert Guiscard when they came to the aid of Pope Gregory VII, who was besieged by the troops of the emperor Henry IV, Paschal II (1099–1118), with the dual aim of reasserting papal power and restoring its ancient dignity to Rome, started an ambitious programme of reconstruction of the city's churches. This was continued by his successors, Honorius II (1124–1130) and Innocent III (1198–1216), under whom the early Christian Renaissance reached its apex. Among the most important buildings reconstructed during the twelfth century and inspired by the architectural designs of the early Christian basilicas were Santa Maria in Cosmedin, Santi Quattro Coronati, San Crisogono, San Clemente and Santa Maria in Trastevere.

Santi Giovanni e Paolo, campanile, c. 1150

Some of the major decorative schemes of the period, including the apse mosaics of San Clemente and Santa Maria in Trastevere, were still influenced by the late-antique repertoire. One of the most innovative areas of the artistic output of medieval Rome is undoubtedly constituted by the thriving activity of the marble-workers, who established family-run workshops that, in the twelfth and thirteenth centuries, specialized in the production of ecclesiastical ornaments and architectural decoration. Their refined art, inspired by the repertoires of antiquity, but reinterpreted with lively imagination and vivid colours, is known as Cosmati work, which is named after one of the leading families—together with the Vassalletto—in this field. The aspiration to greatness of the Roman papacy continued also during the thirteenth century: although, as regards architecture, they were still linked to late and traditional forms and it was difficult for the Gothic style to penetrate the city (the few exceptions include Santa Maria sopra Minerva, the Sancta Sanctorum and Santa Maria in Aracoeli), starting with the pontificate of Nicholas III (1277–1280), the Roman artistic milieu in the years preceding the first jubilee (1300) experienced a period of great vitality. Rome, in fact, not only saw the presence of some of the most innovatory Italian artists of the day, such as Cimabue in 1272, Arnolfo di Cambio from 1275 to 1296 and Giotto, who stayed in the city on a number of occasions in the late thirteenth and early fourteenth centuries, but, above all, it became one of the main centres for the elaboration of an advanced pictorial language aimed at the definitive abandonment of the Byzantine stylistic forms through the rediscovery of space and volume. The protagonists of the renaissance of painting in Rome were the great local masters Pietro Cavallini, Jacopo Torriti and Filippo Rusuti, who designed mosaics and painted frescoes in the main churches. Thanks to these artists, Rome contended with the Florence—where the artistic milieu was dominated by Giotto—for the supremacy for the renewal of painting in a naturalistic sense, obtained through the revival of monumentality of form, as a result, above all, of a new interest in the art of antiquity. The death of Boniface VIII in 1305, the removal of the papal seat to Avignon from 1308 to 1376 and, after the return of the papacy to Rome, the schism in the West (1378–1418) constituted one of the most difficult and confused periods in the history of the Church, leading to a notable hiatus in Rome's artistic output.

Behind the Trajan Markets stands the Torre delle Milizie, thirteenth century

Pietro Cavallini
Life of the Virgin: Annunciation
1291
Santa Maria in Trastevere

CROSS OF JUSTIN II

570 AD
Museo del Tesoro, St Peter's, Vatican

One of the most interesting of the precious objects kept in the treasury of St Peter's, is the *Crux vaticana*, donated by the Byzantine emperor Justin II to the Church of Rome, perhaps as an *ex voto* to be venerated on Peter's tomb. The portraits of the emperor and his wife Sophia, who are also mentioned in the inscription, are chased on the back of the cross. Entirely covered with silver gilt foil, the reliquary, which contains fragments of the Holy Cross, is studded along the edges with precious stones of different colours and types—such a emeralds, jaspers and aquamarines—and glass paste.

DALMATIC OF CHARLEMAGNE

Ninth–fourteenth centuries ?
Museo del Tesoro, St Peter's, Vatican

Erroneously believed to be the robe worn by Charlemagne when he was crowned as emperor in 800, this precious dalmatic in Turkish silk is embellished with polychrome, gold and silver embroidery representing the Transfiguration: in the centre, Christ ascends to heaven in a fiery aureole, flanked by Moses, with the tables of the Law, and Elijah. In the lower part, the apostles Peter, John and James watch the event, while, amid the outcrops of rock, and on the sleeves, there are other scenes from the Gospels. A motif of Greek crosses covers the rest of the robe. The dating of the splendid vestment is open to debate: some believe it to be the work of Roman embroiderers in the ninth or tenth centuries, others that it is a Byzantine product of the fourteenth century.

ENTHRONED VIRGIN AND CHILD WITH ANGEL AND DONOR

(known as the "Madonna della Clemenza")
sixth–eighth centuries
tempera on panel
Santa Maria in Trastevere

This remarkable icon in Santa Maria in Trastevere portrays, in the centre, an immobile and hieratic Madonna in the guise of a Byzantine empress, with rich robes studded with precious stones, like the throne on which she is seated. Kneeling at her feet is the donor, while two angels disposed symmetrically on either side, but with slight variations in their positions and poses, lend vitality to the central figure, which has the evocative power of an idol. The function of some icons was, in fact, to substitute the real presence of the imperial family: in this case the queen of the earth, the empress of Constantinople, is identified with the Queen of Heaven. Believed to be the work of western artists, probably Roman, but strongly influenced by the Byzantine manner, the icon is datable to a period extending from the sixth to the eighth centuries.

Panel Paintings

The majority of panel paintings in medieval Rome consisted of icons portraying the Virgin Mary. Large-format, painted in tempera on panel or else on canvas that was then laid on a panel, the oldest examples —traditionally believed to be of eastern origin— are datable to a period extending from the sixth to the eighth centuries. Their production was often linked to a special occasion, such as the re-consecration of a church, and they quickly became the object of popular devotion, which attributed supernatural and thaumaturgic powers to them. The oldest prototypes, deriving from Byzantine iconography and stylistic features, albeit interpreted in the western manner, were repeated with innumerable variations in the following centuries. With the exception of this type of image with a liturgical function, until the beginning of the thirteenth century paintings executed specifically for the altars of churches and basilicas were rare.

ICON OF THE VIRGIN HODEGETRIA

c. 609
panel
Pantheon

Of the four ancient icons of the Virgin present in Rome believed to have been painted by St Luke, this work is the only one that can be dated with certainty: it was, in fact, executed around 609, when the Pantheon was converted into the Church of Santa Maria ad Martyres. The almost supernatural vitality of the image depends on the way the Virgin and Child appear to gaze intently at the spectator. The modulation in the light and shade of the Child's head has been executed very skilfully in.

Masters Giovanni and Nicola

LAST JUDGEMENT

late twelfth–early thirteenth centuries
panel
Pinacoteca Vaticana, Vatican

Signed by the Roman painters Giovanni and Nicola, this remarkable work, one of the few on panel paintings dating from this period, is well orchestrated both from the point of view of the composition, divided into horizontal registers, and the variety of the colours used. Although the Byzantine stylistic forms still predominate, there is new fluency in the rendering of some of the figures.

The Towers of Medieval Rome

The skyline of medieval Rome was dominated by the tall Romanesque campanili of the churches, the ancient monuments and, above all, the numerous towers that rose above the dense urban fabric, as may be seen in the fresco with a famous view of Rome painted by Masolino da Panicale in the Baptistery at Castiglione Olona, in Lombardy, in 1435. An old history of the city records almost nine hundred towers, built exclusively by the leading noble families in order to flaunt their power, as well as for defensive purposes. Now isolated or in ruins, the imposing medieval towers, built from the eleventh to the fifteenth centuries, crowned with swallowtail or square merlons, once formed part of fortresses that were later destroyed or converted into aristocratic residences. One of the districts with the largest number of towers is the Rione Monti, where the thirteenth-century Torre del Grillo, the Torre dell'Arcioni and, above all, the Torre delle Milizie are all located. The last of these is a massive brick construction erected at the beginning of the thirteenth century by the Conti family; located in a commanding position on the Quirinal Hill, it is one of the most imposing medieval buildings remaining in Rome.

MEDIEVAL BUILDINGS AND THE TORRE DELLE MILIZIE

thirteenth century

This colossal tower, formerly attached to an edifice known as the *militiae palatium*, was once part of a fortified quarter comprising various buildings standing around a courtyard in the centre of which the lofty tower stood. The medieval building incorporates the remains of a previous structure, perhaps built during Augustus's or Trajan's reign to dominate and defend the forum extending below it.

TORRE DELLE MILIZIE

thirteenth century

Only two-thirds of the tower, formerly three storeys in height, remains, with an overall height of over 50 metres. The solid, square first storey, in which there are marble-framed loopholes, is surmounted by a re-entrant second storey; adorned with slender buttresses, it has rounded corners and is crowned by battlements. The tower's original appearance may be seen in the famous view of Rome painted by Cimabue in one of the vaults of the upper Church of San Francesco in Assisi.

HOUSE OF THE CRESCENZI

eleventh century

The inscription over the front door, stating that the house intended to revive the splendour of Rome, attests to the owner's desire to restore the magnificence of ancient Rome in the context of a private building. The use of brick demi-columns engaged in the wall and alternating with architraved pilasters echoes the models of antiquity and is typical of Roman architecture of this period. The entablature and the brackets with volutes, sphinxes and lacunars are composed of fragments taken from ancient buildings.

Campanili

In the period from the tenth to the thirteenth centuries there were no major innovations in architecture in Rome: the buildings were, in fact, very classical in style and the religious architecture was still closely linked to the traditional type of the basilica. The real change consisted, however, in the richness of the church ornaments, the construction of splendid cloisters and in the great variety of the campanili. Although influenced by the Lombard Romanesque style, the Roman campanili are characterized by the division of the storeys, which is stressed by string-courses. The division is further emphasized by the cornices corresponding with the springing line of the arches over the one- and two-light windows in the façades of the bell-towers. An original feature is the frequent insertion of ceramic bowls in various colours (red, green, yellow) in the wall surrounding the windows.

SANTI QUATTRO CORONATI

entrance tower
ninth–twelfth centuries

This massive bell-tower was originally built for defensive purposes.

SANTA MARIA IN COSMEDIN

façade and campanile
twelfth century

This bell-tower is one of the most interesting structures of medieval Rome: with two rows of two-light windows and five of three-light ones separated by string-courses, it is adjacent to the simple gable-topped façade with three round-headed windows. In front of this is the entrance porch. The fountain in the foreground dates from the early eighteenth century.

SANTI GIOVANNI E PAOLO

campanile
twelfth century

At the side of the monastery adjacent to the Basilica of Santi Giovanni e Paolo stands this majestic campanile, built during the pontificate of Paschal II (1099–1118) by Cardinal Teobaldo, who also reconstructed the monastery, which had been destroyed by the Normans. Built on a massive base of travertine, the bell-tower is divided into different storeys by elaborate string-courses: on the last six storeys numerous coloured ceramic bowls and inlays of porphyry and serpentine have been inserted in the wall, in accordance with the taste of the period. The massive structure is lightened by the numerous two-light windows on its sides: on the four highest storeys the openings are two on each side. The use of bare brick for the construction of Romanesque campanili is, in effect, the continuation of the building traditions of the reigns of Trajan and Hadrian, when the workers were particularly skilled in the use of this material.

TRIUMPH OF THE CROSS

1128
mosaic
apse semi-dome, San Clemente

Blue and green acanthus scrolls starting from a bush at the foot of the cross stand out against the glittering gold ground. Amid the vegetal arabesques, animals of a symbolic nature (doves and deer) and sacred objects give the work greater vitality and stress its message of redemption.

MIRACLE OF THE BLACK SEA

late eleventh–early twelfth centuries
fresco
San Clemente

One of the most outstanding of the precious works of art in San Clemente, this important fresco cycle devoted to the lives of Saints Clement and Alexis is located in the lower church.

CHRIST AND THE VIRGIN ENTHRONED WITH SAINTS AND POPE INNOCENT II

1140–1143
mosaic
apse semi-dome, Santa Maria in Trastevere

The huge mosaic in the apse semi-dome of the basilica is an example of the revival of classicism and the return to the themes and iconography of the early Christian period that characterized the artistic output of Rome from the eleventh to the mid-twelfth centuries. Below the narrow band with the Lamb of God and Twelve Sheep, an allusion to the apostles, are recognizable, between the windows, some of the scenes of the remarkable *Life of the Virgin* executed by Pietro Cavallini in 1291 or, according to some scholars, 1296.

SANTA MARIA IN TRASTEVERE

façade
twelfth century

Traditionally considered to be the first church to officially open for Christian worship, the basilica, founded by St Callistus at the beginning of the third century, has been rebuilt on numerous occasions, as is evident on the exterior: the portico was designed by Carlo Fontana (1702), while the façade crowned by a pediment and the massive campanile are in Romanesque style (twelfth century).

CLIVO DI SCAURO

Fifth–thirteenth centuries

On the left side of the Church of Santi Giovanni e Paolo, this striking sequence of seven arches serving as buttresses spans the Clivo di Scauro—the Clivus Scaurus of the ancient Romans—leading to the apse of the church. The dating of the arches varies from the fifth to the thirteenth centuries.

SANTI GIOVANNI E PAOLO

exterior
fourth–thirteenth centuries

Like many of the oldest basilicas in Rome, also the one dedicated to Saints John and Paul is the result of additions and rebuilding over the centuries: the architraved portico was built in the twelfth century to replace the old narthex; the gallery above it dates from the beginning of the thirteenth century; the upper part of the façade is dominated by five blind arches with re-used columns of the third century AD. The dome visible on the right over the Chapel of San Paolo della Croce was built in the nineteenth century.

SAN LORENZO FUORI LE MURA

exterior
thirteenth centuries

The medieval appearance of the basilica dates from the pontificate of Honorius III, who, between 1216 and 1227, combined two adjacent buildings by demolishing the apses. The thirteenth-century portico in front of the façade was probably built by the Vassalletto family: a series of marble columns with Ionic capitals of antique origin support an architrave adorned with mosaics and roundels in porphyry and serpentine, techniques and materials typical of medieval Rome. The use of the lion protomes on the eaves is of classical derivation. The three round-headed windows in the upper part of the façade were returned to their original form by the restoration of a "purist" type that eliminated the subsequent alterations.

ST JOHN LATERAN

cloister
1215–1230

One of the most outstanding cloisters of thirteenth-century Rome is the one at St John Lateran, a masterpiece by Niccolò di Angelo and Pietro Vassalletto, members of one of the leading families of marble workers in city.

SANTI QUATTRO CORONATI

cloister
early thirteenth century

This elegant cloister is surrounded by a series of round arches supported by coupled colonnettes.

SAN PAOLO FUORI LE MURA

detail of the decoration of the cloister
late twelfth–early thirteenth centuries

"Doctissimi magistri": this is how the old sources described the marble workers active in the twelfth and thirteenth centuries in Rome, drawing attention to the explicit use of the styles of antiquity by these outstanding artists. Like the one at St John Lateran, this cloister was built by the famous Vassalletto family: the typical decoration known as Cosmati work is evident in the entablature above the round arches, adorned with porphyry discs and mosaic made of small, coloured tesserae.

SAN PAOLO FUORI LE MURA

cloister
late twelfth–early thirteenth centuries

Small in size, but remarkably rich in decorative elements, the cloister at San Paolo fuori le Mura is composed of groups of four small arches separated by pilasters. Pairs of smooth, octagonal and twisted columns, many decorated with inlaid mosaic, alternate along the sides, giving the complex great vitality with regard to both form and colour, but without losing the taste, of classical derivation, for well-balanced, harmonious architecture.

CHRIST IN MAJESTY AND FIVE APOSTLES

1198–1216
embossed, engraved and gilded copper, pearls and enamel
Museo Pio Cristiano, Vatican

One of the most important exhibits in the Museo Pio Cristiano is this series of statues made with what is known as the appliqué technique: they are figurines in copper that has been embossed, engraved, gilded and decorated with pearls and precious Limoges enamel. Stylistically similar to each other, the statues formed part of the antependium of St Peter's tomb in the Vatican. In the centre of a group of five apostles, is the figure of Christ blessing, wearing a splendid crown **embellished with gems.**

following page
SANCTA SANCTORUM

floor with Cosmati work
last quarter of the thirteenth century

This beautiful floor in the Sancta Sanctorum is a splendid example of Cosmati work. In the centre is a series of roundels in porphyry on a white ground, surrounded by inlaid serpentine with the characteristic decorative motifs, while, by the walls, are aligned rectangular slabs of porphyry, also surrounded by decorative motifs in Cosmati work. The overall effect is that of sort of visual route drawn on the floor, from the entrance to the altar, for the benefit of the processions coming to this holy place from the papal palaces.

Sancta Sanctorum

On the architrave separating the apse from the rest of the chapel is the following short inscription: "Non est in toto sanctior orbe locus" (There is no holier place in all the world), which stresses the special significance of the old palatine chapel of the Lateran Palace intended to house the most precious relics of western Christianity. Possibly founded as early as the sixth century and dedicated to St Lawrence, the Sancta Sanctorum was given its present appearance by the reconstruction carried out by Pope Nicholas III (1277–1280), who consecrated it in 1279. The layout is very simple: a large square hall is covered with a pointed cross-vault, supported by four corner columns; two architraved columns mark the entrance to the square apse and frame the venerated *acheiropoeitis* ("made without hands") image of the Saviour. The encounter between the technique of the Roman marble workers (the Cosmati-work decoration of the chapel is signed by "Magister Cosmatus") and the Gothic style of the anonymous architect has produced a space combining, in an organic manner, tradition and innovation.

SANCTA SANCTORUM

lunette in the east wall
last quarter of the thirteenth century
fresco

The east wall has one of the most important scenes of the fresco cycle adorning the chapel: on the left of the high window Saints Peter and Paul are portrayed together with Pope Nicholas III, who built the chapel and is shown kneeling as he offers the model of the Sancta Sanctorum to Christ, represented in the panel on the right enthroned and flanked by two angels.

NON·EST·IN·TOTO·SANCTIOR·ORBE·LOCVS

SANCTA SANCTORUM

interior of the chapel facing the altar
last quarter of the thirteenth century

The walls of the Sancta Sanctorum are covered with a high marble dado, consisting of slabs of antique origin, above which is a blind arcade composed of small trefoil arches supported by elegant twisted colonnettes: each niche is frescoed with figures of saints, apostles and popes.
This is clearly influenced by the Rayonnant style of French Gothic, which is combined with the wholly classical spirit of the capitals of the large columns and the decoration in general.
The fresco decoration also extends above the row of saints.

SANCTA SANCTORUM

lunette in the east wall
last quarter of the thirteenth century
fresco

One of the large lunettes in the chapel is frescoed with two panels containing, on the left, the *Crucifixion of St Peter* and, on the right, the *Beheading of St Paul*, surmounted by two figures of angels placed symmetrically on either side of the window. Although both scenes are clearly inspired by Cimabue's work, with specific quotations from this, the solid volumes of the figures —influenced, above all, by a careful study of early Christian models—are innovatory.

SANCTA SANCTORUM

vault of the apse
last quarter of the thirteenth century
mosaic

The apse of the Sancta Sanctorum is covered by a barrel vault decorated with a mosaic on a gold ground against which a clipeus with a bust of Christ Blessing, borne by four angels, stands out. While the figure of Christ, with sunken cheeks, appears to be hieratic and immobile and is influenced by Byzantine models, the angels are more animated, as is evident in their positions and the rendering of the fluttering drapery of their robes.

Santa Maria in Aracoeli

Standing on the highest point of the Capitoline Hill, the church may have been founded by St Gregory the Great on the site where, according to legend, in the presence of Augustus, the Tiburtine Sibyl foretold the coming of Christ: it is from the prophetess's words, "Ecce ara primogeniti dei" (Here is the altar of God's first-born"), that the name of the church is said to derive. Originally served by Greek monks and then by Benedictine ones, the church was handed over to the Franciscans by a bull of Innocent IV (1243–1254): it is from this period that its transformation into the Romanesque-Gothic style dates; terminating in 1320, this may have been based on design by Arnolfo di Cambio. One of the most important alterations was the addition of a vast transept to the pre-existing basilican building; the simple brick façade, crowned by a squat flat-topped tower, dates from the late thirteenth century.

SANTA MARIA IN ARACOELI

staircase
1348

Built in 1348 as an *ex voto* after two scourges that afflicted Rome, an earthquake and an epidemic of plague, the Aracoeli stairs comprise 125 marble steps, grouped in series of 8, in accordance with the mystical concepts of medieval mathematics. The staircase formed part of the urbanistic and architectural programme of Cola di Rienzo (1313–1354), the Roman notary who took the title of tribune in 1347 and 1354, and wanted to transform the entire hill into the city's secular centre.

SANTA MARIA IN ARACOELI

façade
thirteenth century

Beyond the rigid marble statue of one of the Dioscuri standing next to his horse—a work of the imperial period located on the balustrade in front of the Piazza del Campidoglio, at the end of the *cordonata* (the monumental ramp designed by Michelangelo)—the brick façade of Santa Maria in Aracoeli is visible. The tall two-light windows on the lateral wings and small rose-windows with patterned tracery are typically Gothic.

LAST JUDGEMENT AND LIFE OF CONSTANTINE

1246
fresco
oratory of San Silvestro, Santi Quattro Coronati

The oratory of San Silvestro has one of the most important fresco cycles of thirteenth-century Rome devoted to the lives of Emperor Constantine and Pope Sylvester. This cycle, executed in 1246, evidently had political significance: in the same year, in fact, Pope Innocent IV confirmed, with a bull, the validity of the donation of Constantine and the legitimacy of the dominion of the church. Below the huge *Last Judgement* a number of the scenes in the cycle are recognizable.

LIFE OF CONSTANTINE

1246
fresco
oratory of San Silvestro, Santi Quattro Coronati

The explicitly political value of this fresco cycle is confirmed by this scene portraying the bareheaded emperor Constantine kneeling before Pope Sylvester—who is handing him the papal tiara—with a gesture of submission alluding to the supremacy of the pope, from both the temporal and the spiritual points of view. Despite the narrative tone of the scene—and the cycle as a whole—the figures are rigid and expressionless, still very much influenced by the Byzantine style and the tradition of early medieval painting in Rome.

The Roman School

The last thirty years of the thirteenth century were a period of great importance and vitality for painting in Rome, and coincided with the climate of renewal that affected the city as a whole. The most outstanding feature of this change was the gradual abandonment of the Byzantine figurative tradition, to which the painting was still inseparably bound: the innovatory impetus was undoubtedly connected with the contact between the Roman artistic milieu and the upper Church of San Francesco in Assisi, then under construction, where artists from both Tuscany and Rome developed a style characterized by a new plastic power in the form that was destined to change the course of western painting. One of these artists working in Assisi was, in fact, Jacopo Torriti (active in Rome between 1291 and 1300), a leading exponent of painting in Rome, who obtained the most important commissions in the city at the end of the century. In the mosaics in Santa Maria Maggiore (c. 1295), together with elements that are still Byzantine, there is solemn majesty deriving from a profound study of the art of antiquity. In 1297 Filippo Rusuti (active in Rome between 1288–1297 and in Naples around 1320) also worked in Santa Maria Maggiore; a painter and mosaicist who was influenced by the innovations in Assisi, in 1308 he moved to the court of the king of France. The third great exponent of the classicizing and cultured current of late-thirteenth-century Roman art was Pietro Cavallini (active in Rome and Naples between 1273 and 1308), who, at the same time as Giotto, attained new plasticity of the figures and a new sense of space, thus revolutionizing the style of Italian art as a whole.

Filippo Rusuti

LIFE OF POPE LIBERIUS

detail
1292–1297
mosaic
façade, Santa Maria Maggiore

The mosaics on the façade of Santa Maria Maggiore are devoted to the life of Pope Liberius, who founded the basilica. In the rendering of the three-dimensionality of the space, especially in a sense of depth, Filippo Rusuti shows that he had been influenced by the revolutionary works attributed to Giotto in Assisi.

overleaf
Jacopo Torriti

CORONATION OF THE VIRGIN

DEATH OF THE VIRGIN

1295
mosaic
apse, Santa Maria Maggiore

Directly below the *Coronation*, the large central field with the *Death of the Virgin* is the most remarkable of the scenes from the life of the Virgin along the lower edge of the apse semi-dome.

MARIA VIRGO ASSVPTA
EXALTATA EST SANCTA
SYON

Pietro Cavallini

A leading figure in the artistic milieu of Rome in the late thirteenth and early fourteenth centuries, Cavallini (active between 1273 and 1321) is now at the centre of critical debate because he is believed to be either the main precursor of Giotto's art or one of the earliest and most attentive followers of the Tuscan master. Apart from the question of which of the two artists preceded the other, the innovatory significance of Cavallini's style is undeniable: in his works solemn and majestic forms, influenced by careful study of antique art, are accompanied by the artist's own personal range of colours. As well as in Rome, where his most important works were the mosaics of the *Life of the Virgin* in Santa Maria in Trastevere (1291 or 1296) and the frescoes in Santa Cecilia in Trastevere (c. 1293), the artist also worked at the Angevin court in Naples.

Pietro Cavallini

VIRGIN AND CHILD WITH SAINTS PETER AND PAUL AND THE DONOR BERTOLDO STEFANESCHI

c. 1296
mosaic
Santa Maria in Trastevere

This dedicatory mosaic panel represents Saints Peter and Paul presenting Cardinal Bertoldo Stefaneschi—who commissioned the mosaic cycle of six scenes of the life of the Virgin in the basilica—to the delicate Virgin. Evident here is the innovatory way in which the artist has rendered the volume of the figures, the three-dimensionality of which is obtained thanks to gradual, soft passages of colour and light.

Pietro Cavallini

LAST JUDGEMENT

c. 1295
fresco
Santa Cecilia in Trastevere

One of the most outstanding Italian paintings of the late thirteenth century, this fragmentary *Last Judgement* by Cavallini combines the old Byzantine iconography of the *deësis* (the representation of Christ between the Virgin and St John the Baptist) and Christ in a *mandorla* surrounded by angels in what has now become a mature style, influenced also by French art of the same period.

The artist's remarkable mastery of the fresco technique allowed him to model, with subtle passages of colour, solid plastic masses, which he inserted confidently in compositions with a monumental structure.

Arnolfo di Cambio

The leading protagonist of the renewal of Italian sculpture at the end of the thirteenth century, Arnolfo di Cambio (Colle Val d'Elsa c. 1245–Florence c. 1302) trained in Nicola Pisano's workshop, where he assimilated the Gothic element in his master's art and, above all, the profound classicism that led him to create solemn, well-balanced forms in his sculptural works. After working in the service of Charles of Anjou, Arnolfo went to Rome, where he ran his own workshop from 1275 to 1296: the most outstanding works he executed in this period include an imposing statue of Charles I of Anjou (1277, Musei Capitolini, Rome), the tomb of Cardinal Annibaldi in St John Lateran (c. 1276) and the two large ciboria in San Paolo fuori le Mura (1283–1284) and Santa Cecilia in Trastevere (1293).

Arnolfo di Cambio

ST PETER

c. 1300
bronze
St Peter's, Vatican

Located on the last pier on the right of St Peter's, the statue reveals that Arnolfo had made a careful study of the art of antiquity.

Arnolfo di Cambio and assistants

NATIVITY

c. 1291
marble
Chapel of the Sacramento
Santa Maria Maggiore

It is difficult to reconstruct the original appearance of the Oratorio del Presepe (Oratory of the Crib) and the precise position of the various figures, because the old chapel, rebuilt by Arnolfo in 1291, was dismantled and reassembled in the sixteenth century, the period from which the Virgin and Child date. In all likelihood, Arnolfo had based the whole composition on the carefully created relationship between the figures, inspired by the solid volumes of the statues of antiquity, and the real space in which they were located.

opposite
Arnolfo di Cambio

CIBORIUM

1293
marble
Santa Cecilia in Trastevere

Influenced by the Rayonnant Gothic style prevalent in France, especially as regards its structure with pinnacles at the corners and a pediment with a small rose-window in the centre of the trefoil arch supported by colonnettes, the ciborium of Santa Cecilia also reflects the art of antiquity with its harmonious proportions and rigorous rhythm. The elegant structure extends horizontally in space, without the dizzying upward thrust of the ciborium in San Paolo fuori le Mura, which Arnolfo had executed nearly ten years before.

The Jubilee and Giotto

In the last quarter of the thirteenth century and the first few years of the following century Rome was an important centre for the elaboration of a new artistic style: this great period in the history of art in Rome began during the pontificate of Nicholas III (1277–1280), who started a series of decorative schemes that were then continued under his successors. This renewal was linked, above all, to the desire to exalt the papacy that culminated in the proclamation of the first jubilee by Pope Boniface VIII (1294–1303) in February 1300. Because it attracted immense crowds of pilgrims to the city, this event was an important occasion for asserting the power and universality of the Church. It is extremely likely that Giotto's sojourn in Rome was related to the works of art commissioned for the celebration of the Holy Year, although doubts have been raised concerning this visit due to the lack of reliable documentation and the fragmentary state of the works attributed to the Tuscan artist in the city. The works in Rome ascribed to Giotto include the fresco portraying Boniface VIII in St John Lateran, executed around 1300, and the mosaic of the *Navicella*, formerly in the atrium of Old St Peter's and executed during his second visit, around 1307–1313. The only surviving fragments of this work, known to us thanks to copies and old reproductions, are two busts of angels in clipei. However, the large polyptych commissioned by Cardinal Stefaneschi for St Peter's and now in the Pinacoteca Vaticana dates from a later period, probably the third decade of the fourteenth century.

BONIFACE VIII ISSUING A BULL

fresco from the Benediction Loggia
c. 1300
third pier in the first aisle on the north side,
St John Lateran

Traditionally assigned to Giotto—but recently attributed to Cavallini—this fragment formed part of the pictorial cycle that decorated the old Benediction Loggia of the Lateran Palace. Standing between two members of the Curia, Boniface VIII appears on the loggia, giving a blessing. A drawing in the Ambrosiana Library in Milan allows the whole scene to be reconstructed, with a crowd of faithful acclaiming the pope. This work has been interpreted as representing the proclamation of the jubilee of 1300 by the pope, whose assistant is reading the bull; alternatively, it may depict Boniface VIII taking possession of the Lateran in 1295.

opposite
Giotto and assistants

STEFANESCHI ALTARPIECE

front (above) and reverse (below)
1320–1330
Pinacoteca Vaticana, Vatican

Commissioned by Cardinal Stefaneschi, this large triptych by Giotto was intended for the high altar of St Peter's. The reverse represents, in the centre, St Peter enthroned, while at his feet, on the left, the kneeling donor is offering him a model of the painting and, on the right, Pope Celestine V is presenting a codex. The central panel of the front portrays Christ blessing, surrounded by angels with, once again, the donor, while the side panels depict the crucifixion of Peter (left) and the beheading of Paul (right).

Once Again th

Michelangelo, *Creation of Adam,* 1508–1512. Ceiling of the Sistine Chapel, Vatican

e Centre of the World

The Return of the Papacy and the Renaissance

The election by the Council of Constance of Pope Martin V (1417–1431), who received a triumphal welcome in Rome in 1420, marked the end to a long and difficult period in the history of the city that had begun with the removal of the papacy to Avignon from 1308 to 1377 and continued with the thorny problem of the Great Schism (1378–1418).

When the papacy was brought back to a city that had for too long been left to its own devices, the situation was one of total desolation: there were now only a few thousand inhabitants, the buildings were in ruins and all productive and cultural activity had come to a halt. Thus Martin V and his successors turned their efforts to the complete reorganization of the city, starting with its civil and religious life, and initiating an ambitious programme of cultural renewal that reached its climax in the first two decades of the sixteenth century. And it was only then that Rome regained its position of supremacy over the other Italian courts. With regard to the artistic output, in this period the popes obtained the services of the most important artists from outside Rome. Thus the principal exponents of the still vigorous International Gothic style, including Gentile da Fabriano (1427) and Pisanello (1427–1432), worked in St John Lateran; from 1423 to 1428 the Tuscans Masaccio and Masolino were in Rome, working in San Clemente and on the Santa Maria Maggiore

Raphael
Loggia di Psiche
1517–19
Villa Farnesina

Raphael
dome of Sant'Eligio degli Orefici
1509

Statue of Pasquino
classical period
Piazza di Pasquino
(corner of the Palazzo Braschi)

Altarpiece. The Roman artistic milieu gradually opened up to Florentine humanism through the fundamental presences of Leon Battista Alberti, Bernardo Rossellino and Fra Angelico, who was commissioned by Pope Nicholas V (1447–1455) to decorate his new chapel in the Vatican.
The systematic transformation started by this pope, who wished to assert the continuity between Christian Rome and that of the ancients, was carried on by Sixtus IV (1471–1484), known as the *restaurator urbis* due to the fervour of his commitment to the renewal of the city. The most famous Umbrian and Tuscan painters, such as Perugino, Botticelli, Signorelli and Ghirlandaio were summoned to decorate the Sistine Chapel, while both secular and religious architecture enjoyed a period of great development, assimilating the most up-to-date forms elaborated by the Tuscan humanists and paving the way for the golden age of the High Renaissance. The period of the great patronage of Julius II (1503–1513) and Leo X (1513–1521) was one of the absolute cultural supremacy of Rome thanks to the presence of outstanding artists with an intuitive capacity to interpret the ambitious policies of the popes, who sought to display their power and authority, both spiritual and temporal, and revive the splendours of ancient Rome. Thus Bramante, Michelangelo, and Raphael managed to create a magnificent new style that was harmonious, wholly classical and unaffected by local variations.
Thanks to them, Rome enjoyed a period of renewal that was unrivalled in the rest of Europe: Julius availed himself of the services of Bramante for the urbanistic renovation, while he commissioned fresco cycles from Michelangelo and Raphael, who created some of the greatest masterpieces of western art with, respectively, the vigorous images of the Sistine ceiling and the harmonious scenes in the papal apartments in the Vatican.
The primacy of Raphael, whose deep interest in the culture of antiquity was reflected in all his creative activities, from architecture to the decorative cycles, continued with great success under Leo X. The artist's early death in 1520 left a gap that could not be filled, and this coincided with profound changes from a historical point of view: with the start of the Lutheran schism and the dramatic Sack of Rome in 1527 the universal ideals of the Renaissance waned and artists began to take a fresh look at their approach in a difficult search for new forms and modes of expression.

Raphael
Villa Madama
designed in 1518
exterior

Vatican Palace

After the papacy was brought back from Avignon in 1377, the papal residence was moved by Gregory XI (1370–1378) from the Lateran Palace to the Vatican. Although the various successors to Saint Peter sought to embellish their new seat, it was only during the pontificate of Nicholas V (1447–1455) that an important chapter opened in the history of the huge complex, which was gradually transformed into a magnificent residence. It is not known who drew up the project, which involved a square palace, fortified externally, arranged around what is now the Cortile dei Pappagalli.
In 1473 Sixtus IV (1471–1481) built what was to be known as the Sistine Chapel, while the villa on the Belvedere hill, dating from the pontificate of Innocent VIII (1484–1492), was then linked by Bramante to the rest of the complex by the splendid stage-set-like Cortile del Belvedere. Bramante was also responsible for the construction of the loggias overlooking the Cortile del San Damaso, which were completed by Raphael. New buildings were subsequently added to the huge palace, including Antonio da Sangallo's Cappella Paolina, Pirro Ligorio's extensions, Domenico Fontana's library and the Scala Regia designed by Bernini. From the end of the eighteenth century onwards, part of the complex was converted into a museum housing the important papal collections of paintings and archaeological finds.

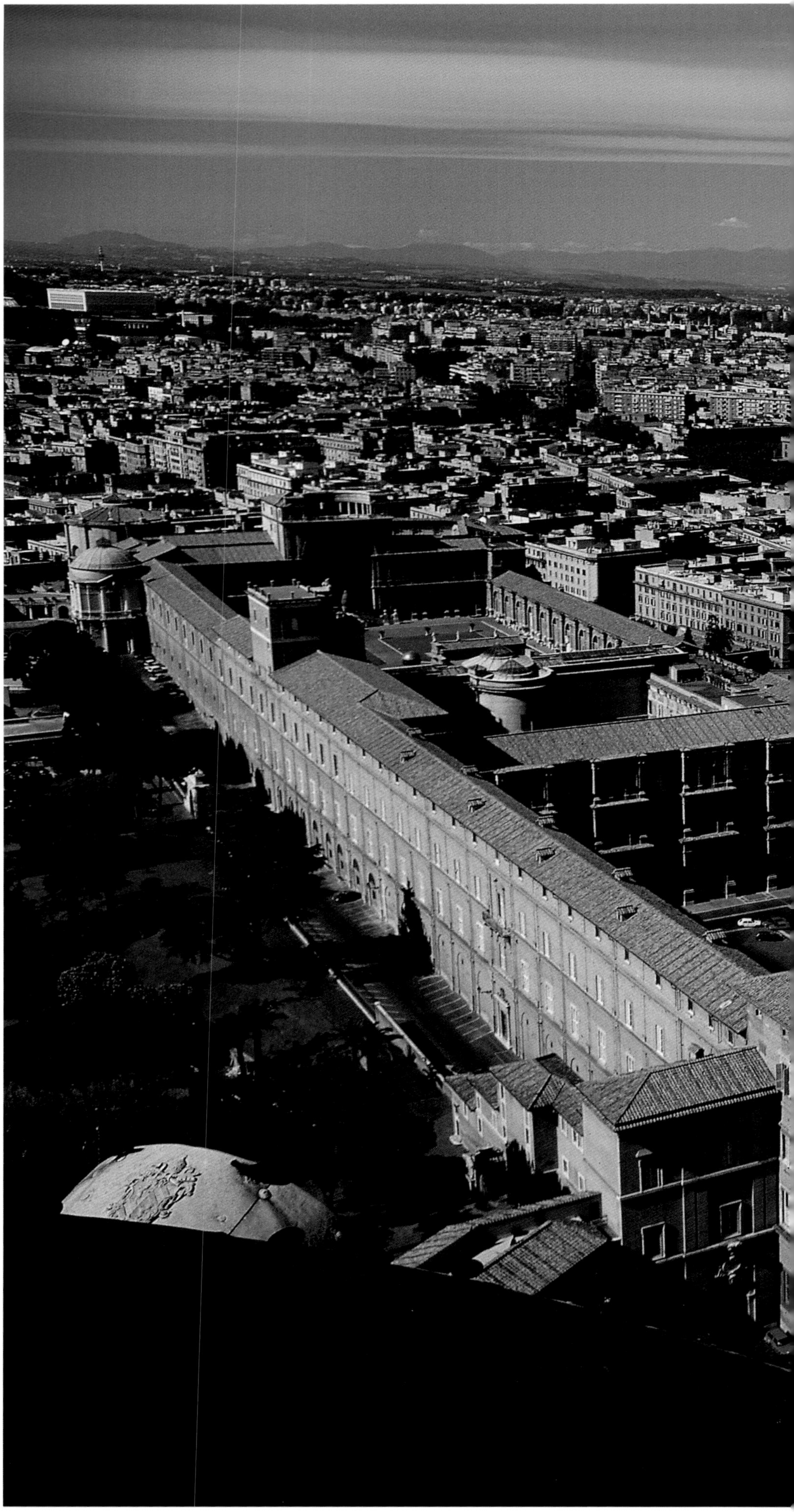

VATICAN PALACE

overall view
Vatican

The imposing structure of the Vatican Palace is the result of numerous extensions and improvements carried out by various popes over the centuries, from the middle of the fourteenth century onwards. Immediately evident in this photograph is the grandeur of the complex, in which there are three different courtyards: the large rectangle of the Cortile del Belvedere, the smaller space of the library courtyard, enclosed between the transverse structures of the Salone Sistino and the Braccio Nuovo, built (1817–1822) to a design by Raffaele Stern and identifiable thanks to the large hall with an apse, and, lastly, the Cortile della Pigna with the enormous exedra, wrongly said to be by Bramante. The rectangular building in the foreground is the Sistine Chapel.

Fra Angelico

ST SIXTUS CONFIDES THE TREASURES OF THE CHURCH TO ST LAWRENCE

1447–1450
fresco
Chapel of Nicholas V
Vatican Palace, Vatican

Called to Rome by Eugenius IV in 1446, Fra Angelico was then commissioned by Nicholas V to paint frescoes in several rooms, unfortunately now lost, and his private chapel. On the walls of the small chapel the artist painted scenes from the life of the protomartyrs Stephen and Lawrence; this masterpiece is an ideological manifesto of Nicholas V's Christian humanism. The splendour of the range of colours is particularly remarkable in this scene, with the pink of St Lawrence's dalmatic, shading, with delicate passages, to the light blue of the papal cloak, and the green and orange of the armour of the soldiers on the left, who stand out against the yellow background of the wall.

Fra Angelico

THE DISPUTE IN THE SYNEDRION

1447–1450 fresco
Chapel of Nicholas V
Vatican Palace, Vatican

The solemn, measured gestures of the figures give this scene a sense of stately classicality and composure that is also found in the rest of the cycle, which is regarded as the most important series of paintings executed in the period immediately before the jubilee of 1450.

Fra Angelico

ST LAWRENCE ORDAINED DEACON BY ST SIXTUS

1447–1450
fresco
Chapel of Nicholas V
Vatican Palace, Vatican

This scene, one of the most important of the whole fresco cycle, is set in an imposing basilica and alludes to the forms of worship at the court of Nicholas V, whose features are those of Sixtus II's face, seen in profile. The vestments of the figures—the clerics on the right, the deacons in the background and the cardinals with rich copes on the left—are rendered with great precision.

Fra Angelico

ST LAWRENCE DISTRIBUTING ALMS TO THE POOR

1447–1450
fresco

Chapel of Nicholas V
Vatican Palace, Vatican

The gesture of Lawrence, who is distributing alms to the poor, as part of a programme of ecclesiastical celebration promoted by Nicholas V, refers to the Church—to which the nave in the background alludes—seen as the bestower of grace on the faithful, symbolized by the beggars gathering with dignity around the deacon. It is likely that, as in other scenes in this cycle, Angelico was helped to paint this fresco by his assistant Benozzo Gozzoli.

PALAZZO VENEZIA

exterior
1455–1467

The first important example of secular Renaissance architecture in Rome, the solemn Palazzo Venezia, realized according to a project inspired by the models of Leon Battista Alberti, was built on the initiative of the Venetian Cardinal Pietro Barbo from 1455 onwards. After he had been elected pope with the name of Paul II, the prestigious residence was extended, incorporating the nearby church of San Marco, the titular of which, Marco Barbo —who was the pope's nephew— completed the work in 1467.

Divided horizontally by white string-courses standing out against the dark surface of the walls, the building, with its square forms, is crowned with battlements, giving it a medieval flavour. There is a series of imposing windows framed with marble on the first floor—the piano nobile—which now houses the important Museo di Palazzo Venezia. On the façade giving onto Piazza Venezia, above the elegant Renaissance portal, is the balcony from which Benito Mussolini spoke to the crowds assembled below during the Fascist period.

Melozzo da Forlì

SIXTUS IV APPOINTING PLATINA PREFECT OF THE VATICAN LIBRARY

1447
fresco, transferred to canvas
Pinacoteca Vaticana, Vatican

In this solemn event, taking place in a majestic, wholly Renaissance architectural setting, with a ceiling formed by blue and gold coffers, the humanist Bartolomeo Sacchi, called Platina, kneeling in the centre, is appointed prefect of the Vatican Library by Sixtus IV. The other members of the papal court present at the ceremony are, on the right, the cardinals Raffaele Riario and Giuliano della Rovere, and, on the left, the laymen Giovanni della Rovere and Girolamo Riario, all members of the pope's family.

Melozzo da Forlì

ANGEL PLAYING A MUSICAL INSTRUMENT

1480–1484
fresco detached from the apse of Santi Apostoli
Pinacoteca Vaticana, Vatican

An artist of fundamental importance for the diffusion of humanistic art in Rome, Melozzo da Forlì (1438–1494) was commissioned by Giuliano della Rovere, the future Pope Julius II, to decorate the apse of the Church of Santi Apostoli, where he executed a splendid illusionistic composition representing Christ and angels playing musical instruments, of which only a few fragments remain. The bright colours and the monumentality of the forms of this angel clearly attest to the influence of Piero della Francesca.

The Sculpture of the Quattrocento

In the early stages of the Renaissance a truly Roman school of sculpture did not exist: as in the case of painting and architecture, in this field, too, the most outstanding works were executed by Tuscan artists. While Donatello's sojourn in the city (1432–1433) made no impact on the local artistic milieu, of greater importance were Filarete, who made the bronze doors of St Peter's (1434–1435), Mino da Fiesole and Isaia da Pisa, both active together with their workshops around the middle of the century, sculpting tombs, altars and reliefs. Also in the second half of the Quattrocento, the most important figures were still from outside Rome, including the Lombard Andrea Bregno, who tempered the realistic vigour of his earlier works with Mino da Fiesole's classicism, the Tuscan Antonio del Pollaiuolo, the Dalmatian Giovanni da Traù and, lastly, Mino del Reame, from southern Italy.

Antonio del Pollaiuolo

TOMB OF INNOCENT VIII

1498
bronze, partially gilded
south aisle
St Peter's, Vatican

Destined to be very popular with the popes, the model of the wall tomb designed by Pollaiuolo for Innocent VIII is innovative because the deceased is portrayed twice, alive and dead. At the bottom the pope is recumbent on his sarcophagus, while above he appears in all his majesty.

Andrea Bregno

ST PETER

fragment of the tomb of Cardinal di Cusa
c. 1494
marble
San Pietro in Vincoli, Vatican

The figures are framed by severe architectural elements in the composed classical style of Andrea Bregno, one of the leading sculptors in fifteenth-century Rome.

opposite
Matteo del Pollaiuolo

DELIVERY OF THE KEYS TO PETER AND THE HEALING OF THE CRIPPLE

FALL OF SIMON MAGUS AND THE DISPUTE BEFORE NERO

CRUCIFIXION OF ST PETER

bas-reliefs on the ciborium of Sixtus IV
c. 1471–1478
marble
storerooms of the Reverenda Fabbrica
St Peter's, Vatican

An antiquarian taste and the reference to the styles, iconography and techniques of monuments of classical antiquity, especially Trajan's Column, characterize these bas-reliefs that formerly adorned the ciborium of Sixtus IV.

Filarete

BEHEADING OF ST PAUL

1434–1435
bronze
central door
St Peter's, Vatican

The bronze doors of St Peter's, which Pope Eugenius IV (1431–1447) commissioned from Filarete, have four large elongated compartments, two for each leaf, representing Christ enthroned, St Paul, the Virgin and St Peter, while below are two square panels: the one on the left shows the martyrdom of St Paul. On the left of the panel, in a classical aedicula carefully reconstructed in accordance with the artist's antiquarian taste, a Roman magistrate and soldier appear, while, on the opposite side, Paul is being beheaded. Higher up, the saint's soul appears to Plautilla, returning the veil that the woman had lent him so he could be blindfolded during his execution.

Filarete

CRUCIFIXION OF ST PETER

1434–1435
bronze
central door
St Peter's, Vatican

This crowded scene of the martyrdom of St Peter, who was crucified upside down because he did not regard himself as worthy of dying on the cross in the same position as Christ, occupies the panel at the bottom right of the central door. The use of stylistic and iconographic motifs drawn from both late Roman friezes and early Christian ivories make Filarete's doors, consisting of a wooden core covered with sheet metal, one of the first examples of Renaissance art in Rome.
In this scene it is possible to recognize some of the monuments of ancient Rome.

Sistine Chapel

The most important undertaking in the feverish process of renewing the city promoted by Pope Sixtus IV (1471–1484) was the construction, at the Vatican Palace, of a new chapel, named "Sistine" after him, which was intended for the most solemn ceremonies of the papal court. The project was attributed to the Florentine architect Baccio Pontelli by Giorgio Vasari. Built on the site of an old chapel, the Sistine Chapel, which was started in 1477 and consecrated in 1483, is a simple rectangular hall covered with a barrel vault. The side walls are divided by string-courses into horizontal bands: in the lower one are depicted fictive hangings with the papal coat of arms; the middle one is occupied by a cycle of frescoes representing the life of Christ on the right and the life of Moses on the left (1480–1481), while the third band, interrupted at regular intervals by windows, contains a series of portraits of the first thirty popes. The famous decoration of the ceiling with frescoes by Michelangelo dates from 1508–1512, while the *Last Judgement* on the altar wall was painted by Michelangelo from 1535 to 1541.

opposite, above
Sandro Botticelli

THE PUNISHMENT OF KORAH, DATHAN AND ABIRAM

1482
fresco
Sistine Chapel
Vatican Palace, Vatican

In close correspondence with Perugino's *Delivery of the Keys to St Peter*, located opposite, the scene alludes to the punishment inevitably awaiting those who challenge the pope's authority. Although the composition is arranged around the monumental arch of Constantine, dominating the centre of the scene, it is fragmentary and without the capacity for synthesis that is a characteristic of Perugino's fresco.

opposite, below
Cosimo Rosselli and Biagio d'Antonio

THE LAST SUPPER
1482
fresco
Sistine Chapel
Vatican Palace, Vatican

The Florentine artist Cosimo Rosselli, who also painted other scenes in the Sistine cycle, often in collaboration with his pupil Piero di Cosimo, dwells on prosaic and anecdotal details, such as the fight between the cat and dog at bottom right.

SISTINE CHAPEL

1477–1481
interior
Vatican Palace, Vatican

The dimensions of the hall of the Sistine Chapel (41 × 13.5 m) are the same as those attributed in the Bible to the temple of Solomon. The medieval basilicas were, however, the source of inspiration for the mosaic floor and the marble screen, finely decorated with classicizing motifs by Mino da Fiesole, Andrea Bregno and Giovanni da Traù.

Pietro Perugino

DELIVERY OF THE KEYS TO ST PETER

1481–1482
fresco
Sistine Chapel
Vatican Palace
Vatican

Of the numerous artists that Sixtus IV summoned from Tuscany and Umbria to fresco the side walls of the new chapel, there is no doubt that one of the most important was Pietro Perugino. In fact, it was this artist and not Botticelli, as Vasari maintained, who had the role of coordinating the prestigious team of painters working in the Sistine Chapel. In addition to the *Assumption of the Virgin* on the altar wall, destroyed to make way for Michelangelo's *Last Judgement*, and a number of portraits of popes in the upper band, three panels were painted by Perugino: the *Baptism of Christ*, *Moses Leaving Egypt* and the *Delivery of the Keys to St Peter*. This fresco may, in fact, be regarded as a résumé of the ideological message of the whole cycle, which was intended to celebrate the historical function of the Church and the papacy through scenes from the lives of Christ and Moses, interwoven with complex symbolic references and allusions to the period when they were painted, also with the inclusion of contemporary personages. The composition, which is extremely well-balanced, is dominated by the bulk of the Temple of Jerusalem, which, with its octagonal structure, is a reminder that the centrally-planned building was a theme that aroused a great deal of interest in the early Renaissance.

SIX TE OPIBVS
DISPAR
RELIGIONE
PRIOR

Religious Architecture

Architecture in Rome during the Quattrocento was notably late in its forms in comparison with the more up-to-date Tuscan style. While the decades following the return of the papacy from Avignon were mainly devoted to the renovation of the old basilicas, which had fallen into disrepair because of neglect, it was only with Nicholas V (1447–1455) that important initiatives were taken with regard to religious architecture, first and foremost the idea of a new Basilica of St Peter's, which the Tuscan Bernardo Rossellino was commissioned to design. Nicholas V's commitment to renewal was maintained under the forceful Sixtus IV (1471–1484); during his pontificate, in fact, various important churches (Sant'Agostino, Santa Maria del Popolo, San Pietro in Montorio, Santa Maria della Pace), porticoes (Santi Apostoli, San Pietro in Vincoli) and cloisters (San Giovanni dei Genovesi, San Cosimato) were built, revealing a new Renaissance spirit, imported from Tuscany, in the harmonious arrangement of the parts and elegant proportions. The most outstanding architects working in this period include Baccio Pontelli and Andrea Bregno.

SANT'AGOSTINO

façade
fifteenth century

Commissioned by the wealthy Cardinal Guglielmo d'Estouteville, the architect Jacopo da Pietrasanta built the church of Sant'Agostino—one of the most important examples of religious architecture of the early Renaissance in Rome—together with the adjacent monastery, from 1479 to 1483. The broad façade, completely covered with travertine, has two superimposed levels of pilasters, separated by pronounced horizontal cornices with an unusual trapezial form. The central part, crowned by a triangular pediment, is linked to the lower side aisles by two enormous volutes, which had been envisaged in the original project and were perhaps inspired by Alberti's designs.

SANTA MARIA DEL POPOLO

interior
1472–1478
(with seventeenth century additions by Bernini)

The interior of the church, consisting of a nave and two aisles with groin-vaults, divided by demi-columns and piers, was modified in the Baroque period by Bernini, who enlarged the windows and added delicate stucco figures of saints to the arches without, however, altering the harmonious sense of space typical of the Quattrocento.

SANTA MARIA DEL POPOLO

façade
1472–1478
(with seventeenth century additions by Bernini)

Founded at the end of the eleventh century, Santa Maria del Popolo was completely reconstructed by Sixtus IV, perhaps according to a project by the Tuscan Baccio Pontelli. The severe façade is divided into three parts by pilasters: the volute-like wall segments between the central section, dominated in the upper part by a large oculus, and the outside bays were added by Bernini.

OSPEDALE DI SANTO SPIRITO IN SASSIA

exterior
1473–1478

The hospital, founded by Innocent III at the end of the twelfth century, was destroyed by fire in 1471: the reconstruction of the building and its extension, from 1473 to 1478, were part of the feverish activity of renewal promoted by Sixtus IV. The façade overlooking the Tiber, with four two-light windows flanked by pilasters and crowned with a pediment containing a rose-window, was restored to its present appearance in the early twentieth century.

OSPEDALE DI SANTO SPIRITO IN SASSIA

octagonal crossing tower
1473–1478

The elegant octagonal crossing tower, located halfway along the arcaded side of the Ospedale di Santo Spirito in Sassia, stands over the former entrance to the building. Possibly designed by Baccio Pontelli, the tower has on each face, alternately, a two-light and a three-light window, flanked by tondos in coloured majolica contrasting with the brick walls, in accordance with a local fashion that was already present in medieval buildings in Rome.

SANTA MARIA DELLA PACE

exterior, rear
second half of the fifteenth century

Of the original Church of Santa Maria della Pace, erected during the pontificate of Sixtus IV, only the rear part has survived; this is constituted by an octagonal building surmounted by a dome, to which a longitudinal nave was then added. It was next to this centrally-planned structure, probably realized by Baccio Pontelli from c. 1480 to 1483, that the famous cloister was built; this was Bramante's first work in Rome (1500–1504).

Pinturicchio

NATIVITY

1485–1489
fresco
Della Rovere Chapel

Santa Maria del Popolo

The Chapel of the Della Rovere family in Santa Maria del Popolo has preserved its fifteenth-century appearance almost intact. Depicting the *Nativity*, the altarpiece—surrounded by an elegant classicizing architectural frame designed by Andrea Bregno, who was also responsible for the antependium—was executed using the fresco technique by Pinturicchio and his assistants, who also decorated the rest of the chapel.

opposite
Pinturicchio

ISIS ENTHRONED BETWEEN HORUS AND MERCURY

ENCOUNTER BETWEEN ISIS AND OSIRIS

1492–1495
fresco
Sala dei Santi
Borgia Apartment, Vatican Palace
Vatican

Pinturicchio, one of the most sought-after painters in the last twenty years of the fifteenth century, created his greatest masterpiece in the decoration of the Borgia Apartment, commissioned by Pope Alexander VI. The artist's exuberant style and his love for antiquity and archaeology are combined with his fertile imagination to produce unexpected, bizarre results.

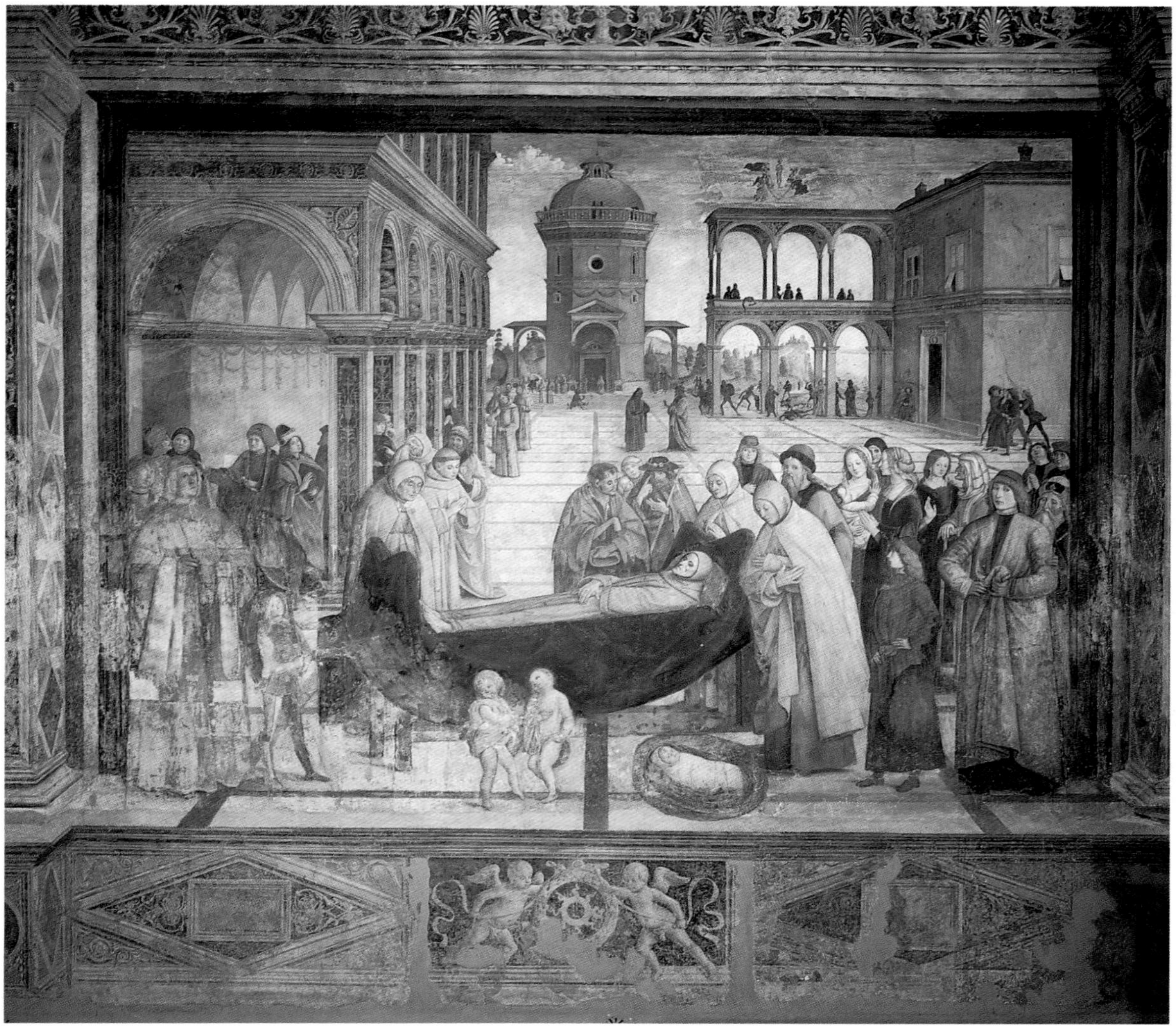

Pinturicchio

FUNERAL OF ST BERNARDINO

c. 1486
fresco
Bufalini Chapel
Santa Maria in Aracoeli

The scene of the funeral of St Bernardino is part of the cycle commissioned from the artist by Manno Bufalini, a consistorial advocate who came from Città di Castello, to commemorate the peace established by the saint between the patron's ancestors and the Baglioni family of Perugia. The scene takes place in a magnificent architectural setting, with a large square overlooked by Renaissance buildings, dominated in the background by an octagonal temple and the elegant house of the Bufalini. With his usual narrative skill, the artist dwells on details, paying particular attention to the costume of the crowd taking part in the funeral rites.

Pinturicchio

SCENES FROM THE MYTH OF ISIS AND OSIRIS

1492–1495
fresco
Sala dei Santi
Borgia Apartment, Vatican Palace
Vatican

The vault of the Sala dei Santi, the most sumptuous room in the pope's private apartments, is devoted to representations of the myths of the Egyptian gods Isis and Osiris, proceeding from their marriage to the tragic death of Osiris, who then reappears as the bull Apis, which was sacred to the Egyptians. The frequent depiction of Apis, alluding to the bull that was an emblem on the Borgia coat of arms, serves to celebrate Alexander VI's family. The daring choice of subject matter reflects the enthusiasm for the rediscovery of the culture of ancient Egypt that was a characteristic of humanism.

The Palaces of the Early Renaissance

The renewal of secular buildings began in Rome around the middle of the Quattrocento: in the Palazzo Venezia (1467–1471), the first example of Renaissance architecture in the city, appear some motifs destined to become an integral part of the local architecture, such as the extension of the elevations in a horizontal direction rather than a vertical one and the asymmetrical tendency of the façades. The secular architecture of this period was, however, still "rustic" in comparison with the contemporary Tuscan palaces: the façades were stuccoed or adorned with sgraffito, the only architectural ornaments were the string-courses in travertine and crenellated towers in medieval style were still present. An important turning point was the Palazzo della Cancelleria (1489), the model of an elegant residence that, with the horizontal division of the front, the use of ashlar and the rhythm imparted to the façade by pilasters and windows, influenced all late Quattrocento and early Cinquecento Roman palaces, starting a new chapter in the city's architecture.

PALAZZO DELLA CANCELLERIA

façade
1485–1513

Constructed for Cardinal Raffaele Riario, nephew of Pope Sixtus IV, the palace is considered to be one of the most outstanding buildings of the early Renaissance in Rome. The imposing and harmonious edifice, inspired by Leon Battista Alberti's Palazzo Rucellai in Florence, is remarkably long (almost 90 metres) and is delimited by shallow projections at each end. The rigorously designed façade is divided into three horizontal bands: the ground floor in smooth ashlar, interrupted only by the arched windows, is the base on which the two upper storeys rest; these are rhythmically divided by two rows of pilasters flanking the large windows, which have different shapes on the two levels. The elegant courtyard was attributed by Vasari to Bramante, and it has been also suggested that he was the architect who designed the whole palace.

PALAZZO TORLONIA

façade
c. 1500–1520

The importance of the Palazzo della Cancelleria as a model for architecture in Rome during the Renaissance is evident in the Palazzo Torlonia: built at the beginning of the sixteenth century for Cardinal Adriano Castelli di Corneto, it is, in effect, a copy on a smaller scale of Raffaele Riario's palace. Possibly designed by the same architect—who may have been Andrea Bregno—and drawing on Bramante's ideas, the Palazzo Torlonia reproduces the rigorous structure of the Palazzo della Cancelleria in its elegant façade: the division into three horizontal bands is similar, as are the two rows of pilasters flanking the windows on the upper storeys. This palace differs, however, from the model both as regards the shape of the windows in the base, which are rectangular, not rounded, and the rhythm with which the different elements are distributed along the façade.

Donato Bramante

After the fall of Ludovico il Moro in 1499, Bramante (Fermignano, near Pesaro, 1444–Rome 1514) left Milan, where he had settled around 1480, to go to Rome. His encounter with Julius II and direct contact with the great monuments of classical antiquity allowed the artist, whom the pope appointed as Superintendent of the papal buildings, to experiment with various themes relating to architectural design, obtaining excellent results in his subsequent career. Although small in size, his first works in Rome, the cloister at Santa Maria della Pace (1500–1504) and the round tempietto at San Pietro in Montorio (1502) paved the way for more imposing projects: the Cortile del Belvedere (1505–1506) and then the new basilica of St Peter's, where his constant interest in the theme of the centrally-planned building is most clearly expressed.

Donato Bramante

TEMPIETTO AT SAN PIETRO IN MONTORIO

c. 1502

One of the first works Bramante realized in Rome is the small building located in a courtyard adjacent to the church of San Pietro in Montorio, on the Janiculum, which may be regarded as one of the earliest examples of "modern" architecture in the context of the Renaissance. With rigorous logic, Bramante drew on elements of the classical architectural vocabulary and composed them in a coherent manner, making his building a universal model, paradigmatic for all the architecture of the Cinquecento. Inspired by the peripteral temple, the building is based on the repetition of circular geometrical forms: the structure is, in fact, cylindrical and surrounded by sixteen Doric columns. Above the balustrade rises a drum, also cylindrical, surmounted by a cupola.
The motif of the circle is also repeated in the concentric steps forming the base.

CORTILE DEL BELVEDERE

detail of the Cortile della Pigna
1504-1505, 1560
Vatican Palace
Vatican

The huge Cortile del Belvedere was designed by Bramante in 1504–1505 to connect the Vatican Palace to the summer residence, the villa of Innocent VIII on the Belvedere hill. The architect had planned a huge space delimited by two long linking corridors, with terraces arranged on three levels, linked to each other by stairs. The court was closed spectacularly towards the north with a huge exedra. The organic, unified nature of the project had already been lost in the second half of the sixteenth century with the construction of the Salone Sistino across it. The northern part of the court, called the Cortile della Pigna after the enormous bronze pine cone at the foot of the niche, is terminated by the exedra, realized in 1560 by Pirro Ligorio by transforming the one Bramante built.

Raphael

The leading protagonist of the Roman artistic scene during the pontificates of Julius II (1503–1513) and Leo X (1513–1521), Raphael (Urbino 1483–Rome 1520) was the great exponent of the Renaissance dream to restore the city's pre-eminence as a cultural centre, especially as regards its architecture, reviving the magnificence of ancient Rome in the imperial period. In addition to his career as a painter engaged in the execution of important fresco cycles, portraits and altarpieces, in which he attained a wholly classical expressive capacity, he worked as an architect (he was appointed architect-in-chief of St Peter's in 1514), was a keen scholar of archaeology and was Superintendent of Roman Antiquities, a position which allowed him to become very familiar with the great buildings of the past. In his architectural and decorative schemes for the Vatican Logge and Villa Madama, the splendour of the classical civilization came alive once again.

Raphael

PORTRAIT OF A YOUNG WOMAN WITH A UNICORN

c. 1506
oil on panel transferred to canvas
Galleria Borghese

In his activity as a portraitist, Raphael was considerably influenced by Leonardo da Vinci: in this case, in fact, there is evidently a resemblance to the *Mona Lisa*, not only in the young woman's pose, but also in the balustrade framing the landscape in background. The presence of the unicorn, a symbol of chastity, suggests this might be the wedding portrait of a young lady whose identity is unknown.

Raphael

CORONATION OF THE VIRGIN (ODDI ALTARPIECE)

1503
oil on panel transferred to canvas
Pinacoteca Vaticana
Vatican

Commissioned by the Perugian noblewoman Maddalena degli Oddi for the family chapel in the church of San Francesco in Perugia, the work displays the influence of Perugino, especially in the facial types. On the other hand, the variety of gestures and expressions and the bright colours are quite innovatory.

Raphael

ENTOMBMENT

1507
Oil on panel
Galleria Borghese

Besides the references to the statues of antiquity and the classical sarcophagi representing the bearing of Meleager, the influence of Michelangelo on Raphael's painting is evident: in fact, the young woman on the right holding up the swooning Virgin is very similar to the Madonna in the *Doni Tondo*.

The statuesque youth bearing Christ—linking, with his dynamic position, the group on the left with the holy women on the right—is perhaps a portrait of Grifonetto Baglioni; the son of Atlanta, the patron of the work, he was barbarously assassinated during the struggle for the signoria of Perugia.

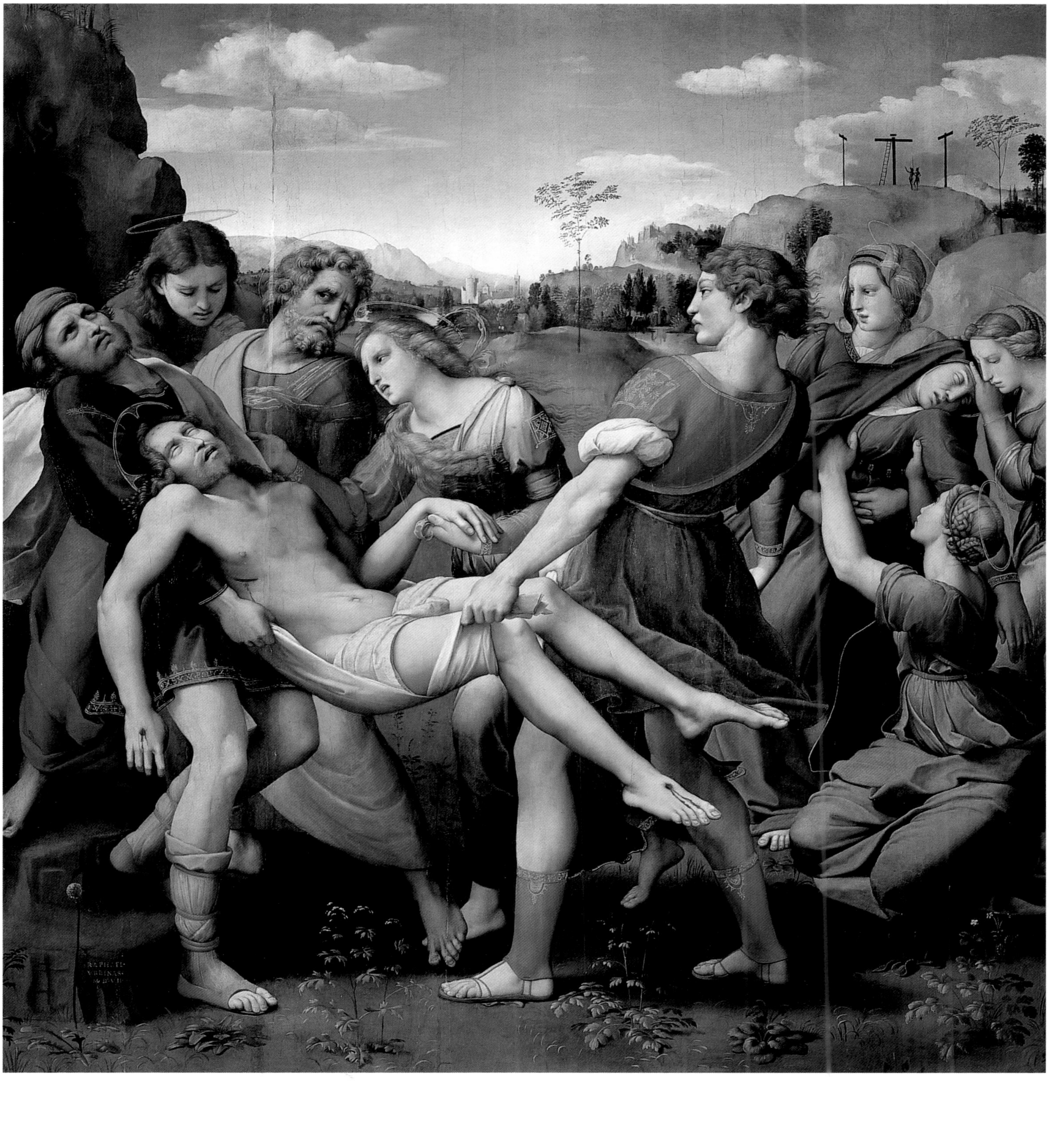

Raphael

PARNASSUS

1509–1510
fresco
Stanza della Segnatura
Vatican Palace, Vatican

The Stanza della Segnatura, which was intended to house the pope's private library in Julius II's new apartments, is frescoed with themes recalling the subjects treated by the books in an "ideal" library. In Parnassus, for example, the immortal value of poetry is celebrated in a meeting between ancient and modern poets, from Ovid and Horace to Ludovico Ariosto, gathered around Apollo, who is playing the cithara accompanied by the Muses.

Raphael

SCHOOL OF ATHENS

1510
fresco
Stanza della Segnatura
Vatican Palace, Vatican

Represented in a majestic architectural setting—the interior of a temple inspired by Bramante's project for St Peter's—the *School of Athens* is not only Raphael's masterpiece, but also one of the greatest achievements of Renaissance art. The rigour and clarity of the composition, arranged around the figures of Aristotle and Plato engaged in a philosophical discussion in the centre of the scene, are combined with a remarkable variety in the attitudes of the powerful figures of the sages and philosophers of antiquity, many of whom are depicted as portraits of Raphael's contemporaries, such as Bramante, Michelangelo and Leonardo da Vinci.

Raphael

LIBERATION OF ST PETER FROM PRISON

detail
1512
fresco
Stanza di Eliodoro
Vatican Palace, Vatican

The most notable features of the scene of the liberation of St Peter from prison are the remarkable light effects depicted by the artist, who creates a fascinating atmosphere: the dazzling light around the angel suddenly rends the darkness of the cell, reflecting on the soldier's armour and illuminating the prison where Peter is still asleep.

Raphael

STANZA DI ELIODORO

1511–1512
fresco
Vatican Palace, Vatican

An evident change from the harmonious atmosphere in the Stanza della Segnatura, replaced by a more agitated and dramatic rhythm.

Raphael

STANZA DELL'INCENDIO *(detail)*

1514–1517
fresco
Vatican Palace, Vatican

Functioning as stage sets, the splendid architectural backdrops transform the scenes in this room into spectacular episodes.

Raphael in the Roman Churches

Most of Raphael's activity as a painter in Rome was linked to commissions from the popes for the decoration of the Vatican Palace. Some churches, however, have important works by this artist: both the frescoes of the funerary Chapel of Agostino Chigi in Santa Maria della Pace, with *Sibyls, Angels and Four Saints* (c. 1511), and the powerful *Prophet Isaiah* in Sant'Agostino (1511–1512) were inspired by Michelangelo's art. As an architect in the fieldof religious buildings, Raphael developed from the clear-cut forms of the small Church of Sant'Eligio degli Orefici (1509) to the sumptuous exuberance of the Chigi Chapel in Santa Maria del Popolo (1513–1516), inspired by the Pantheon and based on an organic relationship between structure and decoration. The only altarpiece that Raphael executed for a Roman church is the famous *Foligno Madonna* (1512), now in the Pinacoteca Vaticana.

Raphael

PROPHET ISAIAH

1511–1512
fresco
Sant'Agostino

Raphael

SIBYLS AND ANGELS

1511–1512
fresco
Chigi Chapel
Santa Maria della Pace

A festive sequence of angels and sibyls extends over the arch of the chapel: that this is an interpretation from a Christian point of view of a pagan subject is underlined by the fact that the prophetic inspiration of the Sibyls comes from the reading of tablets and scrolls brought from heaven by divine messengers.

Raphael

CHIGI CHAPEL

1513–1516
dome mosaic
Santa Maria del Popolo

Entirely designed by Raphael, also as regards its architecture, the sumptuous Chigi Chapel, inspired by the ancient mausolea, is covered by a well-lit dome with coffers decorated with mosaics executed in 1516 by the Venetian mosaicist Luigi da Pace to Raphael's design. In the centre is the daringly foreshortened figure of the Creator setting the celestial spheres in motion, while, in the eight larger panels below, the sun and the planets are represented with the angels propelling them. The frescoes between the windows in the drum were painted by Francesco Salviati.

The Sistine Ceiling

The fifteenth-century decoration of the Sistine ceiling consisted simply of a blue sky dotted with gold stars painted by Piermatteo di Amelia during the pontificate of Sixtus IV. In 1505 Julius II decided to replace this decoration, damaged by the presence of a crack in the ceiling, by promoting an extraordinary undertaking that was destined to start a new chapter in the history of western art. In 1508 the pope commissioned Michelangelo to fresco the ceiling: it took him four years of continuous very hard work to complete it, but he was finally able to give full play to his imagination and creativity after the disappointing affair of Julius II's tomb. The complex iconographic programme required nine scenes from Genesis on the ceiling, from the *Separation of Light from Darkness* to the *Drunkenness of Noah*, alternating larger and smaller panels; surmounted by the figures of *Ignudi* (male nudes) bearing bronze medallions with biblical scenes, *Prophets* and *Sibyls* are seated in monumental thrones along the sides. The *Ancestors of Christ* are portrayed in the lunettes above the windows and the coves linking them to the ceiling. Inserted in an imposing architectural framework linking together the various scenes and, at the same time, dividing them into different levels of interpretation, the magnificent cycle constitutes an apotheosis of the Creation: Genesis, the punishment of man with the original sin and the first salvation of humankind with Noah's Ark are, in fact, the historical premises for the way to redemption.

Michelangelo

SCENES FROM GENESIS

1508–1512
fresco
Ceiling of the Sistine Chapel
Vatican Palace
Vatican

The vitality and energy of the figures created by Michelangelo on the Sistine ceiling are enhanced by the use of a range of colours of remarkable brilliance, which re-emerged only after the recent cleaning: thus the artist managed to imbue two-dimensional images with the plastic power typical of sculpture, the art that he regarded as superior to all the others.

CVMAEA
EZECHIAS
MANASSES
AMON
ESAIAS
DELPHICA

Michelangelo

JONAH

1508–1512
fresco
Ceiling of the Sistine Chapel
Vatican Palace
Vatican

In the overall plan for the decoration of the Sistine Chapel, the figures of sibyls and prophets, because of their function as seers, occupy an intermediate level between the condition of man before the revelation, illustrated in the coves and pendentives, and the biblical scenes of the central area. It was, in fact, commonly believed in the Renaissance that the prophets of the Old Testament and the sibyls of classical antiquity had, with their prophecies, foretold the coming of Christ. The imposing figure of Jonah, located directly above the altar, opposite Zechariah, is depicted next to the huge fish that swallowed him after he was shipwrecked as he fled from the divine command to convert the inhabitants of Nineveh. The vigorous twisting of the body and the unstable pose are indicative of the prophet's restless and rebellious character.

Michelangelo

LIBYAN SIBYL

1508–1512
fresco
Ceiling of the Sistine Chapel
Vatican Palace
Vatican

The fact that the *Libyan Sibyl* is located in the same bay as the *Separation of Light from Darkness*, the first scene painted by Michelangelo, is due to the prophecy that was attributed to her—that the coming of Christ would rend the darkness of paganism—in Filippo Barbieri's treatise devoted to the predictions of the sibyls, which was very popular at the end of the fifteenth century. The brilliant colours of the sibyl's garment augment the joyous vitality of the figure, portrayed in a dynamic twisting position. Her supple bust is, in fact, seen from behind, her face in profile and her legs, covered by violet drapery, are depicted from the side: even the position of her feet is indicative of the sibyl's incredible energy.

LIBICA

Michelangelo

When Michelangelo (Caprese, near Arezzo 1475–Rome 1564) first came to Rome, it was to work as a sculptor: his earliest sojourn in the city, from 1496 to 1501, was an excellent opportunity for the young artist, who had trained in Florence under Lorenzo de' Medici's patronage, to see the works of classical antiquity for himself. The *Pietà* in St Peter's marked the beginning of his successful career in Rome, which then lasted, interrupted only by a number of stays in Florence, until his death. His long career as a sculptor, architect and town planner coincided with the apogee of the Renaissance, but, at the same time, he paved the way for its dramatic demise.

Michelangelo

TOMB OF JULIUS II

completed in 1545
San Pietro in Vincoli

The difficult question of Julius II's tomb, which Michelangelo described as the "tragedy of the sepulchre," concluded with the realization of a simple wall-tomb of the traditional type. The large number of statues originally planned was considerably reduced and some of the figures already sculpted for the work—such as the famous *Slaves*, now in the Louvre—were eliminated.

Michelangelo

MOSES

1515
marble
San Pietro in Vincoli

Michelangelo

PIETÀ

1497–1500
marble
St Peter's
Vatican

Michelangelo

RISEN CHRIST

1519–1521
marble
Santa Maria sopra Minerva

The works executed by Michelangelo during the pontificate of Leo X include the *Risen Christ* in the Church of Santa Maria sopra Minerva, commissioned in 1514 by the canon of St Peter's, Bernardo Cencio, and the Roman nobleman Metello Vari. The execution of the sculpture wasa long and tormented business: the present statue is, in reality, the second version, because Michelangelo stopped working on the first one when he noticeda dark vein in the marble block. The new statue was started in Florence, where, in the meanwhile, the artist had gone to work on the façade of the church of San Lorenzo, and, after it had been roughed out, it was sent to Rome: the task of completing it was given to two assistants, firstly Pietro Urbano and then Federico Frizzi. Since the patrons were not entirely satisfied with the result, Michelangelo personally intervened with a number of finishing touches. Leaning on a large cross, Christ is holding the cane and the sponge soaked in vinegar, attributes of the Passion. The build and vigorous tension of the pose, which is similar to that of *David*, mean that this figure of Christ resembles a classical statue; perhaps because its nakedness was thought to be indecorous, its loins have been covered with a gilded cloth.

Villa Farnesina

Built as a "pleasure villa" for Agostino Chigi, a refined and cultured banker of Sienese origin, the Villa Farnesina (thus called because in 1580 it became the property of the Farnese family) was designed by Baldassarre Peruzzi, who paid particular attention to the relationship between the building and its natural setting. While the south façade of the building, with two storeys divided horizontally by an architrave and vertically by two rows of pilasters, is based on the typical schemes of urban palaces, the opposite side, facing the garden with a U-shaped plan, is composed of a five-arched loggia between two projecting wings.

Baldassarre Peruzzi

VILLA FARNESINA

garden façade
1509–1511

In the garden façade, crowned by a classicizing frieze with putti and festoons, the loggia giving onto the garden with five large arches, formerly the main entrance, was decorated by Raphael and his assistants with episodes from the *Love Story of Cupid and Psyche.* The loggia was transformed into an illusionistic bower beneath a blue sky, thus creating a perfect union between the internal space and the surrounding natural setting.

Raphael

PSYCHE RECEIVED ON OLYMPUS

1517–1519
fresco
Villa Farnesina
Loggia di Psiche

Like the *Wedding of Cupid and Psyche,* this scene simulates a fictive tapestry, framed by festoons of fruit and flowers, hanging from the centre of the ceiling.

Baldassarre Peruzzi

SALA DELLE PROSPETTIVE

general view
1509–1511
Villa Farnesina

Raphael

GALATEA

1512
fresco
Villa Farnesina

Raphael's capacity to bring the ancient myths of the classical age alive is evident in this fresco with its profane subject taken from Ovid, *Galatea*. The most striking feature of this scene, notable for its great vitality, is the delicate beauty of the goddess who, as she rides the waves in a shell drawn by dolphins, is accompanied by a train of Tritons and Nereids. Galatea's "Pompeian" red cloak and the rendering of the surface of the sea clearly indicate that the artist had studied the painting of ancient Rome.

The Vatican Logge

The construction of the loggias, which were intended to form the front of the oldest nucleus of the Vatican Palace, was started by Bramante and completed by Raphael, who realized the two upper storeys and designed the refined pictorial and stucco decoration of the interior. The long intermediate gallery, reserved for the pope, is divided by wide transverse arches into thirteen bays covered by coved ceilings. Each bay is decorated with frescoed panels illustrating scenes relating to such biblical figures as Abraham, Noah and David, while two whole ceilings are devoted to Moses, considered to be the precursor of the pope. Instead, the decoration extending along the pilasters, arches and soffits of the arches consists of a vast series of naturalistic, fantastic and geometrical elements or small scenes inspired by ancient coins, gems and sarcophagi. Stuccoes and paintings are juxtaposed with deliberate variations, but there is always a close relationship with the architectural structure. Raphael was only responsible for the planning of the decorative scheme and, in some cases, for the designs. The decoration was, in fact, executed by a large team of assistants: the stuccoes were mainly the work of Giovanni da Udine, while the frescoes were by various artists, including Giulio Romano, Polidoro da Caravaggio, Perin del Vaga and Giovan Francesco Penni.

Raphael

LOGGE

1516–1519
Vatican Palace, Vatican

The recesses devised by Raphael in the internal wall of the loggia, which is divided into a series of longitudinal arches, sets off the cornices of the large rectangular windows crowned by pediments, thus creating a quasi-sculptural effect. The pilasters and soffits of the arches are decorated with refined grotesques, both in stucco and fresco, a type of ornamentation that was to be widely used throughout the Cinquecento.

Giulio Romano
(after designs by Raphael)

THE SACRIFICE OF NOAH

ABRAHAM AND MELCHIZEDEK

FINDING OF MOSES

CROSSING OF THE RED SEA

ADORATION OF THE GOLDEN CALF

MOSES SHOWING THE TABLETS OF THE LAW TO THE ISRAELITES

third bay
1516–1519
fresco
logge, Vatican Palace, Vatican

Some of the panels in the bays of the logge have been identified, not without difficulty, as being by the hand of Raphael's most important pupil, Giulio Romano, who was also responsible for supervising the work of the other assistants. His style is distinguishable by the range of particularly brilliant colours, the attention given to the landscape and the effects of the backgrounds.

Raphael and assistants

EPISODES FROM THE LIFE OF DAVID

ceiling of the eleventh bay
1516–1519, fresco
logge, Vatican Palace, Vatican

Each of the small cove ceilings in the logge contains four narrative episodes surrounded by richly decorated stucco frames, while the coves are adorned with motifs of an architectural character. In this case the paintings, devoted to episodes from the life of David, were executed by Perin del Vaga and Giulio Romano. The centre of the ceiling is occupied by heraldic devices of the Medici family, in honour of the patron, Pope Leo X (1513–1521), Lorenzo the Magnificent's son.

Sebastiano del Piombo

Together with Raphael and Michelangelo, one of the great exponents of the Roman painting of the Cinquecento was the Venetian Sebastiano Luciani (Venice c. 1485–Rome 1547), who became known as Sebastiano del Piombo after his appointment as Cancelliere della Piombatura pontificia (Keeper the Papal Seals) in 1531. After training in his native city, where he was influenced by Giovanni Bellini and Giorgione, and starting a promising career there, the artist was introduced to the Roman milieu thanks to Agostino Chigi. Invited in 1511 by the wealthy banker to participate in the decoration of the Villa Farnesina (one of the works he painted here is *Polyphemus*, next to Raphael's *Galatea*), the painter decided to stay in Rome, where he immediately made his mark thanks to his capacity to combine the warm tonality of Venetian painting with the sculptural sense of form he had acquired from Michelangelo, with whom he became close friend. His most important works include *Pietà* (1516–1517, Museo Civico, Viterbo), a fresco cycle for the Borgherini Chapel in San Pietro in Montorio, both influenced by Michelangelo's style, and the *Raising of Lazarus* (1517–1519, National Gallery, London), painted in competition with Raphael's *Transfiguration*. After the death of Raphael, Sebastiano continued his activity as a painter very successfully, especially in the field of official portraiture.

Sebastiano del Piombo

THE FALL OF ICARUS

JUNO IN HER CHARIOT DRAWN BY PEACOCKS

SCYLLA CUTTING NISUS'S HAIR

1511–1516
fresco
Villa Farnesina

Sebastiano del Piombo's first works in Rome, the lunettes in the Villa Farnesina, are devoted to mythical episodes based on Ovid's Metamorphoses. While the rendering of the figures clearly shows that he was influenced by Michelangelo's frescoes in the Sistine Chapel (especially in the panel with the *Fall of Icarus*, top), the warm, bright palette of Giorgionesque derivation is linked to the artist's Venetian training.

Sebastiano del Piombo

FLAGELLATION
1516

wall painting
Borgherini Chapel
San Pietro in Montorio

Commissioned by the merchant Pier Francesco Borgherini in the wake of the success obtained by Sebastiano with his Pietà, the cycle in San Pietro in Montorio revolves around the dramatic scene of the *Flagellation*: the vigorous forms of the tormentors and Christ's statuesque body reveal that Michelangelo was responsible for the drawing on which this work is based.

Villa Madama

The result of both theoretical reflections and the first architectural experiments in the Renaissance on the theme of the villa, the project for the Villa Madama was a model for this building type throughout the Cinquecento. Designed by Raphael firstly for Pope Leo X, and later for his cousin, Cardinal Giulio de' Medici (who became pope in 1523 as Clement VII), the villa stands in splendid natural surroundings on the slopes of Monte Mario. Its excellent location was, in fact, exploited in a spectacular manner by the architect, who made the integration between the building and nature one of the fundamental features of the whole complex. Inspired by classical antiquity and the writings of Vitruvius and Pliny, the villa was to comprise various blocks arranged along the natural slope around a circular courtyard: the series of salons, loggias, apartments, baths, pavilions and hanging gardens were to make this the ideal setting for the gatherings of the refined aristocratic society of the day, thanks also to the presence of a hippodrome and a theatre. The project was, however, revised on a number of occasions by Antonio da Sangallo the Younger and Giulio Romano, who, after the death of Raphael in 1520, were given the task of finishing the work. Plundered during the Sack of Rome in 1527, the villa has been considerably modified over the centuries, so only a few fragments remain of the original unified conception based on the perfect harmony between the geometry of the buildings and the beauty of the natural landscape.

opposite
VILLA MADAMA

gardens
designed in 1518

In the conception of Raphael, who planned the gardens of the villa, the building and the surrounding landscape were to be harmoniously linked to each other by a carefully designed series of courtyards, terraces, pools, nymphaea and rows of trees: all these elements were based on the architecture of the suburban villas of antiquity.

VILLA MADAMA

designed in 1518
garden loggia
south-west exedra with decorations by Giulio Romano

After Raphael died the work on the villa was still far from being completed: in all probability the patron decided to entrust the supervision of the building work to Antonio da Sangallo the Younger, while Giulio Romano and Giovanni da Udine were responsible for the execution of the refined decoration of the interior. In this exedra, divided by elegant pilasters with delicate old-fashioned stuccoes, the hand of Giulio Romano is evident above all in the plastic vigour of the figures in the small stucco panels adorning the semi-dome.

Raphael and assistants

VILLA MADAMA

interior of quadripartite vault
c. 1519

The decorative schemes of a number of the rooms in the Villa Madama are dominated by grotesques, influenced by the recent archaeological discoveries that had aroused the enthusiasm of the whole Roman society. Deriving their name from the decorations found in Nero's Golden House, where the underground rooms were called "grotte" (grottoes), grotesques, either in stucco or painted, comprise fantastic and naturalistic motifs such as candelabra, putti, tempietti, shells and animals that became part of the repertoire of the leading Renaissance artists.

Raphael and assistants

VILLA MADAMA

interior of dome
c. 1519

Raphael and assistants

VILLA MADAMA

interior of loggia designed in 1518

The ideal of the rebirth of antiquity that inspired Raphael found one of its most complete expressions in the rooms of the Villa Madama: the project for the harmonious integration between the architectural structure and the decoration in classical style with stuccoes and bas-reliefs, which Raphael had already tried out in the Logge Vaticane, was coherently developed here by his continuators. The numerous niches in the walls of the loggia were intended to house Giulio de' Medici's collection of statues.

VILLA LANTE

exterior
c. 1523–1530

The geometric block of the villa built on the Janiculum by the wealthy Cardinal Baldassarre Turini da Pescia is the first example of an old-fashioned building inspired by the Villa Madama, albeit on a smaller scale. It was probably designed by Giulio Romano, who had recently completed the work on the Villa Madama after Raphael's death. The classical and humanistic ideals of the patron are evident in the choice of the site: this was where a villa belonging to the Latin poet Martial once stood.

VILLA LANTE

loggia
c. 1523–1530

Commanding a splendid view over Rome, from the Vatican to the Alban Hills, the loggia links the interior of the villa to the surrounding landscape. Covered by a barrel vault decorated with elegant stuccoes, the external side of the loggia consists of a Serliana. The same architectural motif is repeated along the internal wall.

Baldassarre Peruzzi (?)

PALAZZETTO LEROY (PICCOLA FARNESINA)

1522–1523

Attributed by some writers to Baldassarre Peruzzi, by others to Antonio da Sangallo the Younger, this small, elegant palace was intended to be the residence of the French Cardinal Leroy. The fleurs-de-lis of France on the façade were wrongly believed to be the lily that was the Farnese family's emblem, which is why the building is also known as the "Piccola Farnesina." Divided into three storeys by conspicuous string-courses, the palace is crowned by an elegant cornice. The curious loggia on the right, which makes the façade asymmetrical, is the result of early twentieth-century remodelling.

Baldassarre Peruzzi

PALAZZO MASSIMO ALLE COLONNE

1532–1536

The skill with which Peruzzi has combined elements of antique architecture is evident, above all, on the ground floor: the rhythm of the pilasters is, in fact, interrupted at the central opening to make way for the monumental Doric columns, which, standing in front of the semi-darkness of the entrance loggia, create a strongly plastic effect. The unusual convex façade is the result of the need to adapt it to the curve of the street.

Castel Sant'Angelo

Intended by Hadrian to be the mausoleum of the imperial family, this building, the construction of which started around ad 135, originally consisted of an imposing circular drum faced with travertine, tufa and peperino marble, to which Antonius Pius added a massive square base. Having lost its sepulchral function in the reign of Aurelian, who transformed it into a fortified bridgehead on the far side of the Tiber, Castel Sant'Angelo maintained this defensive role over the centuries, playing an important part in the control of the whole city. The stronghold of the pope's temporal power at the end of the fourteenth century, this castle, linked to the Vatican by a walkway known as the "passetto," often became a refuge for the pope in the case of danger and, sometimes, even his residence. It was, in fact, the popes who were responsible for the transformations to which the castle was subjected on various occasions: the most important work was carried out under Nicholas V, who built three corner towers, subsequently incorporated in the bastions by Alexander VI, who also added a fourth tower. It was during the pontificate of Alexander, who commissioned Antonio da Sangallo the Elder to supervise the work, that brick curtain wall above the Roman nucleus and the moat around the whole construction were added. Important changes were also made by Julius II, who was responsible for the elegant loggia on the front of the building, and Paul III, who commissioned a large team of architects and artists, including Antonio da Sangallo the Younger and Raffaello da Montelupo, to build his sumptuous new apartment.
Today the building houses the Museo Nazionale di Castel Sant'Angelo, which has an interesting collection of archaeological exhibits, old weapons, paintings and furnishings.

CASTEL SANT'ANGELO

Beyond the ancient Ponte Sant'Angelo, where ten statues of angels designed by Bernini are arrayed, stands the massive cylindrical drum of Hadrian's mausoleum crowned by the eighteenth-century bronze statue of the archangel Michael.

Raffaello da Montelupo

ARCHANGEL MICHAEL

1544
marble
Cortile dell'Angelo
Castel Sant'Angelo

Originally intended for the top of the building, the imposing and melancholic statue of the archangel Michael sculpted by Raffaello da Montelupo for Paul III was then placed in the west courtyard of Castel Sant'Angelo, a fascinating space overlooked by parts of the building of different periods, such as Leo X's chapel with its façade designed by Michelangelo.

LOGGIA OF JULIUS II

1504–1505
Castel Sant'Angelo

The massive fortified structure of the castle is interrupted by Julius II's loggia, with its elegant marble columns. Built in 1504–1505, the loggia replaced an old open balcony overlooking the Tiber. Under the corbel table and directly below the loggia is the huge coat of arms commemorating the end of the work carried out during Alexander VI's pontificate.

Correggio

DANAË

c. 1530
oil on canvas
Galleria Borghese

Among the masterpieces of the classicism of the Cinquecento is this sensual and sophisticated Danaë by Correggio, part of a cycle of four works—now dispersed in various museums in Europe—devoted to Jupiter's loves. It was commissioned by Duke Federico II Gonzaga of Mantua as a gift for Emperor Charles V.

Giovan Gerolamo Savoldo

TOBIAS AND THE ANGEL

c. 1527
oil on canvas
Galleria Borghese

The fascination of this work by Savoldo, a refined exponent of Brescian painting in the Cinquecento, lies in the subtle way the artist uses light effects to enhance the figures' clothes with virtuosic silvery and iridescent reflections which stand out against the thick foliage in the background.

Dosso Dossi

CIRCE

c. 1522–1524
oil on canvas
Galleria Borghese

The imaginative compositions of Dosso, a creative exponent of the mythological and literary current in vogue in the Renaissance courts, fully reflect the sophisticated cultural climate, dominated by the poet Ludovico Ariosto in Ferrara, when it was governed by the Este family. Seen against the luxuriant vegetation of a landscape inspired by Venetian painting, the enigmatic female figure may perhaps be identified as Circe, the sorceress in the Odyssey.

Titian

SACRED AND PROFANE LOVE

1515
oil on canvas
Galleria Borghese

Titian's vital and joyous interpretation of classicism is summed up in this work, which, with its complex allegorical meaning, is regarded as the epitome of the cultural ideals of the High Renaissance. Christian and pagan elements are combined in this composition, where there is a perfect balance between all the components with which the great artist, influenced by Neoplatonic philosophy, celebrates the reflection of divine perfection in earthly beauty.

Faith and Glory: the

St Peter's seen from the Vatican Gardens

Counter-Reformation

From Mannerism to Caravaggio

Francesco Salviati
Bethsheba Goes to David
1553–1555
Palazzo Ricci-Sacchetti

The devastation of churches, palaces and libraries, the destruction of an immense patrimony of artworks and the flight of artists from the city were only some of the tragic consequences of the sack of Rome in 1527. Even more demoralising was the humiliation inflicted on the papacy in the heart of the Catholic world. The end of Renaissance optimism ushered in a period of crisis and disquieting reflections on the destiny of man. All this was enshrined in the art of the age, culminating in Michelangelo's dramatic *Last Judgment*, which reflects the turbulent events of the period. This fresco was to have a decisive influence on the Tuscan artists Jacopino del Conte, Francesco Salviati, Giorgio Vasari and Daniele da Volterra, who painted the series of great Mannerist decorative cycles between the 1530s and the 1550s. The supreme achievements of this phase of Mannerist art are the frescoes in the oratory of San Giovanni Decollato and the Palazzo Ricci-Sacchetti. In these stormy years, when the Church was grappling with momentous religious and political issues, the pontificate of the Farnese pope Paul III (1534–1549) was a first sign of renewal. This appeared in his ambitious building program for Rome, with important plans of urban development and new monuments. The outstanding figures in this task were Antonio da Sangallo the Younger and Michelangelo, who turned his talents to architecture in the refashioning of the Capitol, the construction of St Peter's and the Palazzo Farnese. Michelangelo's architectural achievements late in his life formed the starting point for all the artists active at Rome in the second half of the century. However, Jacopo Vignola reinterpreted his anti-academic experimentalism in

Antonio da Sangallo the Younger
and Michelangelo
Palazzo Farnese
from 1534
exterior

the light of the earlier Renaissance tradition and so produced the design of the Church of the Gesù. This embodied the spirit of the Counter-Reformation and became a model for new places of worship.
At the Council of Trent (1545–1562) the Catholic Church committed itself to a redefinition of its role. Its new agenda included relating works of painting and architecture more closely to specific religious objectives. The new spiritual demands called for greater emphasis on the devotional qualities of religious painting, and the results began to appear as early as the late 1550s. Exponents of this new approach included some Mannerists, such as Daniele da Volterra and Jacopino del Conte, who complied with the new climate of feeling, and also rigorously academic artists like Taddeo and Federico Zuccari. The cycle of frescoes in the oratory of the Gonfalone is the most important achievement of this movement.
The pontificate of Sixtus V (1585–1590) opened a new phase of urban development. Domenico Fontana, with his nephew Carlo Maderno and Giacomo della Porta, created an original synthesis between the new tendencies and the late Mannerism of Michelangelo and Vignola. At the same time a marked reaction against the artificiality of Mannerist painting was spreading. The rediscovery of the "natural" in the late sixteenth and early seventeenth centuries led to a new approach that produced quite different results in the work of two artists from Northern Italy: the Bolognese Annibale Carracci and the Lombard Caravaggio. Their careers ran parallel in post-Renaissance Rome and produced the principal currents of seventeenth-century painting.

Pirro Ligorio
Casina of Pius IV
c. 1568
Vatican

Vatican Gardens
Vatican

The Last Judgement

Between 1533 and 1542 the *Assumption of the Virgin* frescoed on the end wall of the Sistine Chapel was destroyed to make way for Michelangelo's awesome *Last Judgement*. After nearly thirty years the artist returned to the chapel to paint one of the most troubled and intense works in the history of humanity. The traditional iconography of the subject entailed a horizontal division of the scene into separate compartments around the central figure of Christ. However, Michelangelo represented it as a single complex scene that projects a dramatic charge of energy and overwhelms the viewer.

Michelangelo

THE LAST JUDGEMENT

1536–1541
fresco
Sistine Chapel, Vatican Palace, Vatican

Michelangelo freed the scene from its usual architectural frame. In the two upper lunettes the angelic host bear the symbols of Christ's passion. Below them the assembly of saints, patriarchs and martyrs are ranged around the awesome figure of Christ the Judge, before whom even the Mother of God seems to quail in awe. Recognisable among the saints are the majestic figures of St Peter and St Paul.
In front of Christ on the right, St Bartholomew (said to have been flayed alive) holds his skin with the face presenting a tormented self-portrait of Michelangelo. Below these figures a battle rages between devils and angels who struggle for human souls.

Michelangelo

ANGELIC TRUMPETERS

The Last Judgement, particular
1536–1541
fresco
Sistine Chapel, Vatican Palace, Vatican

The last restoration of the fresco was completed in 1994. It removed some of the drapery added by Daniele da Volterra in the later Cinquecento to conceal the nakedness of the figures, judged to be obscene. It also brought to light the splendour and intensity of the original colours by eliminating the layers of dirt that had formed a grey patina over the paintwork. This detail shows the angels blowing trumpet blasts to rouse the dead to life. The Archangel Michael, on the left, holds the scroll of the names of the elect. These bulky forms floating on the wall convey a sense of instability and insecurity that reflects the religious disquiet of the period. The fresco's poetic and moral significance far transcends the confines of art history and sheds light on the spiritual crisis of Michelangelo and his contemporaries.

St Peter's

It was only during the papacy of the Farnese pope, Paul III (1534–1549), that work on the construction of St Peter's picked up again and was triumphantly completed. The idea of a new basilica was first conceived by Nicholas V, who in 1452 appointed Rossellino to produce a design. Construction was soon held up; then in 1506 Julius II gave the commission to Bramante. On his death (1514) responsibility passed to Raphael, assisted by Fra' Giocondo and Giuliano da Sangallo. Raphael suggested the plan should have the shape of a Latin cross instead of Bramante's Greek cross. After further alterations, the task was given to a very reluctant Michelangelo, who restored Bramante's centrally planned church. By the time of Michelangelo's death in 1564, the southern wall, the left apse and the drum of the dome had already been built.

ST PETER'S

interior of the apse
begun in 1546
Vatican

Michelangelo revived Bramante's plan for a "clear, coherent, luminous, freestanding" church but in a simpler, more concentrated form. The plan he designed was a Greek cross inscribed in a square surrounded by an ambulatory and crowned by a majestic dome. While the zone of the apse enshrines Michelangelo's conception, Maderno added three bays to the front of the nave and so turned the plan back into a Latin cross.

ST PETER'S

detail of the dome
begun in 1546
Vatican

The sturdy ribbing seems designed to restrain the buoyant volume of Michelangelo's soaring dome, which rises 137 metres high.

ST PETER'S

view of the dome
begun in 1546
Vatican

Michelangelo's powerfully sculptural and sensuous architecture appears in the interlocking tensions embodied in the design of the dome. The drum is rhythmically ranged with buttresses that take the form of prominent paired columns alternating with pedimented windows. The attic is decorated with festoons of vegetation and rises to the dome, wholly lined with sheets of lead. The final construction work was carried out by Giacomo della Porta (1586–1590). He followed Michelangelo's drawings but altered the curve of the dome to give it a higher profile.

ST PETER'S

detail of the interior
of the dome
begun in 1546
Vatican

The use of two concentric shells instead of a single compact dome reveals Michelangelo's careful study of Brunelleschi's technique in the design of the dome of Santa Maria del Fiore in Florence.

ST PETER'S

interior of the dome
begun in 1546
Vatican

Michelangelo's studies focused on the dome, which was meant to crown the cathedral while uniting its external and internal volumes. The splendour of his conception is clear inside the church: the nave, with its serried interplay of contracted and dilated spaces, leads up to the great open space, flooded with light, beneath the majestic dome. Resting on four enormous barrel-vaulted arches, the drum is set with windows flanked with paired pilasters that support the cornice of the dome. The mosaic tondos in the spandrels (almost 8 metres in diameter) are the work of Cesare Nebbia and Giovanni de Vecchi and depict the *Evangelists*. The mosaics arranged at different heights in the dome were made to cartoons by the Cavalier d'Arpino. They represent popes, doctors of the Church, saints, apostles and angels, rising up to the figure of the *Eternal Father*, his hand raised in blessing, in the lantern.

AEDIFICABO ECCLESIAM

ST PETER'S

begun in 1546
Vatican

The best view of the dome is from the Vatican Gardens. It gives a very good idea of Michelangelo's contribution to St Peter's. Clearly evident is the precise logic that links the sculptural mass of the apses, the modelling of the drum, the tension of the radial ribs and the solid buttresses of the lantern at the top, whose upward thrust seems to liberate all the energy packed into the building.

ST PETER'S

apse and south transept, exterior
begun in 1546
Vatican

Michelangelo designed the wall screen of the basilica as a compact three-dimensional mass. A single giant order of paired Corinthian pilasters runs round the perimeter, alternating with niches and large windows recessed in the thickness of the wall. The serried succession of these colossal elements impresses a sort of dynamism on the three apses, which reappears in the restless and articulated movement of the trabeation and the high attic.

PIRRO LIGORIO

Casina of Pius IV
1558–1562
Vatican Gardens, Vatican

The small complex began by Paul IV and completed by the Medici pope Pius IV is one of the most accomplished examples of the fanciful and bizarre work of the Neapolitan Pirro Ligorio, antiquarian, architect, writer on art and painter of grotesques. Though he used elements rigorously taken from ancient architecture, such as the columns and triangular pediment, the exuberance of the stucco decorations and bas-reliefs covering all the surfaces of the building create an effect that is wholly anti-classical and almost Baroque. The hedonistic spirit of the building is continued in the splendid interior, decorated with frescoes, mosaics, shells, marbles and stucco ornaments.

PIRRO LIGORIO

Casina of Pius IV
1558–1562
Vatican Gardens, Vatican

Pirro Ligorio's imaginative design, typically Mannerist in style, included a refined elliptical court overlooked by two elegant buildings and surrounded by gardens in the Italian style laid out in the sixteenth century. They are set against the backdrop of the majestic dome of St Peter's. The free repetition of motives inspired by antiquity to celebrate the glory and power of the popes appears not only in the revival of the ancient canons of architecture, but also in the refined nymphaeum in classical style enriched with a fountain, statues and obelisks.

Jacopo Vignola

VILLA GIULIA

1551–1553

The suburban residence of Julius III, designed by Vignola with the assistance of Vasari and Ammannati and with advice from Michelangelo, was devised as a place of leisure and festivities. There is a marked contrast between the austere, rectilinear elevation that fronts the city, with its squared, rigid volume, and the highly varied and scenic succession of three courtyards at the back, opening onto the internal garden. The harmonious integration of interior and exterior by means of a semi-circular space was inspired by Raphael's design of Villa Madama.

Taddeo Zuccari

VIEW OF THE ESQUILINE HILL

1553–1555
fresco
Villa Giulia, Room of the Seven Hills

The painted decorations of the rooms in Villa Giulia was supervised by Prospero Fontana. He painted the frescoes on the ground floor, while other artists worked on the upper floors. The Room of the Seven Hills is attributed to Taddeo Zuccari, who painted the delicate landscapes set in ornate frames with grotesque motives and festoons of fruit and flowers.

Bartolomeo Ammannati

NYMPHAEUM

c. 1552
Villa Giulia

Ammannati's elegant nymphaeum is set between the villa and the garden, below a semi-circular balustrade. It was much favoured by Julius III for the refreshing coolness of the water in its spectacular and scenic setting. A nymphaeum was a common feature of classical architecture in Renaissance villas and gardens. This is laid out on three levels with a loggia and enriched with mosaic paving and four caryatids in the form of herms.

The Oratory of San Giovanni Decollato

The Oratory of San Giovanni Decollato was begun together with the adjacent church at the end of the Quattrocento. It belonged to the Rome branch of the confraternity of San Giovanni, founded in Florence in 1488 to bring spiritual comfort to criminals sentenced to death. The elegant interior is wholly decorated with a fresco cycle that is one of the most important examples of Mannerist painting in Rome. Completed in stages between 1538 and 1551, the frescoes represent *Stories of Christ and John the Baptist*. They open with Jacopino del Conte's *Annunciation to Zacharias*. Jacopino also painted the *Deposition* over the altar, designed by Daniele da Volterra. Among the other artists who worked on the cycle, two outstanding figures were the Tuscan Francesco Salviati and the Neapolitan Pirro Ligorio.

Jacopino del Conte

PREACHING OF JOHN THE BAPTIST

1538
fresco
Oratory of San Giovanni Decollato

The Tuscan artist Jacopino del Conte painted a number of episodes of the cycle. He alternated between the model of Raphael (as in the *Annunciation to Zacharias*) and a return, as here, to the manner of Michelangelo, evident above all in the inflated anatomy and the contorted, frozen poses of the figures crammed in around the Baptist till they take up all the available space.

Francesco Salviati

VISITATION

1538
fresco
Oratory of San Giovanni Decollato

In his early works, Salviati's careful study of Raphael is evident in the general composition of the scene, inspired by the architectural background of the *Fire of Borgo* and, above all, in the maiden on the left, whose figure repeats the graceful pose of a Raphael. Other figures, such as the old man with a stick on the right, express the irrational and fantastic vein of Salviati.

Perin del Vaga

VISITATION

c. 1538
fresco
Trinità dei Monti

A pupil of Raphael and a leading painter in Rome under Clement VII, Perin del Vaga's brilliant colouring reflects his Tuscan training and the influence of Rosso Fiorentino.

The typical Mannerist striving for dynamic effects and tensions in the contrived poses of the figures is evident in the group of bystanders on the left.

Perin del Vaga

PSYCHE AND THE OLD WOMAN

1545–1547
fresco
Castel Sant'Angelo, Room of Psyche

Perin del Vaga coordinated the team of artists who decorated the apartments of Paul III in Castel Sant'Angelo. He also painted the frescoes in some of the rooms. In the Room of Psyche he discarded the decorative grotesques begun by Raphael and divided the narrative into panels framed with painted architectural elements. In the episode of Psyche and the old woman the ancient ruins create an atmosphere of nostalgia and melancholy.

Michelangelo

CONVERSION OF ST PAUL

1542–1545, fresco
Pauline Chapel, Vatican Palace, Vatican

SAN MARCELLO AL CORSO

sixteenth century
side chapel

The side chapels in San Marcello al Corso contain numerous Mannerist paintings. In addition to Francesco Salviati, who painted the *Stories of the Virgin* in the Grifoni Chapel, in 1527 Perin del Vaga laid out the scheme of a fresco cycle that was eventually completed by Daniele da Volterra.

Michelangelo

MARTYRDOM OF ST PETER

1542–1545
fresco
Pauline Chapel, Vatican Palace, Vatican

Michelangelo's frescoes in this chapel, built in 1537 by Antonio da Sangallo the Younger for Paul III, are his last intense achievement in painting. They take even further the dramatic innovations evident in the *Last Judgement*: the lack of symmetry, the uncertain organisation of space and the writhing, tangled figures, which reflect the anguished loss of certainties and a world in crisis after the great Renaissance adventure. The cold light and harsh colours create an effect of hallucinatory desolation, expressing an inner torment that permeates all of Michelangelo's late works.

The Capitol (Piazza del Campidoglio)

Paul III's numerous attempts to revive the art and architecture of Rome included a systematic project by Michelangelo for the redesign of the Piazza del Campidoglio in 1538. The pope's decision to erect the equestrian statue of Marcus Aurelius here was the starting point for an ambitious project of urban transformation. Ever since antiquity this square had been the centre of the city's municipal and administrative life. The irregular piazza was conceived as a trapezium-shaped space opening out scenically before the backdrop of the Palazzo Senatorio. The other sides were lined with the Palazzo dei Conservatori and a new, symmetrically placed building, erected for the purpose.

CAPITOL

Cordonata
begun in 1538

The Cordonata (a monumental flight of steps) leading up to the square was included in Michelangelo's plan. He designed an imposing entrance, befitting this important municipal site for all Rome's citizens. In 1583 the rather rigid statues of Castor and Pollux holding their horses were placed at the top of the steps, near the balustrade that surrounds the square.

CAPITOL

view of one of the Dioscuri
begun in 1538

The left side of the square is bounded by the Palazzo Capitolino, which flanks Santa Maria in Aracoeli. It was designed together with Palazzo dei Conservatori by Michelangelo, but only completed in the following century. A giant order of columns is ranged along the front of the building, surmounted by a powerful cornice and a balustrade lined with statues.

MARCUS AURELIUS

copy of the original
from the second centuy AD
the Capitol

The statue of the emperor Marcus Aurelius dominates the piazza on the Capitoline hill. The plinth of the equestrian monument, designed by Michelangelo, is the key to the whole spatial layout of the square. The effect of spatial dilation is amplified by the pattern of the star inscribed in an oval set of the paving.

THE CAPITOL

begun in 1538

Michelangelo's redesign transformed the piazza on the Capitol into a terrace bounded by a balustrade overlooking the city on one side and the Forum on the other.

THE CAPITOL

begun in 1538

This is one of the great examples of an urban project from the High Renaissance. It revived the concept of an ideal city rising above Rome, opening out before the observer who climbs the steps to the top.

Federico Zuccari

PALAZZETTO ZUCCARI

detail of the façade
1592

Bizarre masks with gaping mouths frame the portal and windows of the mansion designed by Federico Zuccari as his home and an academy of painting. Typical of Mannerism, the taste for grotesque and monstrous ornaments is a feature of late-Cinquecento architecture in Rome.

Federico Zuccari

PALAZZO TIZIO DI SPOLETO

detail of the façade
c. 1575

The frescoes with a series of *putti* ranged round the arms of Pius IV are the work of Federico Zuccari. The front elevation is also enriched with elegant stucco decorations framing the windows.

Giulio Mazzoni and Diego de Fiandra

PALAZZO SPADA

detail of the façade
on the courtyard
1560

In the mid-sixteenth century work began on this palace for Girolamo Capodiferro, one of Paul III's cardinals. In 1632 the property passed to Cardinal Spada. The exuberant and joyous decoration of the façade set a new artistic fashion. The elegant, vibrant stuccoes by Giulio Mazzoni and Diego de Fiandra were a true revival of early Cinquecento decorative art: the *putti*, festoons, medallions, statues of emperors and pagan motives are all classical features derived from Raphael.

The obelisks of Sixtus V

Sixtus V (1585–1590) radically reconstructed the city of Rome. The pope decided to link together the seven principal basilicas of the city by laying out broad, straight thoroughfares that would run into each other and create the symbolic form of a star. The main intersections in this scheme, which was only partly completed, were to be marked by fountains and obelisks. The idea of relocating the ancient obelisks was a great novelty, because, in addition to creating a landmark for each space, the pope saw them as charged with symbolic significance. They would express an ideal continuity between the papal city, the Pharaohs of ancient Egypt who had first erected them and the Roman emperors that brought them to Rome. By erecting them in front of the ancient Christian basilicas and surmounting them with bronze crosses, the pope was declaring the triumph of the Catholic faith over these relics of ancient paganism.

FLAMINIAN OBELISK

Piazza del Popolo

The obelisk in Piazza del Popolo came originally from Heliopolis, where it had been erected by Rameses II. It is surrounded by four pools with Egyptian lions placed here by Valadier in 1818. Compared with the other obelisks erected in Rome by Sixtus V, this definitely has the must successful and strategic location, at the convergence of three fine thoroughfares, Via del Babuino, Via del Corso and Via Ripetta.

SALLUSTIAN OBELISK

Trinità dei Monti

The church of Trinità dei Monti was consecrated by Sixtus V, who also began to build the Spanish steps leading up to its façade. The square was completed in 1789 with the raising of the obelisk by Pius VI, who continued Sixtus's urban projects.

VATICAN OBELISK

St Peter's Square, Vatican

The obelisk in St Peter's Square was moved to its present position by Pope Sixtus V. Its earlier location was a square beside the basilica dedicated to the early Christian martyrs. This site was formerly occupied by the Circus of Caligula, who in 37 had the immense obelisk brought here from Heliopolis. The work was supervised by Domenico Fontana, who made a wooden spire to study the effect of its new location. This obelisk was the first to be set up since ancient times; it was soon followed by the erection of Sixtus's other obelisks at key points of the city.

ESQUILINE OBELISK

Piazza dell'Esquilino

This obelisk was brought from the mausoleum of Augustus in the Campus Martius, where it lay broken in four pieces together with its twin, now at the Quirinal. This is the smallest of the four obelisks of the Sistine period. Sixtus V decided to erect it behind the imposing apse of Santa Maria Maggiore (instead of in front of the church) because the entrance to the papal villa was close by and it would be enhanced by the new monument.

LATERAN OBELISK

Piazza San Giovanni in Laterano

The immense obelisk of red granite, the tallest (47 metres) in Rome, was carried off from Thebes by order of the emperor Constantius II, who set it up in the Circus Maximus. Excavated in 1587 by Sixtus V, who found it broken into three parts, it was then raised in 1588 by Domenico Fontana, who also designed the new Palazzo del Laterano.

Tomaso Laureti

THE TRIUMPH OF RELIGION

c. 1568
fresco
Sala di Costantino, Vatican Palace, Vatican

The vault of the Sala di Costantino was frescoed by Tomaso Laureti, a painter from Palermo. He created a rigorous perspective scheme with a boldly foreshortened representation of a majestic church interior. The focal point of the illusionistic perspective is the Crucifix, symbolising the Church's triumph over paganism, represented by the shattered idol in the foreground.

Federico Zuccari

PIETÀ

c. 1567
oil on canvas
Galleria Borghese

As the capital of the Catholic world, Rome developed a new style of art based on the Counter-Reformation guidelines for sacred imagery. In the late Cinquecento a number of painters used their skills to embody a strongly religious content in a simplified style, based on the work of the great masters but stereotyped into devotional forms. An example is this rigorous and austere *Pietà* by Federico Zuccari, a copy of one by his brother Taddeo (now in Urbino).

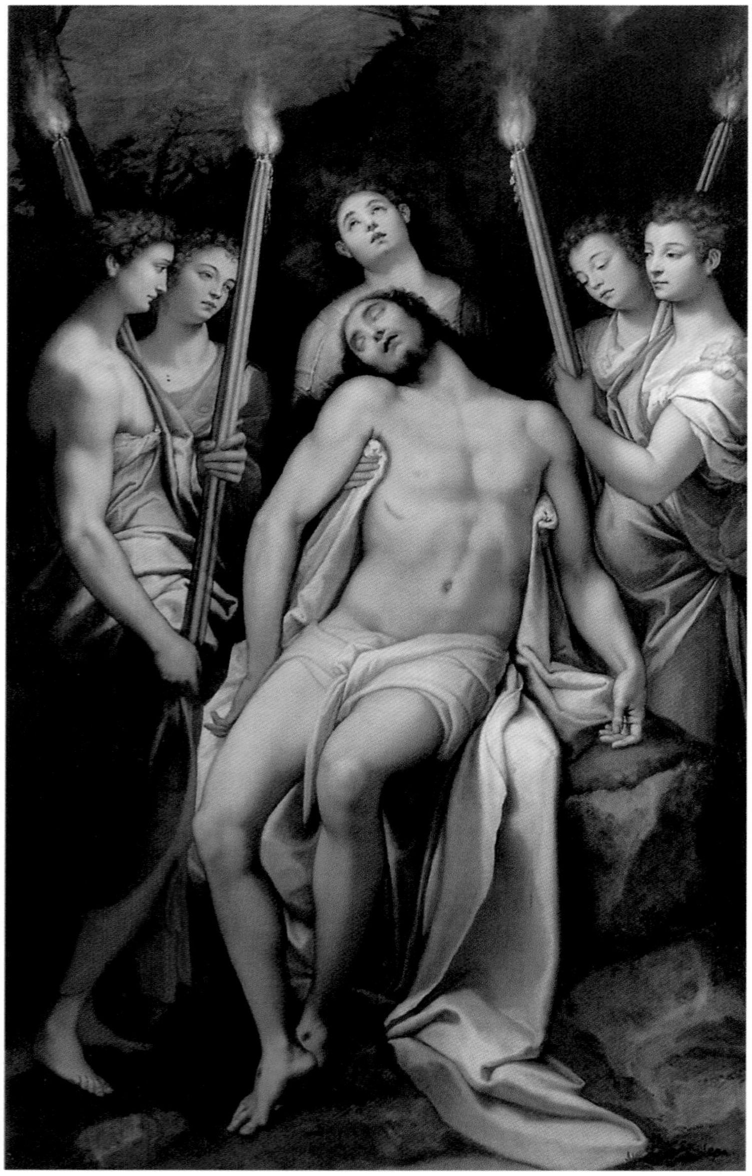

Domenico Fontana

SALONE SISTINO

1587–1589
Biblioteca Apostolica Vaticana, Vatican

The five years of the pontificate of Sixtus V (1585–1590) were notable for numerous new urban projects and monumental buildings. They ranged from a renewal of the city's urban fabric to the construction of the Lateran Palace. The Vatican Palace was also modified by his projects. The pope built out a massive extension facing the suburbs and St Peter's Square, known as the Sistine Wing, and new premises for the Vatican Library. The architect was Domenico Fontana, coming from the Swiss Ticino: this block was set at right angles to the palace, intersecting the Cortile del Belvedere and dividing it in two. The new structure consists of a long gallery and a splendid internal salon covered with frescoes.

Domenico Fontana

SALONE SISTINO

1587–1589
Biblioteca Apostolica Vaticana, Vatican

The main chamber of the new Vatican Library was the great Salone Sistino, divided into a nave and side aisles by massive pillars completely covered with frescoes like the rest of the interior. The team of painters was supervised by Cesare Nebbia and Giovanni Guerra, who also worked on the pope's other new buildings. Nebbia, from Orvieto, had close links with Tuscan-Roman and Lombard art, while Guerra was from Modena; his more refined, elegant style tended to offset Nebbia's harsher manner. Giovanni Baglione has recorded the names of a large number of artists, all more or less famous, who worked under them. They included Paul Bril, Giambattista Pozzo, Paris Nogari, Andrea Lilio and Orazio Gentileschi. The cycle of decorations represents four themes: the great libraries of antiquity (as in Babylon, Athens and Alexandria), the ecumenical councils, the inventors of the alphabets of the various languages and, finally, the achievements of Sixtus V in Rome and the papal state. The vaults are decorated with grotesque motives derived from the Renaissance.

Federico Barocci

The work of Federico Barocci (Urbino 1535–1612) marks the final development of Renaissance art and the transition to Baroque. The reasons lie not just in the chronology of his paintings but, above all, in their new contemplative and spiritual sensibility. The works of his maturity, in particular, herald the nascent art of the seventeenth century. Barocci was trained in the artistic milieu of Urbino, deeply imbued with the legacy of Raphael. Another important influence was Correggio, from whom he derived the graceful movement and sweet expressiveness of his figures, enlivened by a palette that owed much to the Venetians. A rather isolated artist in the panorama of Italian painting, Barocci first appeared in Rome in 1561–1563, when he worked with Taddeo Zuccari on the decorations of the Pius IV's Casina in the Vatican Gardens. In 1565 Barocci returned to Urbino but kept in touch with his numerous clients in various parts of Central Italy. He also sent some works to Rome, such as the *Visitation* and the *Presentation at the Temple* for Santa Maria in Vallicella (Chiesa Nuova).

Federico Barocci

VISITATION

1583–1586
oil on canvas
Santa Maria in Vallicella
(Chiesa Nuova)

In Rome Barocci was particularly patronised by the religious orders and confraternities intent on fostering a radical renewal of the Catholic Church. The narrative clarity and direct feeling in his works complied with the new rules for religious art laid down by the Council of Trent. His *Visitation* in Santa Maria della Vallicella (also called the Chiesa Nuova) was the favourite work of St Philip Neri, the founder of the Oratorian confraternity. Its refined handling of light and colour, which involve the viewer emotionally, already suggests a Baroque sensibility.

Federico Barocci

REST ON THE FLIGHT INTO EGYPT

1573
oil on canvas
Pinacoteca Vaticana, Vatican

The gentle expressions and the delicate looks and gestures express the close affection linking the figures, while also revealing the artist's careful study of composition. Barocci heightens the impression of intimacy and closeness, enhanced by the subdued lighting and soft colouring, with subtly shaded tones of pale pink.

The Farnese Gallery

In 1595 Annibale Carracci (Bologna 1560–Rome 1609) was summoned from his native Bologna to Rome by Cardinal Odoardo Farnese to decorate his private study ("Camerino"). In Rome, where he stayed till his death, Annibale devoted close study to ancient art and the great Renaissance masters, Raphael and Michelangelo, giving his own style a more markedly classical imprint. The Camerino Farnese was followed by Annibale's biggest commission in Rome, the decoration of the gallery of Palazzo Farnese, which he completed early in the seventeenth century. In his quest for a beauty that was both ideal and natural, Annibale drew freely on tradition, recreating the grace and joyous vitality of the ancient myths and fables.

Annibale Carracci

MERCURY DELIVERING THE GOLDEN APPLE TO PARIS

c. 1592–1600
fresco
the gallery, Palazzo Farnese

Annibale Carracci

HOMAGE TO DIANA

1597–1602
fresco
the gallery, Palazzo Farnese

In Annibale Carracci's plan for the decoration of the gallery, the interior was covered with a *trompe l'oeil* collection of ancient paintings: gilt cornices, richly decorated with imitation stucco work and motives from classical art, frame the scenes and create the illusion of a gallery of paintings hung on the vault. Inspired by Virgil's *Georgics*, this painting depicts Pan presenting a precious white veil to the goddess Diana.

Annibale Carracci

VAULT OF THE FARNESE GALLERY

1597–1604
Palazzo Farnese

Underlying this extraordinary *trompe l'oeil* pictorial space created for the Farnese Gallery is the artist's vital rediscovery of the classical world and the free evocation of antiquity derived from his study of Michelangelo and Raphael. Certain scenes are set in illusionistic gilt and stucco frames; others are bounded by great Atlas-figures, simulating ancient stone statues and alternating with young, flesh-coloured nudes holding medallions and garlands.

Annibale Carracci

TRIUMPH OF BACCHUS AND ARIADNE

1597–1602
fresco
the gallery, Palazzo Farnese

In a radiant, luminous world, a bevy of satyrs, nymphs, maenads and bacchantes accompanies the triumph of Bacchus and Ariadne, at the centre of the barrel vault, in a celebration of love and sensuous beauty.

Annibale Carracci

CAMERINO FARNESE

view of the whole
1595–1597
Palazzo Farnese

The decoration of this small private chamber was the first of Annibale's works in Rome. He here showed his full command of the powers of expression. The decoration of this small chamber celebrates the client who commissioned them, the learned Odoardo Farnese, a humanist and librarian. The cycle, which comprises stuccos, frescoes and a large canvas, represents scenes from mythology exemplifying the virtues.
The centre of the vault formerly contained a painting of *Hercules at the Crossroads*, now replaced by a copy. The original is in the Museo Capodimonte in Naples.

Annibale Carracci

LANDSCAPE WITH THE FLIGHT INTO EGPYT

1604
oil on canvas
Galleria Doria Pamphilj

Landscape was used from ancient times as a simple background to episodes from sacred or profane history. It was cultivated as a self-sufficient art form only in the early seventeenth century, firstly in the work of Annibale Carracci. This lunette of the *Flight into Egypt*, originally painted for the chapel of the Palazzo Aldobrandini, was a new way of representing nature, interpreted in the light of the classical ideal. This balanced and rational view of the natural setting, in which figures and landscapes blend harmoniously, was later developed and became an established genre in the work of the French artists Nicolas Poussin and Claude Lorrain.

Annibale Carracci

VENUS WITH SATYR AND CUPIDS

c. 1588
oil on canvas
Palazzo di Montecitorio

This painting, now in the Palazzo di Montecitorio, comes from the Palazzo Farnese, where it is recorded in a seventeenth-century inventory of the family's collection. This valuable document reveals that the collector and art patron Odoardo Farnese favoured works by the Carraccis and their followers, a number of which could be seen at strategic points of the family palace in Rome. The long partnership between Annibale and the cultured cardinal probably began even before the artist was invited to Rome, since this work was painted before that date. The sensuous pose of Venus clearly derives from Titian. The erotic charge of the painting and the vitality of the scene anticipate the themes of the Farnese Gallery.

Caravaggio

After his early training in Lombardy, the young Michelangelo Merisi (Milan or Caravaggio 1571–Porto Ercole 1610) appeared in Rome in about 1590. There he entered the workshop of the Cavalier d'Arpino. In these early years at Rome he produced his celebrated still-lifes with flowers and fruit. The canvases painted in 1599 for the Church of San Luigi dei Francesi marked a breakthrough in his career; they first embodied his dramatic and highly innovative conception of sacred art and his new handling of light. They were followed by a series of altarpieces painted for the most important churches in Rome. Some of them were actually rejected by his clients as "indecorous." After committing a murder in 1606, Caravaggio was forced to flee from Rome. The last years of his life were spent in Naples, Malta and Sicily.

Caravaggio

BOY WITH A BASKET OF FRUIT (THE FRUIT-VENDOR)

1593–1594
oil on canvas
Galleria Borghese

Painted in his early years in Rome, this painting reveals Caravaggio's analytic and descriptive powers. With a delicate, naturalistic sensibility that reflects his training in Lombardy, he endows the fruit and flowers in the basket with a silent life of their own.

Caravaggio

BACCHINO MALATO

1593–1594
oil on canvas
Galleria Borghese

The celebrated "Bacchino Malato" is actually a self-portrait, probably painted after a lengthy illness, as suggested by the livid hue of the face and lips.

Caravaggio

THE FORTUNE TELLER

1593–1594
oil on canvas
Pinacoteca Capitolina

In the 1590s, Caravaggio turned to a range of subjects that had been previously neglected, with figures taken from everyday life and humble settings.

Caravaggio

REST ON THE FLIGHT INTO EGYPT

1595–1596
oil on canvas
Galleria Doria Pamphilj

This early painting lacks the dramatic chiaroscuro typical of Caravaggio's later work. The scene is luminous, the atmosphere peaceful and bucolic, and the composition is dominated by the pure white robe of the elegant angel-violinist.

Caravaggio

JUDITH BEHEADING HOLOFERNES

c. 1599
oil on canvas
Galleria Nazionale d'Arte Antica, Palazzo Barberini

The dramatic force of the episode is heightened by the red curtain, which amplifies the colour of the blood soaking into the white sheet.

San Luigi dei Francesi

The cycle painted in 1599–1602 for the Contarelli Chapel in San Luigi dei Francesi was Caravaggio's first important public commission. The success of the display of his canvases had placed the artist in the limelight. By the good offices of Cardinal del Monte, Caravaggio was given the important commission to complete the decoration of the French chapel. This had been purchased much earlier, in 1565, by Cardinal Mathieu Contarel and left unfinished by the Cavalier Arpino, who frescoed the vault. After the success of his first canvases, the *Calling* and *Martyrdom of St Matthew*, the artist was also asked to paint an altarpiece of *St Matthew and the Angel* to replace a statue by Cobaert, who was then at work on the commission.

SAN LUIGI DEI FRANCESI

1518–1589
exterior

Caravaggio

THE CALLING OF ST MATTHEW

detail
1599–1600
oil on canvas
Contarelli Chapel, San Luigi dei Francesi

This painting illustrates the moment when the tax-gatherer, sitting at a table with his companions in a bare room, is summoned by Christ.
The lighting is carefully calculated and provides the key to the picture's interpretation. A shaft of light falls from the right from the dusty window across the bare wall, leading the viewer's gaze from the beckoning figure of Christ to the astonished, questioning expression of Matthew, who rises to follow the Master.
The light has a symbolic value: it enshrines the divine grace that bursts quite naturally into the sphere of everyday life bringing salvation. This painting was one of those most often copied by Caravaggio's numerous followers.

Caravaggio

ST MATTHEW AND THE ANGEL

1602
oil on canvas
Contarelli Chapel,
San Luigi dei Francesi

This is the second version of the subject painted by Caravaggio for the cycle. The first was rejected because the poses of the saint and the angel were considered undignified and lacking in decorum. In the version accepted by his client, the evangelist, still in an unconventional pose, receives inspiration from the hovering angel, God's messenger.

Caravaggio

MARTYRDOM OF ST MATTHEW

1599–1600
oil on canvas
Contarelli Chapel,
San Luigi dei Francesi

This is the most dramatic episode of the cycle in the Contarelli Chapel. In the middle, his body illuminated by the harsh glare of the light, emerges the sculptural figure of the executioner. The reactions of the bystanders culminate in the figure of the young man, who turns to flee in terror.

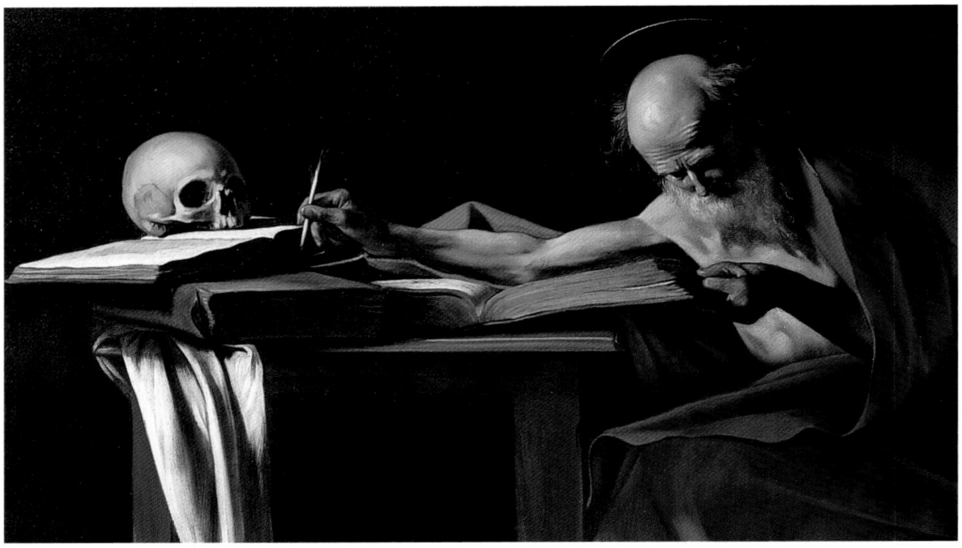

Caravaggio

ST JEROME

1605–1606
oil on canvas
Galleria Borghese

Painted at the end of the Roman period, this work represents a phase of meditation by the artist. It portrays the saint, who was especially cherished by the Counter-Reformation, engaged on his translation of the Bible surrounded by open books and a skull as a memento of the precariousness of life.

Caravaggio

CRUCIFIXION OF ST PETER

1600–1601
oil on canvas
Cerasi Chapel,
Santa Maria del Popolo

Caravaggio received a commission for two paintings in the Cerasi Chapel after the success of his work in the Contarelli Chapel. They were a further step in his revolutionary approach to sacred painting. In the *Martyrdom of St Peter* Caravaggio was influenced by the composition of Michelangelo's painting of the same subject in the Pauline Chapel. The focus of the painting is on the martyr's bewildered gaze and the exertions of his executioners, whose actions are represented with lucid realism.

Caravaggio

THE CONVERSION OF ST PAUL

1600–1601
oil on canvas
Cerasi Chapel,
Santa Maria del Popolo

Here, too, the events of sacred history are interpreted with clear-eyed freedom and set in the context of everyday events. The saint is blinded by the light of divine revelation in the obscurity of a stable, under the indifferent gaze of a stable hand, who is intent on quieting the great horse that looms over the scene. As with *St Matthew and the Angel*, Caravaggio was forced to paint a second version of the work when his client rejected the first.

Caravaggio

ST JOHN THE BAPTIST

1602
oil on canvas
Musei Capitolini

When required by his clients, Caravaggio frequently replicated some of his paintings, at times making slight changes. Among the most often repeated subjects, both by Caravaggio and his followers, was *John the Baptist.* In painting the saint as a vital and joyous young man, Caravaggio was measuring himself with the great Renaissance artists. The twist of his body repeats the pose of Michelangelo's *Ignudi* in the ceiling of the Sistine Chapel.

Caravaggio

MADONNA OF THE PILGRIMS

c. 1604–1606
oil on canvas
Sant'Agostino

Caravaggio's fearless reinterpretation of the traditional iconography is particularly evident here.
The allusion to the Holy House of Loreto, for which this was painted as an altarpiece, is limited to the depiction of Mary on the threshold. The Virgin, who tenderly clasps the Christ child, is represented as a simple woman of the people. The two ragged wayfarers kneeling before her are tender, moving figures without being idealised.

Caravaggio

THE DEPOSITION

1602–1604
oil on canvas
Pinacoteca Vaticana, Vatican

Painted for the chapel of Santa Maria in Vallicella, the church of the Oratorians of St Philip Neri, this *Deposition* is generally considered as representing a "classical" phase in the artist's work, at the very end of his stay in Rome.
The stark rendering of Christ's body, sculpturally modelled by light, is an explicit tribute to the art of Michelangelo. The sharp corner of the tombstone, placed obliquely to the rest of the scene in the foreground, forms a natural plinth for the drama as it unfolds, with the expressive gestures of grief of the figures emerging powerfully from the dark background. Caravaggio's realism is evident in the rendering of the feet and legs of Nicodemus.

Caravaggio

ST FRANCIS IN MEDITATION

1606
oil on canvas
Galleria Nazionale d'Arte Antica, Palazzo Barberini

St Francis is a frequent subject of Caravaggio's religious paintings, where he is portrayed in ecstasy, prayer, meditation or penitence. The exploration of these inner states does not reflect an urge to comply with Counter-Reformation rules for devotional paintings, but is a sign of Caravaggio's deep religious feeling.

Caravaggio

NARCISSUS

1597–1599
oil on canvas
Galleria Nazionale d'Arte Antica, Palazzo Barberini

The fascination of this painting lies in its unusual "playing card" composition. The light falls on the knee of the youth, at the centre of the painting, and his mirror image appears, inverted, in the water. The scene is centred wholly on the personal tensions of Narcissus, whose inner drama is at the centre of interest.

Caravaggio

MADONNA DEI PALAFRENIERI

1605–1606
oil on canvas
Galleria Borghese

Painted for the Chapel of the Palafrenieri in St Peter's, this is one of Caravaggio's works that were rejected by the client. It was displayed for just a month on the altar before being moved to the church of the confraternity of Sant'Anna and then sold to Cardinal Borghese. As before, it was condemned for its lack of "decorum."

Caravaggio

ST JOHN THE BAPTIST

1609–1610
oil on canvas
Galleria Borghese

This melancholy interpretation of a subject represented as vital elsewhere suggests this was one of Caravaggio's last, intense works. The sketchiness of parts of the painting (especially the fleece of the goat) is typical of his late production. Unlike the young, athletic figure in the painting in the Musei Capitolini, here the saint sits wearily and gazes sadly out at the viewer.

Caravaggio

DAVID WITH THE HEAD OF GOLIATH

1609–1610
oil on canvas
Galleria Borghese

The theme of the bodiless head returns in this painting from Caravaggio's sojourn in Naples. Inspired by ancient statuary, the body of David emerges dramatically from the dark background as he holds out Goliath's head, still dripping blood, with a triumphant yet weary gesture. This tragic image enshrines a tormented self-portrait of the artist himself, perhaps in penitence for the murder that forced him to flee from Rome, or only for his violent, misspent life.
The simplified, rapid brushwork, especially in the rendering of David's shirt and sword, is typical of Caravaggio's late work.

Baroque, the

Giovanni Antonio Mari (after a sketch by Bernini), Fountain of the Moor, 1654, Piazza Navona

Spectacle of the City

From the Seventeenth Century to Neoclassicism

In seventeenth- and eighteenth-century Rome, the streets and squares swarmed with artists from all over Europe, who flocked to the Eternal City by different paths. The more fortunate ones lived comfortably on the patronage of the nobility and the cardinals of the Church, or were supported by generous study grants. Many others were content to lead a hand-to-mouth existence, with little money but many adventures with their friends and fellow-artists, glorying in the Mediterranean sunshine and the city's history. In these two centuries, almost every artist, whether the founder of a school or a modest jobbing painter, felt the urge to see Rome. Flemish and German painters, Rubens, Velázquez, Van Dyck and Poussin, all the Baroque artists of Europe, gathered in Rome, where they compared notes and absorbed the city's artistic vitality, which retained its magnetic power until the start of the nineteenth century.

Early in the seventeenth century, there were three main strands in the figurative arts. They emerged first in Rome and then spread to the rest of Europe. These strands had an almost "political" significance, or at least they embodied a definite cultural orientation. They were: the naturalism of Caravaggio, based on chiaroscuro effects and a profound grasp of reality; the classicism of the great Bolognese and later French masters, whose limpid compositions drew their inspiration from Raphael and ancient art; and finally the most sumptuous and theatrical current, the Baroque proper, which achieved a dynamic fusion of architecture, painting and sculpture to create a richly powerful decorative whole.

The stage where these three currents merged and clashed was the Rome

Francesco Borromini
San Carlo alle Quattro Fontane
(San Carlino)
interior
1638–1667

Stefano Maderno
St Cecilia
1600
Santa Cecilia in Trastevere

Pauline Chapel
detail of the dome
with frescoes by Cigoli
1612
Santa Maria Maggiore

Piazza San Pietro

of the popes and princes, the great cross-roads of international artistic culture. The main force in the long golden age of Roman Baroque was the many-sided genius of Gian Lorenzo Bernini.
A master at evoking the sense of wonder that was the defining quality of Baroque art, Bernini worked eclectically in a wide range of different materials. Effortlessly, he draws the viewer into his spectacular inventions with their seductive ambiguities. Then, in the eighteenth century, when the sparkle and brilliance of Bernini's Baroque had died away, Rome created a new, more reflective and refined art, certainly less spectacular but perhaps more subtly poetic. The revival of classical antiquity was veiled with nostalgia for a lost civilisation, whose monumental remains survived but whose values seemed lost. The slow process had begun that led to the birth of a new international style, neo-classicism, with Rome setting the style for Europe.

The Face of the City, between Ancient and Modern

In the late sixteenth and the seventeenth century the face of Rome changed. Any occasion (a Holy Year, the election of a new pope, the pageantry surrounding the princes or new religious orders, even popular festivals) might be seized to rebuild the squares, the churches and the façades of houses. Extensive changes were made to the urban décor, with new fountains, monuments and obelisks. The Baroque aesthetic strove above all to create theatrical effects, so that the city as a whole became like a gigantic stage. It was a city of construction sites, manned by teams of labourers, stone-cutters, masons, stucco-workers and decorators, nearly all of them hailing from Lombardy. The most skilled and successful master builders became a force in this new Rome; they worked not only on mansions and churches but also on some highly original architectural genres, such as the monstrous figures that decorated the aqueducts.

opposite
Giovanni Battista Soria

SANTA MARIA DELLA VITTORIA

façade
1626

The church contains Bernini's celebrated carving of the *Ecstasy of St Teresa*. It has an elegant marble façade with a double order of columns and is an impressive work of evident classical inspiration. Outside it is the Fountain of Moses, a notable architectural work from the late Cinquecento, designed by Domenico Fontana to display the water of the Acqua Felice.

Flaminio Ponzio

COURTYARD OF PALAZZO BORGHESE

1605–1614

Nicknamed "il cembalo" (the harpsichord) because of its shape, this palace has a spectacular courtyard with a colonnade (containing no fewer than ninety columns) and is decorated with ancient statues.

Flaminio Ponzio,
Giovanni Fontana

FOUNTAIN OF THE ACQUA PAOLA (CALLED THE "FONTANONE")

1608–1612
Janiculum

SIXTVS
AQVA
VIA P
MVLTAR
DVCTV S
MIL XX
FELICEMQ D
MARE PER TERRA
COEPIT PONT
SCIPIO S RE CARD BVRGHESIVS M POENITEN ANNO MDCXX VI

Maderno and Classicism

A memorable undertaking of the period was the remodelling of many squares and streets, which included the erection of colossal relics (such as Egyptian obelisks and great basins from Roman thermal baths), which formed new urban landmarks. Yet the remains of antiquity were not always treated so respectfully: many important edifices were simply torn down, stripped of their materials or unceremoniously refashioned to provide new spaces.
This was the fate of the bronze decorations of the Pantheon, melted down by Bernini and recast as the baldacchino in St Peter's, despite angry protests by intellectuals and even the populace. One of the most active architects of the day was Carlo Maderno, a tireless designer whose work evoked classical architecture.

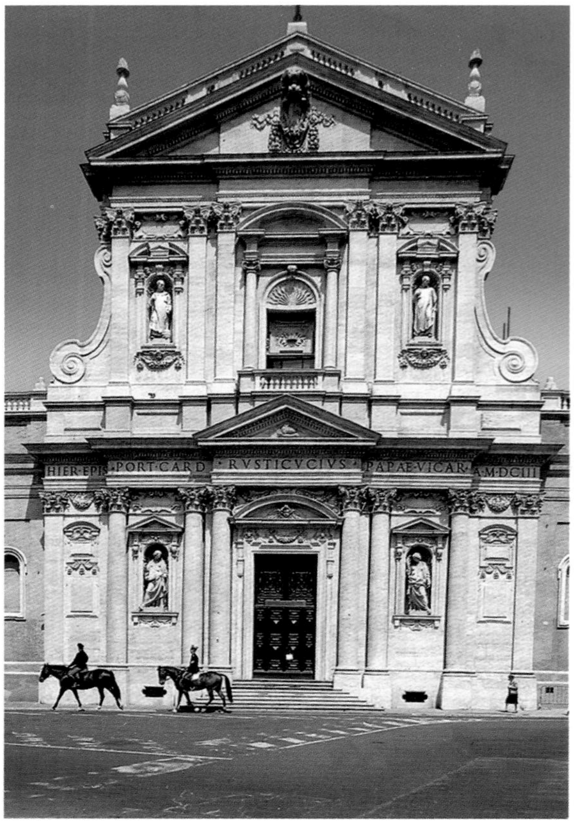

Carlo Maderno

SANTA SUSANNA

façade
1603

An important achievement in the history of architecture, this tall and very beautiful façade is an early example of the harmonious combination of architecture and sculpture.

Carlo Maderno

COLUMN OF THE BASILICA OF MAXENTIUS

1614
marble from Mount Hymettus
Piazza di Santa Maria Maggiore

Carlo Maderno was from the Swiss Ticino. He worked in the tradition of the master builders from the region of the Lombard lakes. He would excavate fragments of ancient Rome and transform them into eye-catching landmarks amid the urban development and new buildings commissioned by the popes, so creating an ideal continuity between the classical world and the Christian city. This Roman column was erected on a tall base bearing the heraldic animals of Pope Paul V and surmounted by a statue of the Virgin.

Carlo Maderno

ST PETER'S

façade
1607–1612
Vatican

This illustration records the state of the façade of St Peter's before the controversial restoration work that "added" a coat of colour to it. Behind and around the solemn, rather monotonous screen of columns by Maderno, the walls now sport a pinkish hue. This was added by the restorers on the basis of uncertain traces that still survived and the recorded purchase of a large number of paint brushes towards the end of the building work carried out under Maderno, completed in 1612. The point of all those brushes is not clear, but they were not necessarily used by squads of house-painters working on the façade. The effect is definitely unexpected, but has a certain appeal. The façade formed a striking backdrop to the solemn ceremonies of the Holy Year in 2000. The colour also brings out the superimposition of an ancient temple front on a triumphant Counter-Reformation building, which was certainly one of Maderno's objectives

CAMPO DE' FIORI

the market and the monument to Giordano Bruno

A busy, popular open space, the market of Campo de' Fiori hardly matches its lugubrious reputation. For centuries this was the chosen spot for the fires and scaffolds used in public executions. On this spot Giordano Bruno, convicted of heresy, was burned alive on 17 February 1600. He is commemorated by a monument dating from the end of the nineteenth century. His death has long been a stain on the conscience of Baroque Rome, a cruel memory continually repressed but always resurfacing.

Carlo Lambari

SANTA FRANCESCA ROMANA

façade
1615
the Forum

Erected by Carlo Lambari, the façade of this fine Benedictine church adds a note of white travertine to the monumental scenario of the Forum. The façade was completed a few years after the saint was canonised in 1608, and was part of a broad redevelopment scheme begun towards the end of the Cinquecento.

Pietro da Cortona

SANTI LUCA E MARTINA

1635–1664
the Forum

The church is a masterpieces of Pietro da Cortona. It belonged to the guild of painters, whose patron was St Luke.
Annexed to it was the building of the Academy of Art, demolished in 1931 to make way for Via dei Fori Imperiali. Despite this eyesore, we can still appreciate the way the architect inserted a dynamic Baroque church in the setting of the Forum, directly opposite the Arch of Septimius Severus (the side of the arch can be made out on the left in the photo).

A City of a Hundred Nations

Multitudes of artists from every part of Europe settled in Rome. They were all there to learn; few of them received commissions or official appointments. To find work, most of them relied on the good offices of their fellow countrymen. A few of them were adventurers in search of fortune. This rich and bewildering humanity offered many opportunities for meeting, exchanging opinions, and developing competing styles against a backdrop of ancient monuments and the masterpieces of Raphael and Michelangelo.

Valentin de Boulogne

ALLEGORY OF ITALY

1628–1629
oil on canvas
Galleria Nazionale d'Arte Antica, Palazzo Barberini

Curiously, this allegorical painting celebrating the glory of Italy, painted by a French artist, belongs to the Finnish Cultural Institute. It is temporarily on display at Palazzo Barberini.

opposite, above
Valentin de Boulogne

THE LAST SUPPER

c. 1625–1626
oil on canvas
Galleria Nazionale d'Arte Antica, Palazzo Barberini

Among all the French painters with official appointments in Rome, Valentin is perhaps now the most admired. In his hands the realism of Caravaggio was transformed into a forceful and often stark vision of reality, represented with unusual energy.

opposite, below
Valentin de Boulogne

CHRIST CLEANSING THE TEMPLE

c. 1618
oil on canvas
Galleria Nazionale d'Arte Antica, Palazzo Barberini

Like many other French artists, Valentin arrived in Rome when he was still young, about twenty. He was at once drawn into the orbit of Caravaggio, frequented the noisy gatherings of Flemish and Dutch painters, representatives of an unbridled realism, just at a time when the taste of collectors was turning towards the classicism of the Bolognese school. Valentin succeeded in carving out a niche in the art market, thanks to his evident technical skill and the immediate sense of human truth it conveys. He died tragically in 1542, when he was just forty years old.

Valentin de Boulogne

MARTYRDOM OF SAINTS PROCESSUS AND MARTINIAN

1629, oil on canvas
Pinacoteca Vaticana, Vatican

Valentin's most important sacred painting was originally intended for an altar in St Peter's, not far from Poussin's *Martyrdom of St Erasmus*, whose composition it imitated.

opposite, above
Simon Vouet

THE FORTUNE TELLER

c. 1618
oil on canvas
Galleria Nazionale d'Arte Antica, Palazzo Barberini

The Parisian Simone Vouet was a child prodigy, a skilled portraitist by the age of fifteen. He arrived in Italy in 1613, when he was just twenty-three. The first city he visited was Venice, where he mastered the rich colouring of Titian and his followers. Once in Rome he soon entered the orbit of Cardinal Barberini, later Pope Urban VIII, and received important commissions. His style was elegant and refined.

opposite, below
Simon Vouet

ST CATHERINE

MARY MAGDALEN

c. 1614–1615
oil on panel
Palazzo del Quirinale

The two half-length figures of saints in the Palazzo del Quirinale are exquisite examples of Vouet's refined style: they display Caravaggesque lighting effects, certainly, but also an eager relish for full-bodied paintwork, which combines reminiscences of Venice with the Baroque influence. The painter had a brilliant career. In 1627 he reached the apex of the hierarchy of painters working in Rome by winning election as the president of the Accademia di San Luca. On returning to France Louis XIII appointed him "First Painter in Ordinary to the King," lodged him in the Louvre and gave him a substantial annual pension. He died in Paris in 1649.

Giovanni Baglione

SACRED AND PROFANE LOVE

1602
oil on canvas
Galleria Nazionale d'Arte Antica, Palazzo Barberini

A stylistic competitor and adversary at law of Caravaggio, Baglione was distinguished more for his important writings on art than for his rare paintings. This work, his masterpiece, fails to conceal the effort it cost him to cope with the great changes then taking place.

Hendrick Terbrugghen

CONCERT (HEARING)

c. 1620
oil on canvas
Galleria Nazionale d'Arte Antica, Palazzo Barberini

A leading representative of the school of Utrecht, Terbrugghen played an important part in the development of Dutch painting. He guided the transition from late-Cinquecento Mannerism to the breakthrough associated with Caravaggio, updated by drawing on the whole panorama of European art.
In 1604 he moved to Rome, where he met Caravaggio. He stayed in Italy for ten years, during which he acquired a remarkable mastery of the production of intensely dramatic works, painted on the grand scale with striking contrasts of light and shade. The subjects, lighting and composition of his works are borrowed directly from Caravaggio, but the Dutch artist added a characteristic interest in exploring physiognomy, with figures that recurred from one painting to another in different settings. On returning to Utrecht in 1614, Terbrugghen became the driving force behind the local school, inducing all the young artists to spend a period of study in Italy. He himself returned to Rome around 1620 and found a new artistic climate, in which the clear and luminous palette of the Bolognese school was dominant. Terbrugghen's own art then took on these lighter hues, and he revealed a significant interest in genre scenes, or at least the interpretation of sacred subjects with a more homely and realistic touch.

Carlo Saraceni

MADONNA AND CHILD WITH ST ANNE

c. 1610
oil on canvas
Galleria Nazionale d'Arte Antica, Palazzo Barberini

The Venetian artist Carlo Saraceni was one of the most interesting yet least known artists in Baroque Rome. His fame has suffered from the fact that he painted no monumental frescoes, yet his canvases strike the modern viewer as among the most intelligent and enjoyable mediations between the different schools.

Carlo Saraceni

ST CECILIA AND THE ANGEL

c. 1606
oil on canvas
Galleria Nazionale d'Arte Antica, Palazzo Barberini

The basic handling of light in this painting is clearly borrowed from Caravaggio, but Saraceni never forgot the vivid colouring of the art of his native Venice. He also revealed his skill in working with the domestic naturalism typical of the masters of the "Schilderbent," the community of Dutch painters resident in Rome.

Bartolomeo Manfredi

BACCHUS AND A DRINKER

c. 1610
oil on canvas
Galleria Nazionale d'Arte Antica, Palazzo Barberini

Manfredi was the first painter to seek a method to tone down Caravaggio's harsh realism and give it a more pleasurable form with a wider commercial appeal.

Orazio Borgianni

HOLY FAMILY WITH ST ELIZABETH, ST JOHN AND AN ANGEL

c. 1609
oil on canvas
Galleria Nazionale d'Arte Antica, Palazzo Barberini

This is one of the most charming works from early seventeenth-century Rome. It is a remarkable synthesis of realism with a meticulous rendering of details.

Guido Reni

CRUCIFIXION OF ST PETER

1604–1605
oil on canvas
Pinacoteca Vaticana, Vatican

The martyrdom of St Peter, crucified head down, is obviously one of the most frequent scenes in Roman art. This book contains many versions of it, from the Middle Ages on. Guido Reni, born in Bologna in 1575, was a pupil of the Carracci brothers; when they moved to Rome, he followed them in 1601. In painting this great altarpiece for St Peter's he clearly had in mind the moving canvas by Caravaggio, installed in Santa Maria del Popolo not long before. However, though in close contact at this time with the realism of Caravaggio, Guido Reni never lost the poise of his intellectually controlled, restrained and supremely elegant art.
The traditional values of painting, which he rediscovered through patient study of classical sculpture and the art of Raphael, became his guiding code, which was not just artistic but also moral.

Guido Reni

AURORA

1612–1614
fresco
Palazzo Rospigliosi Pallavicini

Guercino

AURORA

1621
fresco
Casino Ludovisi

Comparison of the two paintings shown on this page, similar in subject, technique and purpose, reveals the results of the close and fruitful competition between noble art collectors and patrons in Baroque Rome. In 1612 the Rospigliosi family commissioned Guido Reni to paint an *Aurora* for the ceiling of the "casino" (lodge) of their villa. The Bolognese painter adhered scrupulously to the example of his master Annibale Carracci in the vault of the Farnese Gallery, with a *trompe l'œil* painting on the ceiling.
Nine years later Guercino made his dazzling entry on the Roman scene: with almost brutal energy he painted this version of *Aurora* for the Casino Ludovisi, in a wholly different style from Guido Reni. He simulated an architectural space open to the sky framing the flight of the chariot of Aurora, drawn by two great, dappled coursers, viewed from below as they hurtle across the immense celestial vault.

Guercino

BURIAL AND GLORY OF ST PETRONILLA

1623
oil on canvas
Pinacoteca Capitolina

Guercino arrived in Rome in 1621. There he became the favourite painter of the Rospigliosi pope, Gregory XV. He was a violent thirty-year-old from the provinces, ready to crush all competition with the "great machine" of his compositions. Though he came from the same region of Italy as the artists of the Bolognese school, he had little in common with them. But once in Rome, Guercino came to realize that art was not just the direct expression of powerful feelings: it was also calm inner reflection and communication at the highest levels of awareness. His spectacular altarpiece of St Petronilla is one of the peaks of Guercino's art, precisely because of the balance he achieved between chiaroscuro and formal analysis. It is a very large and very beautiful painting, which one can gaze at endlessly, always discovering new points of interest. An example is the highly original detail of the hands emerging from below to support the body of the splendid saint as it is laid in the grave, evoking a space outside the painting.

Domenichino

COMMUNION OF ST JEROME

1614
oil on canvas
Pinacoteca Vaticana, Vatican

The inspiration for this painting was drawn from a similar composition by Agostino Carracci. The large altarpiece was painted for St Peter's.

Domenichino

THE HUNT OF DIANA

1616–1617
oil on canvas
Galleria Borghese

One of the earliest and most brilliant followers of Annibale Carracci, the Bolognese painter Domenichino made his debut while still very young, working at his master's side on the frescoes in the Farnese Gallery. When Domenichino moved to Rome, he lived as in a dream world. Enchanted by the beauties of classical art and enamoured of Raphael, he evoked the golden age of painting in his sophisticated and highly self-conscious art. This work was commissioned by Cardinal Aldobrandini as a pendant to Titian's *Bacchanal*, which had recently arrived in Rome from Ferrara.

Domenichino

THE SIBYL OF CUMAE

c. 1610
oil on canvas
Galleria Borghese

The comparison between these two seductive sibyls brings out the different spirits of classicism in the work of the Bolognese masters who had moved to Rome. Domenichino exalts the memory of Raphael, with a limpid composure of gesture and feeling in a perfect harmony of lighting, colour and composition.

Guercino

THE PERSIAN SIBYL

1647
oil on canvas
Pinacoteca Capitolina

Guercino by this time had firmly curbed the forcefulness of his youthful handling of chiaroscuro; yet this painting hints at disquieting feelings, not just in the pose of the melancholy young woman but also in the dense and shadowy folds of the drapery.

SIBILLA PERSICA

The Debut of Bernini and the Galleria Borghese

Gian Lorenzo Bernini fully enshrined the splendour of the age, a historical and artistic period that had attained complete expressive and emotional development. A gifted, precocious child, he was born into a family of artists in Naples in 1598 and after a long career he died in Rome in 1680. In his spectacular, imaginative, virtuoso inventions the whole universe seems to be filled with life and vertiginous movement, bursting into a thousand slivers of brightness, splendour and action. He was a great sculptor, certainly, but also an architect, painter, designer of pageants and inventor. In short, as has been said, Bernini stage-managed the great festival of art in Baroque Rome.

Many of his early works, which already reveal his extraordinary talent, are to be found in the Galleria Borghese. Most of them are inspired by classical myths and legend.

The opportunity of a lifetime came when Bernini was about thirty. He was given the commission to complete and decorate the basilica of St Peter's. It was Bernini who set the seal of his personality on it.

Gian Lorenzo Bernini

APOLLO AND DAPHNE

1622–1624
marble
Galleria Borghese

This sculpture depicts the melancholy myth of the nymph who fled from Apollo's embrace and was saved by being transformed into a laurel bush. Sculpture vies with poetry in Bernini's version. With his astonishing skill at modelling the surface of the marble, Bernini renders the roughness of the trunk and the softness of flesh, the nymph's flowing hair and the laurel leaves, slender and delicate as in nature, that sprout from her fingers. The expressions on the faces of the two figures are unforgettable: the astonishment of the god, thwarted as he grasps at his prey, and the unexpected metamorphosis of the nymph.

Gian Lorenzo Bernini

THE RAPE OF PROSERPINA

1621–1622
marble
Galleria Borghese

Giovanni Vasanzio

CASINO BORGHESE

1613–1615
entrance to the garden
of Villa Borghese

Gian Lorenzo Bernini

DAVID

1623–1624
marble
Galleria Borghese

Gian Lorenzo Bernini

THE HERMAPHRODITE

restoration of an ancient statue
(first century AD): Bernini carved
the mattress and parts of the figure
marble
Galleria Borghese

Bernini in St Peter

The St Peter's Basilica in the Vatican is the biggest church in Christendom. Early in the Cinquecento Pope Julius II commissioned Bramante to begin construction of the immense fabric of a new church. This entailed the destruction of the early Christian basilica. The work took over a century and included the construction of the gigantic dome designed by Michelangelo, an extension to the nave and the Baroque façade designed by Carlo Maderno. Consecrated in 1626, the immense basilica stood on a vast open piazza with a solitary Egyptian obelisk in its middle. The effect of the whole must have been highly impressive though rather bare, a sequence of empty spaces. At this point Bernini was called in to give the square its definitive urban form, a task that took more than thirty years. He gave the basilica and square of St Peter's their strikingly symbolic emphasis, creating a spectacular stage for the supreme celebrations of the Catholic Church. Before all other considerations, one should note the difficulty created by the size of the space: the church is 186 metres long (equal to two football fields), and the dome is 132 metres high. Yet such was the power of Renaissance architecture and the subtle visual adjustments introduced by Bernini, especially in the most sacred part of the building, that the immense whole appears well-proportioned and harmonious in its blending of styles, colours and lighting. Inside the church, Bernini's first commission centred on the high altar. It was essential to give worshippers a precise focal point when they entered its doors.

Gian Lorenzo Bernini

BALDACCHINO OF ST PETER'S

1624–1633
St Peter's, Vatican

Set at the focal point of the vista of the nave of St Peter's, the baldacchino (or canopy) over the high altar is an immense yet slender structure of partly gilt bronze fashioned in 1633. To furnish the material required, Pope Urban VIII decided to melt down the valuable bronze decorations of the Pantheon.

The use of a baldacchino to protect and mark the high altar of a church was common in Roman churches from late classical and mediaeval times. Bernini reinvented its form: four tall "barley-sugar" columns spiral upward and support a fretted, open-work canopy. To enhance the sense of lightness, the sculptor varied the inclination of the suspended friezes above to suggest the idea of the silk or woollen canopies carried in processions. This impression of dynamism enlivens the interior of the basilica and alludes to the mission of the Church, which reaches out to embrace the faithful.

VIT TIBI
DIC

opposite
Gian Lorenzo Bernini

ST PETER'S

detail of the decoration of the pillars in the nave Vatican

In St Peter's Bernini sought to achieve the effect of a total work of art, which would overwhelm and enthral the viewer by combining architecture, painting, sculpture and the decorative arts. Even the congregation moving through the nave or gathering in prayer in the solemn ceremonies helped to create an idea of rich and emphatic solemnity and grandeur. This could have been attained only by a many-sided creative genius with a theatrical flair, capable of "stage-managing" these special effects.

Gian Lorenzo Bernini

ST LONGINUS

1629–1638
marble
St Peter's, Vatican

The principal part of the basilica, surmounted by Michelangelo's dome, rests on four immense pillars erected by Bramanate. Bernini transformed these structural elements with complex decorative schemes rich in doctrinal significance.
In the upper part of the pillars he set loggias (with spiralling columns like the baldacchino). They display to the worshippers the four principal relics of Christ's passion, preserved in the basilica. Beneath them four statues of saints support the corresponding relics. Bernini himself carved the figure of *St Longinus*, who exhibits the spear that pierced Christ's side on the cross. The remaining three sculptures were executed by others. The total effect is richly symbolic, an assertion of the Church's triumph over the Protestants: it exalted the cult of relics, ascribing to them a mystic value of testimony and stressing the role of the saints as intermediaries and interpreters.

Gian Lorenzo Bernini

BALDACCHINO AND THRONE

1624–1633
1657–1666
St Peter's, Vatican

The mystical-symbolical path begun in the piazza was concluded with the group of statuary placed by Bernini in the conch of the apse at the end of the basilica. Framed between the twisted columns of the baldacchino, the throne of St Peter, commissioned by the Chigi pope Alexander VII, seems to gleam like a mystical apparition.

Gian Lorenzo Bernini

THRONE OF ST PETER

1657–1666
marble and gilt bronze
St Peter's, Vatican

From the gathering of the faithful in the square, worshippers advanced along the path to salvation, guided by saints and relics towards the celebration of Christ's sacrifice under the baldacchino. The culmination of this progress is the exaltation of the role of the pope, the "vicar of Christ," by an object charged with symbolic significance: the "throne of St Peter," an early mediaeval seat decorated with plaques of ivory. (It was probably the throne of Charles the Bald, crowned in the old basilica in 875). The seat, encased in an imaginative and flamboyant bronze cover, seems to rise off the ground amid ribbons of clouds and a rejoicing angels, supported by the figures of the four doctors of the Church. Using a powerfully theatrical device, Bernini exploited the light streaming through a window (an allusion to the Holy Spirit) to enfold the throne in light, which seems to illuminate it mystically.

Pietro da Cortona

PORTRAIT OF URBAN VIII

1625–1626
oil on canvas
Pinacoteca Capitolina

The bee motive often appears on the walls of Rome. The bees are in the arms of the Barberini family and testify to Pope Urban VIII's intense activity and his patronage of the arts in the Baroque period.

Gian Lorenzo Bernini

FUNERARY MONUMENT OF URBAN VII

detail
1628–1647
marble and bronze
St Peter's, Vatican

The bronze skeleton emerging from the sarcophagus is one of the most macabre and effective inventions of the darker side of Bernini's imagination.

Pietro da Cortona

THE TRIUMPH OF DIVINE PROVIDENCE

1633–1639
fresco
Palazzo Barberini

In this fresco in Palazzo Barberini, a Baroque masterpiece, the clarity and order of the frescoes painted by Annibale Caracci for the Farnese family are transformed into a sparkling, dilated, dynamic composition in which everything seems to be propelled upwards. Even the painted architecture, with writhing atlantes (the male figures) and garlands stretched almost to breaking point, adds to the powerful thrust of the whole. Pietro da Cortona cites almost literally the solutions adopted a century earlier by Correggio (such as the big flaky clouds and the effects of foreshortening), but wholly new is his ability to create a total artwork, to ravish the viewer's senses and transport him into a new dimension, with a mingling of different subjects: the triumph of divine providence blends naturally with allegorical figures from classical art and the heraldic celebration of the bees in the Barberini arms.

opposite
Pietro da Cortona

THE RAPE OF THE SABINE MAIDENS

1627–1629
oil on canvas
Pinacoteca Capitolina

Pietro da Cortona

VAULT OF THE NAVE

1668–1669
fresco
Santi Ambrogio e Carlo al Corso

Pietro da Cortona

ATTEMPT ON THE FAITH OF ST BIBIANA

1624–1626
fresco
Santa Bibiana, nave, left-hand wall

Pietro da Cortona

MIRACULOUS INTERVENTION OF THE VIRGIN DURING CONSTRUCTION OF THE CHURCH

1650–1665
fresco
Santa Maria in Vallicella (Chiesa Nuova), nave

The paintings by Pietro da Cortona are an important part of the sumptuous decoration of the Chiesa Nuova, erected by the desire of Filippo Neri at the end of the Cinquecento. These frescoes should be interpreted in the light of the powerful impulse given to the work of the orders that were born out of the Counter-Reformation with didactic, missionary and social purposes. The needs and ideas of the new orders were often closely connected with new forms of architecture and original artistic ideas. The churches and oratories erected for the Oratorians of St Philip incorporated interesting developments in acoustics, because of the importance the saint attributed to choral singing.

Pietro da Cortona

ASSUMPTION OF THE VIRGIN

1650–1665
fresco
Santa Maria in Vallicella (Chiesa Nuova), apse

Pietro da Cortona

THE TRINITY IN GLORY

1650–1665
fresco
Santa Maria in Vallicella (Chiesa Nuova), dome

Borromini, the Flash of Genius

Francesco Castelli, called Borromini, came from the Swiss Ticino. His irony and dramatic flair electrified the artistic milieu in Rome. Even the matchless Bernini was troubled by the daring and bizarre architecture of his colleague, who was almost a contemporary. It has now been established that a fundamental stage in the training of the young Borromini was a period spent working on Milan Cathedral. Immersed in that climate of imperishable Gothic, Borromini absorbed a love for the style and the courage to create bold antithetic forms that contrast with the monumental solemnity of Rome's unvarying classical architecture.

Francesco Borromini

SAN CARLO ALLE QUATTRO FONTANE (SAN CARLINO)

facade and detail of the parapet
1634–1638, completed in 1667

NITATIS·ET·D·CAROLI·M·DC

Francesco Borromini

SAN CARLO ALLE QUATTRO FONTANE (SAN CARLINO)

interior with the oval dome
1634–1638, completed in 1667

For an artist from the diocese of Milan, the commission to build a church dedicated to St Charles Borromeo must have been a welcome opportunity. Borromini had to work in a small space and he exploited it to challenge Bernini on his own ground. The plan of San Carlo alle Quattro Fontane corresponds almost exactly to that of the colossal pillars supporting the dome of St Peter's. The interplay of curving surfaces creates an effect of restless movement.

Francesco Borromini

SAN CARLO ALLE QUATTRO FONTANE (SAN CARLINO)

cloister
1635–1636

The miniature cloister, long and narrow, is a prodigy of rhythm and proportions.

Francesco Borromini

ST JOHN LATERAN

interior
1646–1649

The modelling of the interior of the great basilica, ordered for the Holy Year of 1650, was Borromini's largest commission. Unfortunately, the work entailed the destruction of frescoes by Pisanello and Gentile da Fabriano.

Francesco Borromini

VISTA OF THE GALLERY

1635
Palazzo Spada

A highly successful conjuring example of *trompe l'œil* architecture, the gallery simulates a majestic sequence of arches, though it is actually a corridor just nine metres long.

Francesco Borromini

SAN CARLO ALLE QUATTRO FONTANE (SAN CARLINO)

campanile
1653

Difficult to see from the street, the campanile is yet another highly imaginative work.

Francesco Borromini

SANT'IVO ALLA SAPIENZA

dome, interior of the lantern
1642–1650

Set in the Collegio della Sapienza, the premises of the ancient university of Rome (founded in 1303), the Church of Sant'Ivo may well be Borromini's most extravagant creation in Rome. The lantern surmounting the dome, shown on the opposite page, spirals upward in open contrast with the composed Cinquecento arches of the court of the Collegio. Inside, the dome is an exhilarating field of conflicting tensions, with alternating concave and convex lines. The effect is heightened by the light diffused over the white surface of the pilasters and the light stucco decorations, almost an anticipation of rococo style.

Francesco Borromini

SANT'IVO ALLA SAPIENZA

dome, exterior of the lantern
1642–1650

François Duquesnoy

ST SUSANNA

1629–1633
marble
Santa Maria di Loreto

The careers of many French artists in the seventeenth century followed the same path. They settled in Rome and some even Italianised their first names or surnames. Duquesnoy was certainly one of the most interesting Baroque sculptors in Rome, with his harmonious, thoughtful and elegant style.

François Duquesnoy

ST ANDREW

1629–1640
marble
St Peter's, Vatican

This is one of the group of colossal statues placed against the pillars of St Peter's, as part of Bernini's plan. It should be borne in mind that they are 5 metres tall to match the scale of the immense interior.

Alessandro Algardi

TOMB OF LEO XI

1634–1652
marble
St Peter's, Vatican

The roses with the inscription "sic floruit" on the lower part of the monument are the romantic symbol of Leo XI's very short pontificate (less than a month). The bas-relief on the tomb depicts the most important event in the life of the future pontiff: still in his cardinal's robes, he receives the abjuration of Protestantism by Henri IV, king of France. (The scene is associated with the king's famous quip: "Paris is worth a mass.") Composed in keeping up with the classical code for papal tombs from the late Renaissance to the Baroque, the monument is a notable example of the prowess of the sculptor from Emilia Romagna, whose work ushered in a more subdued style after the flamboyance of Bernini.

Alessandro Algardi

INNOCENT X

1649–1650
bronze
Palazzo dei Conservatori

The successor to Pope Urban VIII, the celebrated patron of many of Bernini's projects, was the Medici pope, the Florentine Leo XI. His pontificate is recalled for its brevity, a mere twenty-four days. He was followed by Innocent X, of the Pamphilj family, who was elected in 1644. His ten-year pontificate marked a breakthrough in the history of Baroque art. Innocent showed little sympathy for Bernini and gave his patronage to his rivals: Borromini as architect, Algardi as sculptor, Velázquez as painter. This was a brilliant, varied period, when many innovations were made and Berninini's ascendancy undermined. The pope, not without a polemical intent, commissioned Algardi to execute the large official statue displayed in the Palazzo dei Conservatori, directly opposite that of his predecessor fashioned in marble by Bernini.

Diego Velázquez

PORTRAIT OF INNOCENT X

1650
oil on canvas
Galleria Doria Pamphilj

Velázquez visited Italy for the second time in 1649 and 1651. The most important fruit of his stay was this portrait of Innocent X, which remains in its original place in Rome's Galleria Doria Pamphilj. It is displayed opposite an equally expressive marble portrait of the pope by Bernini. During these years Velázquez achieved a marvellously intense revision of all his own work and, going further back, of the crucial developments in painting in the Cinquecento and Seicento. Following the example of Titian, Velázquez began to build up his paintings out of broad, separate strokes, using a brush laden with pigment and seeking to achieve an expressive intensity. (This is paralleled by the development of Rembrandt, though in a completely different personal and social context.) With his free, open style, Velázquez is of the greatest importance in the history of art. His work was rediscovered by the French painters of the nineteenth century, especially Manet. It was also drawn on by Picasso and the modern movement in general. In particular, the portrait of Innocent X was repeatedly reinterpreted, imitated and transformed in the work of Francis Bacon.

Sculptures in water and stone

Frequent flooding by the Tiber prompted the construction of high embankments at the end of the nineteenth century. The river was effectively concealed from the city; yet Rome remains a city on its river. There are pools, artificial basins, and spurting fountains everywhere, often conspicuously marked with the papal arms. Many fountains bear the unmistakable imprint of the Baroque: in the fountains, Bernini, in particular, made splendid use of the potential for "modelling" water as an extraordinary, glittering, moving, crystalline material.

Gian Lorenzo Bernini

FOUNTAIN OF THE TRITON

1642–1643
Piazza Barberini

This brawny triton fills a rather cramped square with its shrill musical note.

Gian Lorenzo Bernini

FOUNTAIN OF THE BEES

1644
Piazza Barberini

The bees appear on the arms of the Barberini pope, Urban VIII.

FOUNTAINS OF PIAZZA NAVONA

view of the Church of Sant'Agnese in Agone, the Fountain of the Moor and the Fountain of the Rivers

The fountains in Piazza Navona have a long and troubled history. The two pools at the sides (occupied by the fountains of the Moor and of Neptune) were the work of Giacomo della Porta (1576). They were placed here by Pope Gregory XIII.
The Fountain of the Moor, adorned with tritons and mascarons (grotesque faces), is a nineteenth-century copy of a late Cinquecento fountain transferred to the gardens of Villa Borghese. The Fountain of the Rivers in the middle is an extraordinary work by Bernini (1651), illustrated on the following pages. Bernini himself fashioned the hefty figure of the Moor, while with disagreeable asymmetry the fountain of Neptune was left without its statues till 1878 when, following a public competition, the principal group and the sculptures on the outside were added.

Gian Lorenzo Bernini

FOUNTAIN OF THE RIVERS

1651
Piazza Navona

Bernini must have reflected at length before creating this stunning masterpiece.
The commission for the fountain belongs to the only period when Bernini fell from favour, under the Pamphilj pope, Innocent X. To regain the pope's favour, Bernini devised a wholly new work, which almost seems to contradict the laws of physics. The tall, slender obelisk (a Roman imitation of Egyptian work from the time of Domitian) rests on a void, the hollow of the craggy reef that forms the core of the complex. Around it, in the recesses of the rock and the basin, appear animals and plants of various kinds, a fanciful epitome of mid-seventeenth-century botany and zoology. More conspicuous are the personifications of the four great rivers: the Danube, Ganges, Nile, and River Plate, which have been given the supposed somatic features of the continents they represent. Numerous legends surround these statues and the rivalry between Bernini and Borromini, who designed the facade of Sant'Agnese in Agone, opposite. The River Plate, for example, is said to be raising one hand to ward off the imminent collapse of the church, while the Nile (whose source was unknown) covers its face with a veil to blot out the "eyesores" created by Borromini.

The Cornaro Chapel, a Sacred Theatre

The chapel of the Cornaro, a noble Venetian family, is set in the left transept of the Church of Santa Maria della Vittoria. It is laid out like a small but well-equipped theatre. The altar-stage is illuminated from above by a window-spotlight, concealed by the triangular tympanum, while the members of the family look out from boxes on the sides. The effect is heightened by the rays of gilt bronze, all of differing lengths.

Gian Lorenzo Bernini

ECSTASY OF ST TERESA

detail
1645–1652
Cornaro Chapel,
Santa Maria della Vittoria

The scene of ecstasy, or more precisely the "transverberation," of St Teresa of Avila is one of the masterpieces of all time, an inextricable tangle of suffering and enchantment, of languor and ineffable mystery.

Gian Lorenzo Bernini

ECSTASY OF ST TERESA

1645–1652
Cornaro Chapel,
Santa Maria della Vittoria

Gian Lorenzo Bernini

MEMBERS OF THE CORNARO FAMILY

1646–1652
Cornaro Chapel,
Santa Maria della Vittoria

Gian Lorenzo Bernini

CONSTANTINE

1654–1668
marble and stucco
Scala Regia, Vatican Palace, Vatican

Another celebrated figure in the sacred theatre created by Bernini against the immense backdrop of Rome: this is the celebrated equestrian statue of the emperor, who is represented as filled with wonder by the apparition of the Cross.

The vision of Constantine had been represented in the history of art as a silent dream in the night. Bernini, however, chose to create an immense fluttering backdrop of brocade to set off the figures of Constantine and his rearing horse.

A Piazza for All the World

Before Bernini refashioned the area, in around 1660, it could hardly have been described as a city square. Rather it was a large flat extent of level earth surrounded, with no particular coherence, by the façade of the basilica, the complex of Vatican buildings and the working-class district of Borgo. Around the obelisk and two fountains Bernini designed a large ellipse, defined by the two wings of a portico supported on columns ranged four deep. These broad arms lead to the parvis (forecourt) of the basilica, with its shallow flights of steps curving slightly inwards to enhance the view of the façade and focus on the loggia in the middle, where the popes impart their benedictions. The shape and dimensions of the square allude symbolically to the Church's embrace of the faithful.
It provides an ideal gathering place for all the peoples of universal Christendom.
Bernini planned, but never built, a "fourth arm," a stretch of the portico that was meant to enclose the square on the side opposite the façade of the basilica, in front of the humble suburb of the city called Borgo. In 1936, in a highly controversial development, the architects Piacentini and Spaccarelli demolished this ancient and distinctive (but badly decayed) district to lay out a wide new thoroughfare. The work was eventually completed in time for the Holy Year of 1950.

ST PETER'S SQUARE

view from the top of the dome of the basilica, Vatican

The view clearly shows the effect of the massive clearance that gutted the district to create the rectilinear Via della Conciliazione, the main axis leading to the square from Castel Sant'Angelo. The beginning and end of the street are marked by the arms of Pope Pius XII and the city of Rome, dating from 1940.

Gian Lorenzo Bernini

ST PETER'S SQUARE

1656–1667
view from above
St Peter's Square, Vatican

opposite, top
Carlo Fontana

FOUNTAIN

1677
St Peter's Square, Vatican

Two fountains play in the square, set precisely on the transverse axis of Bernini's elliptical colonnade. The one shown here is the later of the two. The other, by Carlo Maderno, dates from 1613.

Gian Lorenzo Bernini

COLONNADE

1656–1666
St Peter's Square, Vatican

284 columns, 88 pillars, 140 statues: these are the statistics of Bernini's extraordinary urban and architectural invention.
The portico consists of a fourfold file of Doric columns. Two circular stones are embedded in the paving of the square between the obelisk and the fountains: viewed from these two points the portico looks as if it is made of a single row of columns. The obelisk in the middle, unmarked by hieroglyphs, was brought to Rome by Caligula in AD 37. Tradition has it that the tip of the obelisk was once surmounted with a bronze sphere containing the ashes of Julius Caesar. For centuries it stood beside the basilica; in 1586 it was erected in front of the façade by command of Pope Sixtus V. The feat of raising the colossal obelisk, over 25 metres high, remains memorable. Some 900 workmen and 140 horses were needed. The pope imposed absolute silence on everyone involved to quell discontent among the workmen compelled to carry out this dangerous, gruelling task.

Poussin and the Revival of Classicism

Around 1620 the influence of Caravaggio yielded to a more subdued, intellectual kind of painting based on the meticulous imitation of classical antiquity and the major Renaissance models. Once more this movement developed in Rome and spread out from it. With extensive international ramifications, it eventually formed the core of the theoretical and practical curriculum of Beaux Arts Academies all over the West. It also became the favoured courtly style for celebrating royal absolutism. Developed by the masters of the Bolognese school, beginning with Annibale Carracci, classicism formed a major strand in seventeenth-century painting. It was mainly the French masters, above all Nicolas Poussin, who completed its development. Classicism was fostered in the academies of painting and design, which gave their pupils a complete education, teaching not only practical skills but also imparting a general culture that acquainted them with Greek and Roman literature and mythology. Classicism may appear over-intellectual, because it emphasised the technical and formal qualities of art rather than the direct and sincere expression of feeling. Yet this interpretation is reductive. Classicism was the indispensable counterweight to the flamboyance of Baroque. In the hands of the most gifted artists it rediscovered absolute values, deeply rooted in human nature and artistic expression. Refinement, good taste, and control of composition in all its parts were other important qualities favoured by the international classicism of the seventeenth century.

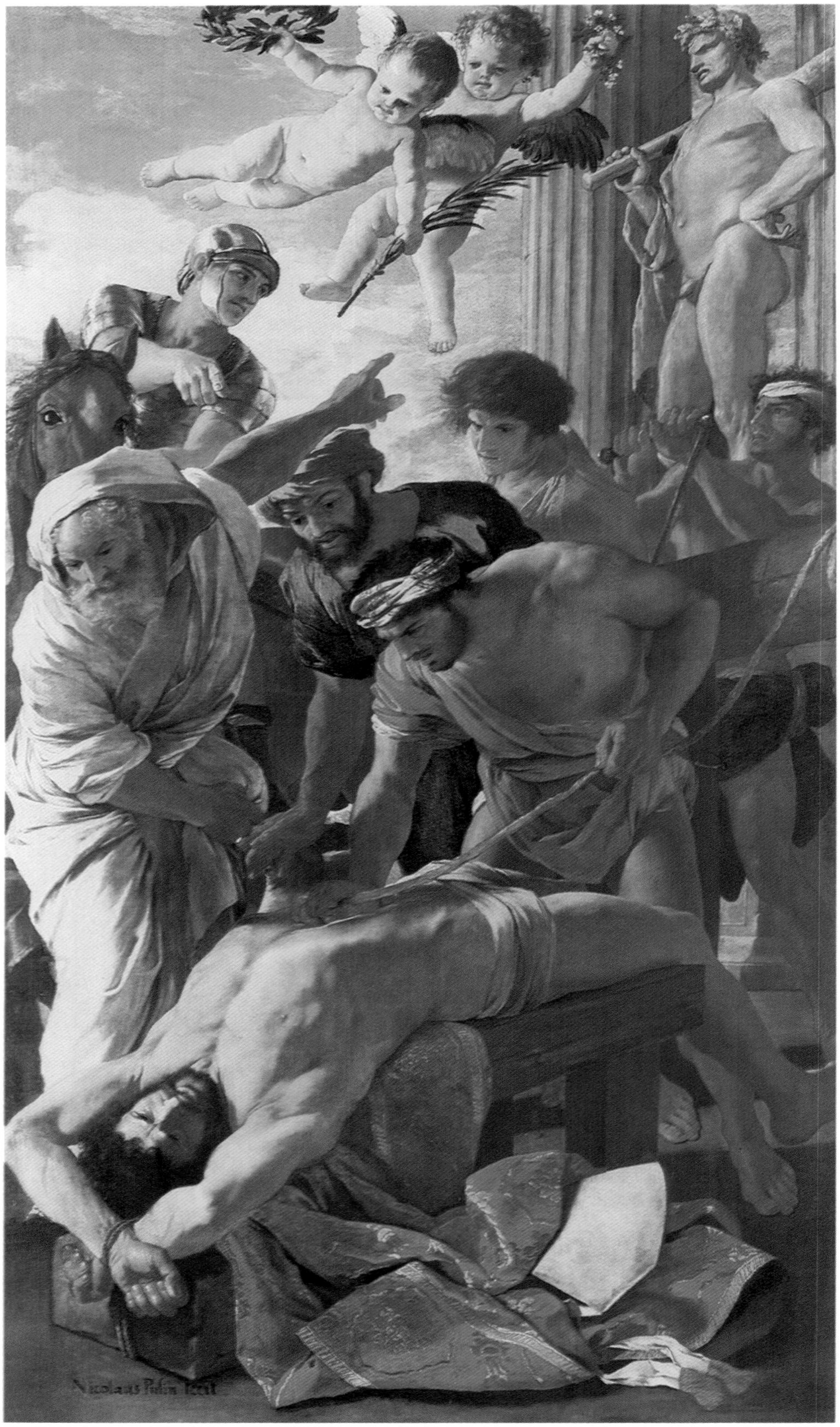

Nicolas Poussin

MARTYRDOM OF ST ERASMUS

1628
oil on canvas
Pinacoteca Vaticana, Vatican

Claude Lorrain

LANDSCAPE WITH APOLLO GUARDING THE HERDS OF ADMETUS

1645
oil on canvas
Galleria Doria Pamphilj

It is erroneous to suppose that classicism took its models only from classical antiquity. The great achievements of the landscape painters show that the classicists were deeply sensitive to the image of the world. Masters like Claude Lorrain had the merit of discovering the poetry latent in the natural scenery and classical ruins of the Roman countryside. Their work has shaped our ideal of a classical landscape. They "corrected" their direct studies of nature by adding figures or architectural elements and carefully calculated effects of light and shade, combining the real with the imaginary. (Here Mercury is shown stealing the herds behind Apollo's back.)

Guercino

ET IN ARCADIA EGO

1618
oil on canvas
Galleria Nazionale d'Arte Antica, Palazzo Barberini

This highly symbolic work offers an unusually elegiac and melancholy interpretation of the *Idylls* of Theocritus. It depicts two Arcadian shepherds discovering a skull accompanied with an admonitory inscription. The phrase, spoken by the Death, signifies, "I too am present in Arcadia," warning of the vanity of the world. However, Guercino dispels the harsh moral into an atmosphere of pure contemplation.

Gaspar Dughet

LANDSCAPE WITH RINALDO AND ARMIDA

c. 1650
oil on canvas
Galleria Corsini

Francesco Albani

SPRING

1618–1622
oil on canvas
Galleria Borghese

The idealisation of antiquity was one of the most important and controversial strands in European art during the seventeenth and eighteenth centuries. To understand it, we have to remember the variety and significance of the different interpretations of the "classical." By the early seventeenth century the nobility had assembled large collections of archaeological relics. They favoured pure, idealised marble sculptures, in which the beauty of the human body (male or female) was unruffled by tensions or violent feelings. Moreover, the Bolognese artists had prompted a rediscovery of the art of the early Cinquecento, especially Raphael, which they presented as a "new classicism": a supreme example of equilibrium, composure and serene expressiveness that more than made up for the complete loss of ancient Greek and Roman paintings. Seventeenth-century classicism was essentially moral. It presented examples of high and refined culture, in contrast with the coarse and violent tone of Caravaggio's painting.

Bernardo Strozzi

THE CHARITY OF ST LAWRENCE

c. 1615–1620
oil on canvas
Galleria Nazionale d'Arte Antica, Palazzo Barberini

Giovanni Serodine

THE PARTING OF ST PETER AND ST PAUL LED TO MARTYRDOM

1624–1625
oil on canvas
Palazzo Barberini, Galleria Nazionale d'Arte Antica

Dramatic, violent, uncouth, Serodine, an artist from the Swiss Ticino, strove to outdo Caravaggio's realism and brought a note of almost desperate animation to early seventeenth-century painting.

Gian Lorenzo Bernini

SELF-PORTRAIT AS A YOUNG MAN

c. 1620
oil on canvas
Galleria Borghese

Bernini produced few paintings, mostly portraits and small chamber paintings.

Gian Lorenzo Bernini

SANT'ANDREA AL QUIRINALE

façade
1658–1670

Bernini's genius revealed itself not just in the design of splendid monuments but also in the meticulous care he lavished on this small church. To cope with the rather cramped site, he created a very simple façade preceded by a semicircular flight of steps. Inside architecture, sculpture and painting are combined to create a wonderfully unified whole.

Gian Lorenzo Bernini

SANT'ANDREA AL QUIRINALE

1658–1670
the inside of the dome

Pietro da Cortona

SANTI AMBROGIO E CARLO AL CORSO

dome
1668–1669

Tall and slender, the dome of the church of the Lombard community in Rome is a landmark in the centre of the city. Michelangelo's influence appears in the alternating columns and windows.

Pietro da Cortona

SANTA MARIA DELLA PACE

façade
1656

This church by Bramante is one of the most important buildings in the history of Renaissance art. Pietro da Cortona completed it by adding the highly refined façade. He was also responsible for the intelligent urban redesign of the street layout in front of it.

The Most Beautiful Bridge

The Emperor Hadrian erected a bridge on the Tiber leading to his colossal mausoleum. Completed in AD 133, three of its arches still survive. Twelve hundred years later, Pope Clement VII placed the statues of St Peter and St Paul on the abutment opposite the mausoleum (turned into a castle in the intervening centuries). From this beginning Ponte Sant'Angelo developed into an open-air gallery of sculpture, a double line of fine Baroque statues rising above the placid river, the forerunner of similar sculptural bridges in other cities, like Prague's Charles Bridge. The row of ten statues of angels bearing the instruments of Christ's passion, was begun in 1688, when the whole bridge was renewed with the addition of new arches and parapets. The work was entrusted to the ageing Bernini, who worked with a select group of assistants. He not only supervised the whole project, which bears the unmistakable imprint of his style, but personally sculpted two of the figures. They were soon replaced by copies and are now in the Church of Sant'Andrea delle Fratte.

PONTE SANT'ANGELO

view from above and vista with Castel Sant'Angelo

At the entrance to the bridge are the Cinquecento statues of *St Peter* (by Lorenzetto) and *St Paul* (by Paolo Taccone).

THE TIBER AND PONTE SANT'ANGELO

The panorama seen from above and views of the side of the bridge that reveal its structure. The three central arches date from the second century, while the arches at either end were rebuilt in 1668 and again altered when the Tiber was embanked in the 1890s.

PONTE SANT'ANGELO

view of the side with Castel Sant'Angelo

Cosimo Fancelli

ANGEL WITH THE TOWEL BEARING THE IMPRESSION OF THE HOLY FACE

after 1668
Ponte Sant'Angelo

The statues on the bridge form a sort of collective exhibition by the Roman sculptors of the late seventeenth century. Though all were followers of Bernini, they succeeded in expressing their distinctive styles. In addition to the sculptors whose carvings are illustrated here, Ercole Ferrata, Antonio Giorgetti, Pietro Paolo Naldini and Domenico Guidi also worked on the project.

Girolamo Lucenti

ANGEL WITH THE NAILS OF THE CROSS

after 1668
Ponte Sant'Angelo

Antonio Raggi

ANGEL WITH THE COLUMN

after 1668
Ponte Sant'Angelo

DALI

BERNABEI

Piazza del Popolo

Before the present, splendid neoclassical layout designed by Valadier, Piazza del Popolo was extensively refashioned by Bernini. To mark the important "trident" formed by Via del Babuino, Via del Corso and Via Ripetta, Bernini completed the twin churches of Santa Maria di Montesanto and Santa Maria dei Miracoli. On the opposite side, next to the Quattrocento Church of Santa Maria del Popolo (Bernini modified the decoration of the interior) stands the classical Porta del Popolo. Bernini added a new façade to this city gate to create a backdrop to the square. The work was completed for the triumphal entry to the city of Queen Cristina of Sweden (1655). Her conversion to Catholicism was the occasion for splendid celebrations with a strong flavour of propaganda.

opposite, top
Carlo Fontana
and Gian Lorenzo Bernini

SANTA MARIA DI MONTESANTO

1673, 1675–1679
Piazza del Popolo

Gian Lorenzo Bernini

PORTA DEL POPOLO

inner façade
1655
Piazza del Popolo

opposite, bottom
VIA DEL CORSO

Vista between Santa Maria in Montesanto and Santa Maria dei Miracoli

Ercole Ferrata (to a design by Gian Lorenzo Bernini)

"IL PULCINO DELLA MINERVA"

obelisk dating from the sixth century BC supported by a marble elephant
1667
Piazza della Minerva

One of the most amusing of the innumerable projects to beautify the city supervised by Bernini.

Late Bernini

The decades went by and Bernini, with his prodigious energy, continued to dominate the artistic scene. There seemed to be no limits to his creativity. His favoured medium of expression remained marble combined with jasper, other kinds of valuable stone and various coloured materials. In his most ambitious projects the sculptor was supported by a large team of assistants, yet his late works include some supreme masterpieces carved with his own hands. In his later years (Bernini died in 1680 at eighty-two), the sculptor frequently explored the themes of the dialogue with the divine, ecstasy, revelation and prayer. The beautifully carved drapery is animated by deeply scored folds framing increasingly contracted and intense faces and gestures, conceptually foreshadowing that art of making "a good death" for which Bernini had been long preparing himself.

Gian Lorenzo Bernini

GABRIELE FONSECA

1668–1675
marble
San Lorenzo in Lucina

Gian Lorenzo Bernini

THE BLESSED LUDOVICA ALBERTONI

detail
1671–1674
marble
Altieri Chapel, San Francesco a Ripa

Baciccio Sails through the Foaming Billows of the Church of the Gesù

The great late-Renaissance Church of the Gesù is the architectural symbol of the Jesuits' piety and their model of architecture. Its interior forms a single large space, evoking the great, united congregation of the faithful. A gigantic space, it forms a single perspective with the no less important space of the sanctuary. The brief for the decoration of the church required that the vault should celebrate the triumph of the Holy Name of Jesus (the symbol of the Jesuit order) and the sacrifice embodied in the Eucharist. The Genoese artist Giovan Battista Gaulli, better known by his quintessentially Ligurian nickname of Baciccio, conceived the painted décor as a coherent scheme, including the windows and architectural elements. The vault scales the heights of Baroque emphasis: the eye is lost in the eddy of angels' wings, dazzling beams of light, the dark clouds under which writhe the defeated forces of Evil, and the final apotheosis of the Mystic Lamb. The sense of involvement is overwhelming and expresses the almost military spirit in which the Jesuits moved to restore the faith.

Giovan Battista Gaulli called Baciccio

TEMPERANCE

fresco
Sant'Agnese in Agone

The spandrels of the dome of Sant'Agnese in Agone were almost a trial run for the colossal achievement of the Gesù. Compared to the *Glory of Paradise* frescoed in the vault of the dome by Ciro Ferri, a rather pedestrian pupil of Pietro da Cortona, Baciccio's allegorical figures have a buoyant lightness: they seem poised to soar out of their frames and dance over larger and freer spaces.

Giovan Battista Gaulli
called Baciccio

TRIUMPH OF THE NAME OF JESUS

1679
fresco
Church of the Gesù

Carlo Maratta, Prince of the Academy

In the late seventeenth and early eighteenth century, under the Albani pope Clement XI, the art scene was dominated by the ageing Carlo Maratta and more generally by the education imparted at the Academy of San Luca. In 1700 Clement XI stimulated the revival of the Academy. Artists from different backgrounds were trained in a curriculum that included copying from the antique, study of Raphael, the imitation of the Carracci and Guido Reni, rigorous instruction in composition, clarity of design and brightness of colouring. The result was a wide shared vocabulary that made Maratta's manner the prevalent style in Italy in the early eighteenth century. Maratta, rhetorically praised as "the Raphael of our times," wielded immense influence. Even when he had practically given up painting he controlled the work of his numerous followers, pupils and assistants.

Carlo Maratta

PORTRAIT OF POPE CLEMENT XI

1700
oil on canvas
Pinacoteca Vaticana, Vatican

After the death of Bernini (1680), Maratta dominated official art in Rome. In the early decades of the eighteenth century, his altarpieces, portraits and frescoes, both sacred and profane, drew largely on the work of Bernini, but he toned down its excesses and corrected them by studying its Cinquecento predecessors, from Raphael to Correggio. The art of Maratta was smooth, unexceptionable, stylistically controlled, yet richly coloured and brilliant. It remained the ideal of good taste, not only in Rome but all the academies of Italy, large and small, down to the mid-eighteenth century.

Carlo Maratta

ASSUMPTION WITH THE DOCTORS OF THE CHURCH

1689
oil on canvas
Santa Maria del Popolo

Composed, unruffled, serene: Maratta mitigated the vehemence of Roman Baroque with a sort of "return to order" in the wake of Raphael.

Carlo Maratta

MADONNA AND CHILD ENTHRONED WITH ANGELS AND SAINTS

1680–1690
oil on canvas
Santa Maria in Vallicella (Chiesa Nuova)

Comparison between these two altarpieces reveals Maratta's eclecticism. He combined reminiscences of Venetian art with his usual striving for harmony.

Gazing up at Paradise

The work of Baciccio in the Church of the Gesù was not yet complete when the other great Roman church of the Jesuit order, dedicated to St Ignatius Loyola, was frescoed with equally imaginative decorations. The vault of the Church of Sant'Ignazio was the work of a Jesuit, Padre Andrea Pozzo. An excellent architect, Pozzo designed the vault to heighten the sense of perspective. The fresco presents a most effective illusionistic doubling of the real architectural members and employs a degree of artifice better suited to stage design than devotional painting. The space is dilated and seems to explode in a dazzling outburst of light and glory. The groups of saints, angels and allegorical figures epitomise a whole encyclopaedia of the geographical and technical learning of the day, while the floating clouds accentuate the virtuoso effect of the whole. It looks exuberant and spontaneous, though it is actually all carefully calculated with almost scientific rigour. Though Pozzo's work still embodies the richness and freedom of seventeenth-century art, we feel that a new season is approaching, in which imaginative freedom will be curbed by intellectual clarity.

Andrea Pozzo

***TROMPE L'ŒIL* DOME**

1691–1694
oil on canvas
Sant'Ignazio

Andrea Pozzo

GLORY OF SAINT IGNATIUS

1691–1694
fresco
Sant'Ignazio, vault

AFRICA

Andrea Pozzo

FRESCOES IN THE CORRIDOR OF THE CHAMBERS OF ST IGNATIUS

view of the whole
1682–1686
Professed house at the Gesù

The decoration of the chambers of the founder of the Jesuit order was one of Pozzo's first works in Rome.
His style soon became a model for others, as appears from the altar illustrated on the opposite page.

ALTAR OF SAN LUIGI GONZAGA

1699
polychrome marble
Sant'Ignazio

Andrea Pozzo

ALTAR OF ST IGNATIUS

1696–1700
Church of the Gesù

The extraordinary altar is like a juggling trick performed with silver, gold, bronze, lapis lazuli, malachite and precious marbles. Its bizarre opulence, a numbing exhibition of power, recalls the sumptuousness of "colonial Baroque," the Portuguese *talha dourada*.

Pietro Bracci

FUNERARY MONUMENT OF MARIA CLEMENTINA SOBIESKA

1735
polychrome marbles
St Peter's, Vatican

An effective example of the free combination of different materials in late Roman Baroque: the curtains are carved in alabaster, the portrait of the queen of England is mosaic.

Work in Progress on the Highest Hill of Rome

One of the most important urban developments of the eighteenth century was the urban design of "Montecavallo," the popular name for the hill of the Quirinal. 61 metres high, it is the most elevated point of Rome. The centrepiece of the piazza is an obelisk flanked by the colossal sculptural group of the twin gods Castor and Pollux, tamers of horses, with a large marble horse trough. The obelisk was only added in 1786, when the square was gradually given its definitive form, largely as a result of the pleasant eighteenth-century buildings that flank the principal palace. The Palazzo del Quirinale, originally the residence of the popes and later the kings of Italy, is now the official residence of the Italian president. A monumental edifice, it enshrines many centuries of the history of the city and of Italy. It houses an impressive collection of art works that make it one of the richest palaces in Europe. It is open to the public.

PIAZZA DEL QUIRINALE

The obelisk was taken from the Mausoleum of Augustus and erected between the Dioscuri, Castor and Pollux, shown holding horses (5.6 metres high). They are imperial Roman copies of Greek originals, dating from the fifth century BC.

PALAZZO DEL QUIRINALE

1573, continued and extended down to 1740
Piazza del Quirinale

The finishing touches to the large palace were added by Ferdinando Fuga, who also designed the adjacent Palazzo della Consulta.

Alessandro Specchi,
Ferdinando Fuga

STABLES OF PALAZZO DEL QUIRINALE

1722–1730

Gae Aulenti restored the stables and converted them into a fine venue for large art exhibitions.

Gaspar van Wittel

PANORAMA OF ROME FROM TRINITÀ DEI MONTI

PANORAMA OF ROME FROM VILLA MEDICI

1713
tempera on paper
private collection

The movement known as *vedutismo*, or the painting of views of the city, began around 1675 with the arrival of the Dutch artist Gaspard van Wittel (1651–1736). He settled in Italy, where he italianised his name as Vanvitelli. In the Netherlands the painting of urban scenes was already an established genre, with a faithful rendering of spaces and light. Jan van der Heyden (1637–1712) was well-known for his views of Amsterdam. They were painted with the help of the *camera obscura*, an optical instrument fitted with a lens and mirror that captured complex urban scenes by projecting them onto a flat surface. This training in optics and the scientific approach are evident in van Wittel's painting; they distinguish it from the practice of the Italian and North-European "bamboccianti" working in Rome. The realism of Dutch landscape in the later seventeenth century shunned any classical idealisation.
The views of Rome, Tivoli, the countryside of Latium, Naples, and the other places depicted with great exactness by van Wittel were an immediate success. They fascinated art-lovers by their impression of fidelity, of objective, documentary truth, their effective rendering of light and shade, the natural setting, and their lively figures.
The views chosen by van Wittel became canonical and continued to be represented for travellers on the Grand Tour as for modern tourists. Van Wittel often produced several replicas of his most successful views to supply the growing international demand.

Gaspar van Wittel

CASTEL SANT'ANGELO

detail
c. 1680–1690
tempera on parchment
Pinacoteca Capitolina

Domenico Paradisi
and Luigi Barattoni

SANTA CECILIA IN TRASTEVERE

façade and interior 1724

Restoration and modernisation of the ancient basilicas continued into the eighteenth century, with a constant effort to balance ancient and modern. On the advice of Ferdinando Fuga, the splendid columns of red granite and African marble were preserved in the façade of Santa Cecilia. Inside, the huge nave opens out to form one of the most graceful and luminous eighteenth-century interiors in Rome.

Nicola Salvi, Giuseppe Pannini

FONTANA DI TREVI

1732–1751, 1751–1762

The memorable backdrop to a scene in *La Dolce Vita*, this is the celebrated fountain where tourists toss a coin to make sure they will return to Rome.
The water comes from the Aqua Virgo, an aqueduct completed by the Roman emperor Agrippa for the baths he built. Begun by Bernini but left incomplete, the fountain is the last spectacular Baroque creation in Rome.
The fundamental idea was to create the "Palace of Ocean," a triumphal arch set in the side of a mansion (Palazzo Poli), from which emerges the bearded figure of Ocean, drawn by two sea horses. Numerous other statues crowd the impressive complex.

POSITIS SIGNIS ET ANA

Ferdinando Fuga

Rome's eighteenth-century architecture is far less renowned that that of the seventeenth. While the seventeenth century was the model for the spread of the Italian style to the rest of Europe, sacred and secular buildings from the eighteenth are generally considered the tail end of the Baroque, as its energy petered out, or else as the precursor of neoclassicism, which had yet to reach its full development. But a more detached view will discover works of great beauty and significance in the architecture of the period. Outstanding among them are those by the Florentine architect Ferdinando Fuga, often masterpieces of good taste, restraint, a carefully measured balance between structure and decoration, with great respect for the existing buildings.

Ferdinando Fuga

SANTA MARIA MAGGIORE

façade 1741–1743

The façade designed by Fuga for this ancient basilica fully reflects the restraint and moderation of Prospero Lambertini, who became pope as Benedict XIV. The design of the loggia above the portals was a stroke of genius: the iridescent hues of the ancient mosaics glimmer in the broad apertures.

Filippo Rusuti and assistants

EPISODE FROM THE LEGEND OF POPE LIBERIUS AND THE PATRICIAN JOHN

late thirteenth century
mosaic
Santa Maria Maggiore, loggia

Ferdinando Fuga

SANTA MARIA MAGGIORE

façade
1741–1743

This night view reveals the cycle of mosaics in the loggia, fortunately preserved in the eighteenth-century reconstruction. By Filippo Rusuti and assistants, this is a notable cycle from the late thirteenth century. It was part of a general renewal of Roman painting that continued in the work of Pietro Cavallini and Jacopo Torriti.

Filippo Raguzzini

PIAZZA SANT'IGNAZIO

1727–1728

SANT'AGATA DEI GOTI

courtyard

Overshadowed by more celebrated buildings, there are many quiet corners of Rome that preserve the atmosphere of the eighteenth century.

Francesco de Sanctis

THE SPANISH STEPS (SCALINATA DI TRINITÀ DEI MONTI)

1723–1726

The steps rising in flights to the obelisk and façade of Trinità dei Monti is one of the most celebrated and successful urban developments of late Baroque Rome. Nowadays it forms an incomparable backdrop for the most varied events. It also has the merit of recording a delightful architectural work, unfortunately destroyed: Porto di Ripetta, built some twenty years earlier by Alessandro Specchi. This was a series of arcaded steps leading down to the Tiber.

P.A. Verschaffelt

THE ARCHANGEL MICHAEL SHEATHING HIS SWORD

1752
bronze
Castel Sant'Angelo

Antonio Canevari

SANT'EUSTACHIO

façade 1724

At the top of the facade rises the hart's head with a crucifix between its horns, in allusion of a vision that appeared to St Eustace while out hunting.

Alessandro Galilei

SAN GIOVANNI DEI FIORENTINI

façade 1734

The broad façade added in the eighteenth century forms a dignified conclusion to this fine Renaissance church.

Antoine Dérizet

SANTISSIMO NOME DI MARIA

dome 1736–1738

This eighteenth-century church overlooks the extraordinary panorama of the imperial fora. It was erected to commemorate the liberation of Vienna from the siege of the Turks.
A distinctive feature is the ring of statues crowning the lantern. The form of the dormer windows is a concession to the international taste of incipient rococo style.

Giovan Battista Gaulli
called Baciccio

APOTHEOSIS OF THE FRANCISCAN ORDER

1707
fresco
Santi Apostoli

In the first half of the eighteenth century, Cardinal Ottoboni exerted a great influence over the musical, theatrical and artistic life of Rome. In this context the style of Maratta even influenced the work of artists who worked independently and already had established careers, like Baciccio. In 1707 (two years before his death) he painted the vault of the basilica of the Santi Apostoli. In 1701 the great canvas by Sebastiano Ricci reproduced alongside was placed in the sacristy.

Sebastiano Ricci

THE ASCENSION

1701 canvas
sacristy, Santi Apostoli

The basilica of the Santi Apostoli contains some of the most interesting cycles of decorative painting from the first quarter of the eighteenth century.

Sebastiano Conca

GLORY OF ST CECILIA

fresco
Santa Cecilia in Trastevere

Sebastiano Conca arrived in Rome in 1707. He had a flair for painting huge religious frescoes, like these in Santa Cecilia, a church whose style was already tinged with rococo elegance. He made a brilliant career, receiving a succession of official commissions and requests from various parts of Italy. After 1740, when Cardinal Ottoboni died, a more subdued artistic taste spread at Rome and misgivings were felt about Conca's sparkling style. In 1752 the artist returned to the Kingdom of the Two Sicilies.

Carle van Loo

GLORY OF ST ISIDORE

fresco
Sant'Isidoro

The stimulating cultural milieu in Rome and its busy art market continued to attract not only foreigners but also artists from many parts of Italy. Some of the finest talents were rapidly absorbed into the prevailing Arcadianism and moderate academicism of Maratta, under the intellectual influence of Cardinal Ottoboni. Around the Accademia di San Luca there formed a group of painters with a fairly uniform style, often engaged on parallel, large-scale and rather monotonous commissions.

Francesco Trevisani

CLEOPATRA'S BANQUET

canvas
Galleria Spada

Francesco Trevisani arrived in Rome in his early twenties after an early training in Venice. There he became the favourite painter of Cardinal Ottoboni, the arbiter of taste in the artistic and musical world at Rome in the early decades of the eighteenth century; he was the leading figure in the Academy of Arcadia in Rome for fifty years, from the death of Cristina of Sweden (1690) until his death in 1740. Above all in his profane and mythological works, Trevisani created an equivalent for the literary charm of the Arcadian idyll. With his refined sensibility and subtle colouring, Trevisani assisted the transition from Baroque energy to the more moderate rococo style, restrained and composed. His influence was immense, extending from the French painters who visited Rome on study grants to those at the court of Piedmont.

Marco Benefial

MARGARET DISCOVERS THE BODY OF ARSENIO

1729–1732
oil on canvas
Boccapaduli Chapel,
Santa Maria in Aracoeli

Marco Benefial

LAST UNCTION OF MARGARET OF CORTONA

1729–1732
oil on canvas
Boccapaduli Chapel,
Santa Maria in Aracoeli

Benedetto Salandra and Girolamo Mariani, after a drawing by Antonio Cocciolini

EMBROIDERED ALTAR FACING

embroidery
Reverenda Fabbrica di San Pietro, Vatican

Carlo Marchionni

SACRISTY

1776–1784
St Peter's, Vatican

Construction of the massive sacristy was the last chapter in the long history of the building of St Peter's. The work of enriching and renewing the décor of the interior went on unabated.

Giovan Battista Piranesi

Piranesi excelled as a draughtsman, architect and designer of furnishings. His career also furnishes a key to understanding the development of artistic taste and thought after the mid-eighteenth century. This was a period of growing enthusiasm for archaeological discoveries, especially the systematic excavations (sponsored by the Bourbon monarchy) of the ancient Roman cities buried by the eruption of Vesuvius. Piranesi was born and trained in Venice, in circles close to Canaletto. This background could easily have made Piranesi a key figure in the convergence of Roman and Venetian *vedutismo*; instead, his remarkably original temperament and an acute sense of history led him to strike out a path of his own. It is difficult to fix his exact field of activity. Piranesi preferred engraving to painting; he was a fertile writer of treatises and limited his practice as an architect to a single building, which is of the greatest interest. This is Santa Maria al Priorato in Rome, erected for the Knights of Malta in 1764–1768. In front of it is the parvis (the paved area before the church), which Piranesi designed with a new sensitivity for the urban décor and its rapport with the green spaces around it. He completely rejected the Baroque legacy, but never tried to replace the tradition with a new formal code. In a highly symbolical way, Piranesi brought together elements and reminiscences of the architecture of the past, with an effect of mingling and accumulation. Over everything there hovers a powerful feeling of nostalgia.

Giovan Battista Piranesi

SANTA MARIA DEL PRIORATO

1764–1766

Pierre Subleyras

THE MASS OF ST BASIL

1745–1747
oil on canvas
Santa Maria degli Angeli

Around the middle years of the century, mainly through the work of Batoni and the French artist Subleyras, academic painting acquired a new dignity, an elevated tone that reflected a renewed moral commitment on the part of the artists. Characteristic of this solemn, restrained taste, which eschewed excess and frivolity, was a series of altarpieces commissioned by Pope Benedict XIV (1740–1758) for St Peter's and now in Santa Maria degli Angeli. They date from the years between 1745 and 1755.

Pompeo Batoni

THE FALL OF SIMON MAGUS

1755
oil on canvas
Santa Maria degli Angeli

Pompeo Batoni introduced a new approach towards the work of art. He sought to achieve beauty through the stringent study of figurative models and steady application. He arrived in Rome from Lucca in 1727. In his work he favoured portraits and mythological or allegorical subjects; he recommended restraint and moderation, constant revision and the correction of all excess. He also insisted on the need for a critical approach to the work of the professional artist, based on a profound knowledge of the old masters, whose example should be imitated and even improved by comparisons with other painters. In Batoni's work, formal and intellectual control were the paramount virtues.
He achieved a subdued but never meagre elegance.

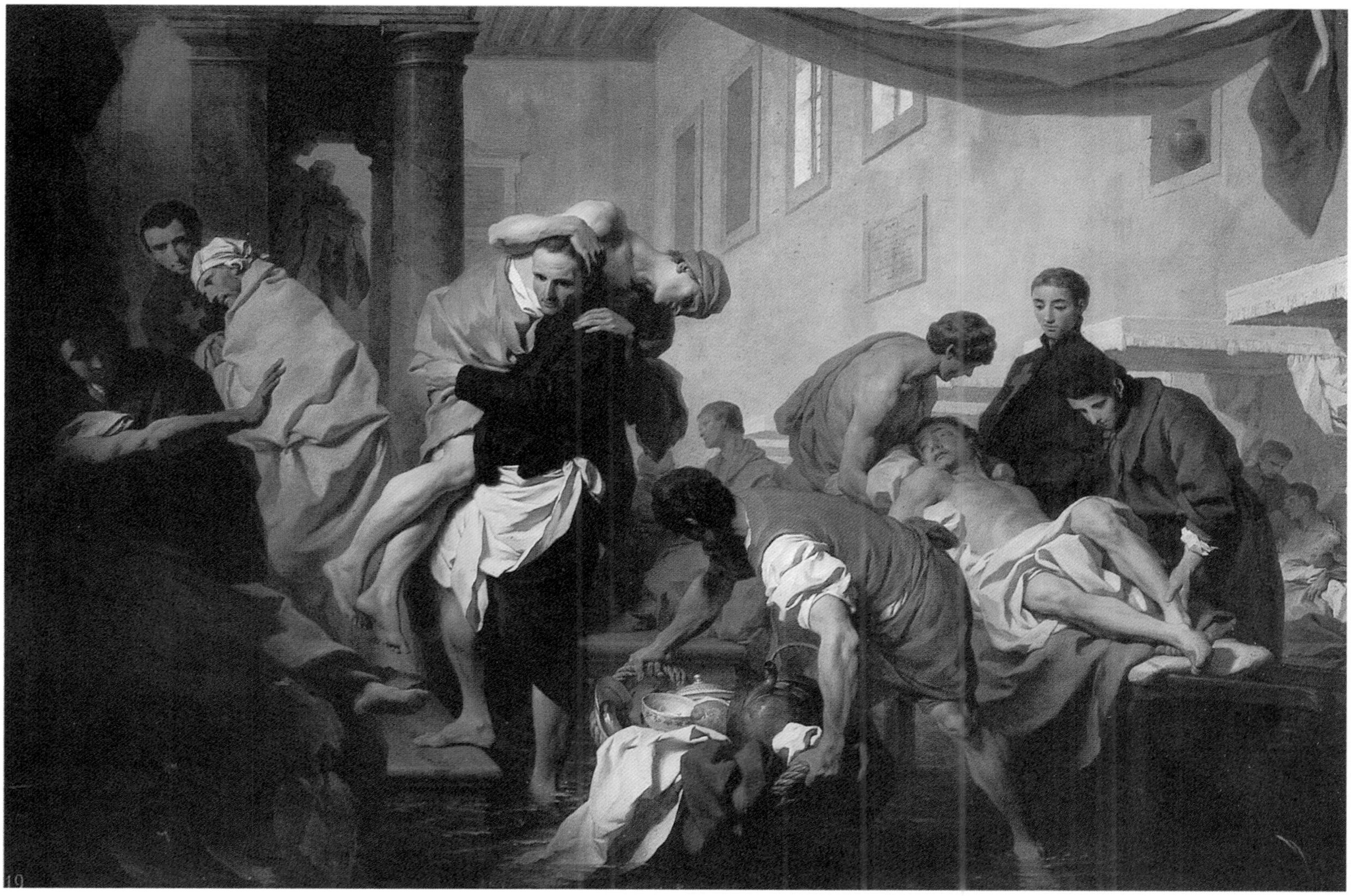

Pierre Subleyras

ST CAMILLUS DE LELLIS SAVING PATIENTS DURING FLOODING OF THE TIBER

oil on canvas
Museo di Roma

THE MYSTIC MARRIAGE OF ST CATHERINE DE' RICCI

c. 1740–1745 oil on canvas
private collection

Giovanni Paolo Pannini

ROMAN RUINS

canvas
Galleria Nazionale d'Arte Antica, Palazzo Barberini

Pannini was the leading representative of Roman *vedutismo* in the eighteenth century. Born in Piacenza, he trained in Emilia, at the flourishing local school of stage design. He proved a virtuoso at handling perspective and foreshortening on large canvases. In 1711 he arrived in Rome as the pupil of Benedetto Luti and in 1719 became an academic of San Luca. Pannini soon developed into the leading painter of urban views: he depicted ancient monuments, Baroque architecture and archaeological remains. Even though the city's glories lay in the past, the Rome of Pannini was an animated, festive city, teeming with life and swarming crowds. His most successful and celebrated works date from 1742–1744: the great, carefully composed views of Piazza del Quirinale and Santa Maria Maggiore that decorate the coffeehouse of the Palazzo del Quirinale.

Giovanni Paolo Pannini

SANTA MARIA MAGGIORE

1744
canvas
Palazzo del Quirinale, coffeehouse

Last Splendours of the Eighteenth Century

The work of decorating the salons of Villa Borghese absorbed some of the finest artistic talents in Rome in the last quarter of the century. Crowds of painters swarmed over the scaffolding creating a complex of great interest, eloquent testimony to the shift in taste from the billows of late Baroque to the quieter and more secluded paths of incipient neoclassicism.
Today Villa Borghese is visited above all for the collection it houses, but it can be considered as essentially a significant monument of the artistic culture of the late eighteenth century.

Antonio Asprucci

TEMPLE OF AESCULAPIUS

1790–1795
Villa Borghese

A landmark for dating couples and strolling lovers, the temple is set on an island in the artificial lake of Rome's biggest and most beautiful public garden.

Mariano Rossi

APOTHEOSIS OF ROMULUS

1775–1778
fresco
Villa Borghese, vault of the main salon

Winckelmann, Mengs and the Fascination of Antiquity

Mengs settled in Rome in 1752. His painting of *The Glory of St Eusebius* on the vault of the Church of Sant'Eusebio dates from 1757. It is the last tribute to the decorative manner used in painting Baroque vaults from Correggio to Baciccio. The arrival of Winckelmann in Rome (1755) marked the beginning of a close collaboration to recover and study ancient art works. Mengs took up this return to a serene, intellectual art based on the classical rules of decorum, harmony and composure. He also gave a didactic application to these precepts as the director of the Accademia Capitolina. The publication of the first volume about the antiquities of Herculaneum (1757) opened a new phase of art. Alongside the severity of a style inspired by Greek art, according to the precepts of Winckelmann, there was also great interest in the sense of the "sublime," the awe inspired by ancient grandeur. Mengs devised a personal aesthetic based on the "sense of beauty." In 1762 he published the first edition of his *Precepts of Beauty*, a theoretical work read in all Europe. In 1763 Winckelmann declared: "We can say that elsewhere beauty in art is only partial, while only in Rome can the sense of beauty be perfect, true and refined. This capital of the world still remains an inexhaustible source of the beauties of art."

Anton Raphael Mengs

GLORY OF ST EUSEBIUS

1757
fresco
Sant'Eusebio

A tribute to the late-Baroque tradition, this is one of Mengs's first important works in Rome.

FUNERARY MONUMENT OF ANTON RAPHAEL MENGS

1778
Santi Michele e Magno

The true start of the neoclassical period was marked by Mengs's return to Rome in 1771 and by a new flow of artists towards the Eternal City. Jacques-Louis David arrived in 1775 and stayed till 1780. This was the prelude to his work on the *Oath of the Horatii* at the Louvre (1784).

Anton Raphael Mengs

JUPITER AND GANIMEDE

Encaustic
Galleria Nazionale d'Arte Antica,
Palazzo Barberini

The imitation of antiquity reached its peak in this work. Winckelmann was actually deceived into supposing it an original from classical times.

Canova, Eternal Beauty

At the end of 1779, Antonio Canova arrived in Rome for the first time. He was just twenty-two. Though he shared the general enthusiasm for ancient sculpture and archaeological excavations, Canova distanced himself from this nascent neoclassicism. His training had emphasised virtuosity and naturalism, and he refused to make marble copies of ancient statues. This exercise, he wrote, curbed an artist's originality, which "can only be achieved by inventing and creating something for oneself." In the stronghold of orthodox neoclassicism he raised a dissenting voice. Another artist who refused to conform was Felice Giani. Giani first revealed his talent in the decorations of Villa Borghese and Palazzo Altieri (1789–1793), with a highly original blending of free Baroque brushwork, love for the antique and a subtly disquieting visionary quality. Despite the presence of Canova and Giani, in the last decade of the eighteenth century art in Rome suffered from the effects of the French Revolution. Commissions began to peter out and 1793 the Académie de France was closed. The many artists from all over Europe dispersed. In the city there were risings, followed by the establishment of a Jacobin Republic and the death of Pope Pius VI in exile.

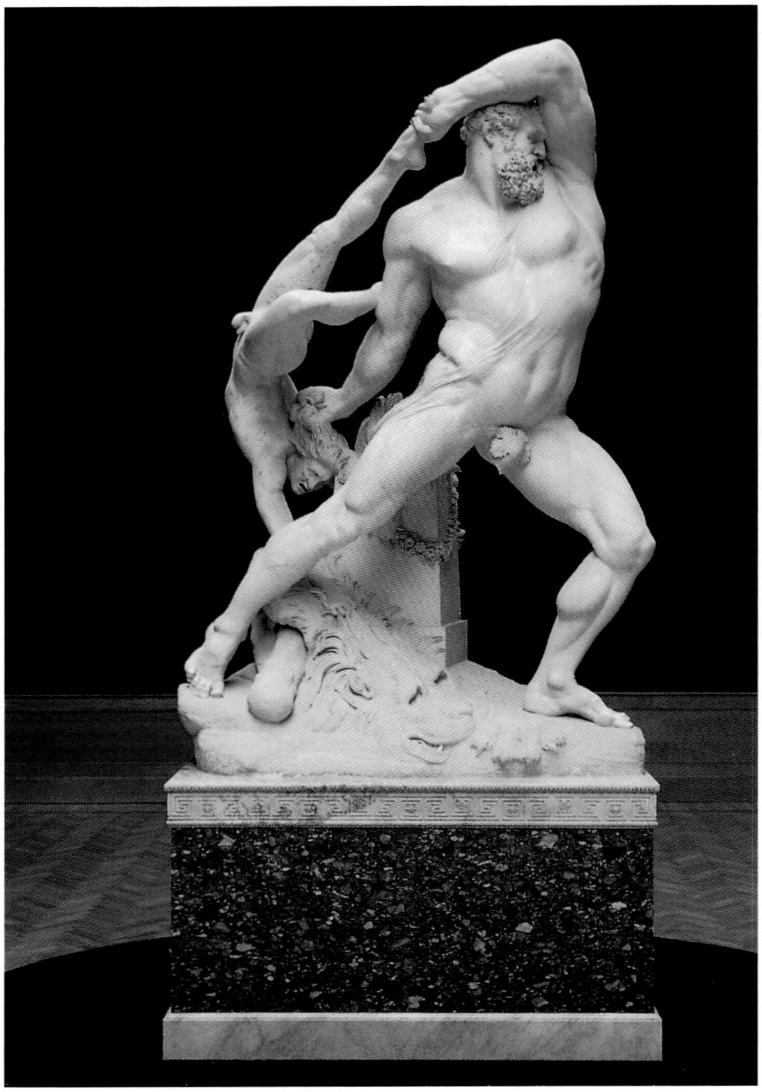

Antonio Canova

HERCULES AND LYCUS

1815
marble
Galleria Nazionale d'Arte Moderna

Antonio Canova

PAULINE BORGHESE

1805
marble
Galleria Borghese

The sculpture of Napoleon's sister Pauline is the epitome of Canova's smoothly sensuous and naturalistic art.

Antonio Canova

TOMB OF CLEMENT XIII

1784–1792
St Peter's, Vatican

Canova's funerary monuments are one of the great achievements of Western art. Arriving in Rome with his rich sensibility and expressive flair, Canova was receptive to the influence of Bernini but he also explored the changeless beauty of ancient art. From this he created his remarkable works, combining the close observation of reality with the serene contemplation of pure beauty, a wonderful fusion of the natural and the ideal.

Rome,

Giacomo Balla, *Villa Borghese, Deer Park*, 1910.
Galleria Nazionale d'Arte Moderna

Always the Capital

From the Nineteenth Century to Rationalist Architecture

At the beginning of the new century, the magnetism of Rome, Eternal City and museum of the classical past, made the city a sampler of all the different versions of neoclassicism. The dominant figure in this field was the architect Giuseppe Valadier, who designed a number of places of worship.
During the French occupation of Italy, Valadier was responsible for a program of urban improvement and archaeological excavations financed personally by Napoleon. His most important project was the redesign of Piazza del Popolo and the nearby Pincian hill. This occupied Valadier for some decades, from the first draft of the project in 1793 to its completion in 1824.
In this period a brotherhood of German artists became active in Rome. Known as the Nazarenes, they established themselves in the convent of Sant'Isidoro. They drew their inspiration from the painters of the early Renaissance, especially Raphael. Their most significant work was the decoration of Villa Massimo in the Lateran, where they frescoed three rooms inspired by the great epics of Dante, Ariosto and Tasso.
When Rome became the capital of the new kingdom of Italy, it developed a neo-Renaissance architectural vocabulary exemplified in works by Gaetano Koch, which include Piazza Esedra and Palazzo Boncompagni (now the American Embassy).
The "stile umbertino" was a decorative historical style of architecture used in Guglielmo Calderini's Palazzo di Giustizia (law courts) and Giuseppe Sacconi's monument to Victor Emanuel II. The latter dominates the city from an artificial hill created by enlarging Piazza Venezia.
At the turn of the century, the international expositions rapidly spread Art Nouveau through Europe. (In Italy it became known as *stile floreale* or *Liberty*). One of its leading practitioners was the Sicilian Ernesto Basile. He designed the extension to Palazzo Montecitorio that contains the present parliamentary chamber and the façade on Piazza del Parlamento.
At the same time as Art Nouveau, a classical and monumental style also developed; an interesting example of it is Cesare's Bazzani's Galleria Nazionale d'Arte Moderna (1911).
After World War I, there were social and political upheavals; the growth of industry caused far-reaching economic changes. One result of this turbulence was a reaction against the experimental movements that had dominated art in the first twenty years of the century. Many artists felt the need to reject the irrationalism and exuberant individualism typical of the avantgarde, especially Futurism. There were calls for a "return to order," meaning to form and tradition. The mouthpiece for this movement was the Roman periodical *Valori Plastici*, published from 1918 to 1922.

Giuseppe Valadier
Church of San Rocco, façade
1834

Following the Fascists' March on Rome in 1922, with Fascism gradually gaining control over the state, the official style in architecture became the "stile littorio." It was invented by the regime's official architect Marcello Piacentini, who mediated between the metaphysical traditionalism of the "Novecento" and the rationalist movement of Edoardo Persico and Giuseppe Pagano, which was incompatible with Fascism's need for a rhetorical style.
In designing the new University of Rome, Piacentini was assisted by architects from both currents. In particular he chose the Rationalists Giuseppe Pagano (Institute of Physics) and Gio Ponti (School of Mathematics).
Among the major urban projects sponsored by the Fascist regime was the Foro Italico. The architect, Enrico del Debbio, sought to emphasise the contrast between the buildings and the landscape, as at Hadrian's Villa. It took nearly thirty years to complete the project and it suffered from a series of alterations that distorted the original design.
In this period there was a marked contrast between different architectural styles. For instance, de Chirico's metaphysical paintings undoubtedly influenced the design of architectural complexes such as the Termini railway station and the buildings erected the Esposizione Universale in 1942. The symmetrical, obsessively repeated vistas of arches in the Palazzo della Civiltà Italiana are the architectural equivalent of the cityscapes in de Chirico's finest metaphysical paintings, though devoid of their remarkable lyricism.

Costantino Costantini
and Enrico del Debbio
Piazza De Bosis with the Mussolini obelisk and the Academy of Physical Educaton
1932
Foro Italico

Eugenio Montuori
Termini Station, main building
1948–1950

Giuseppe Valadier

Giuseppe Valadier (Rome 1762–1839) was the leading neoclassical architect, both under the Napoleonic administration and after 1816, when the pope returned from exile. He carried out important urban development projects. His redesign of Piazza del Popolo and the Pincian hill nearby is scenically very effective.

PIAZZA DEL POPOLO

aerial view

Giuseppe Valadier

PIAZZA DEL POPOLO

1816–1824

The remodelling of the square, which was the principal point of arrival for travellers from the north, linked the city and the Pincian hill with the area sloping down to the Tiber. He expanded the four-sided piazza with two lateral hemicycles to give it a monumental breadth. He built a series of open arcades and loggias on the hillside and laid out a road along the river bank.

Giuseppe Valadier

CASINA VALADIER

1816–1817

On the top of the Pincian, the Casina Valadier, still a café, is both functional and picturesque. It is an original interpretation of the neoclassical style, with front and side elevations that differ markedly. The front entrance has a double staircase curving round a portico of Doric columns surmounted by an incongruous Doric frieze, while Doric loggias stand open at the sides.

The Nazarenes

This was the slightly ironic nickname given to a brotherhood of German painters who established themselves in the convent of Sant'Isidoro in the second decade of the nineteenth century. They lived a communal life and painted biblical subjects with a strong didactic vein. The leading member of the group was Friedrich Overbeck, who had trained at the Vienna Academy. He rejected the neoclassical aesthetic for an inward-looking Christian art based on models from the Tuscan Quattrocento.

Julius Schnorr von Carolsfeld

THE CAPTURE OF BISERTA

1824–1825
fresco
Sala dell'Ariosto, Casino Massimo

Tomaso Minardi

MADONNA OF THE ROSARY

1840
oil on canvas
Galleria Nazionale d'Arte Moderna

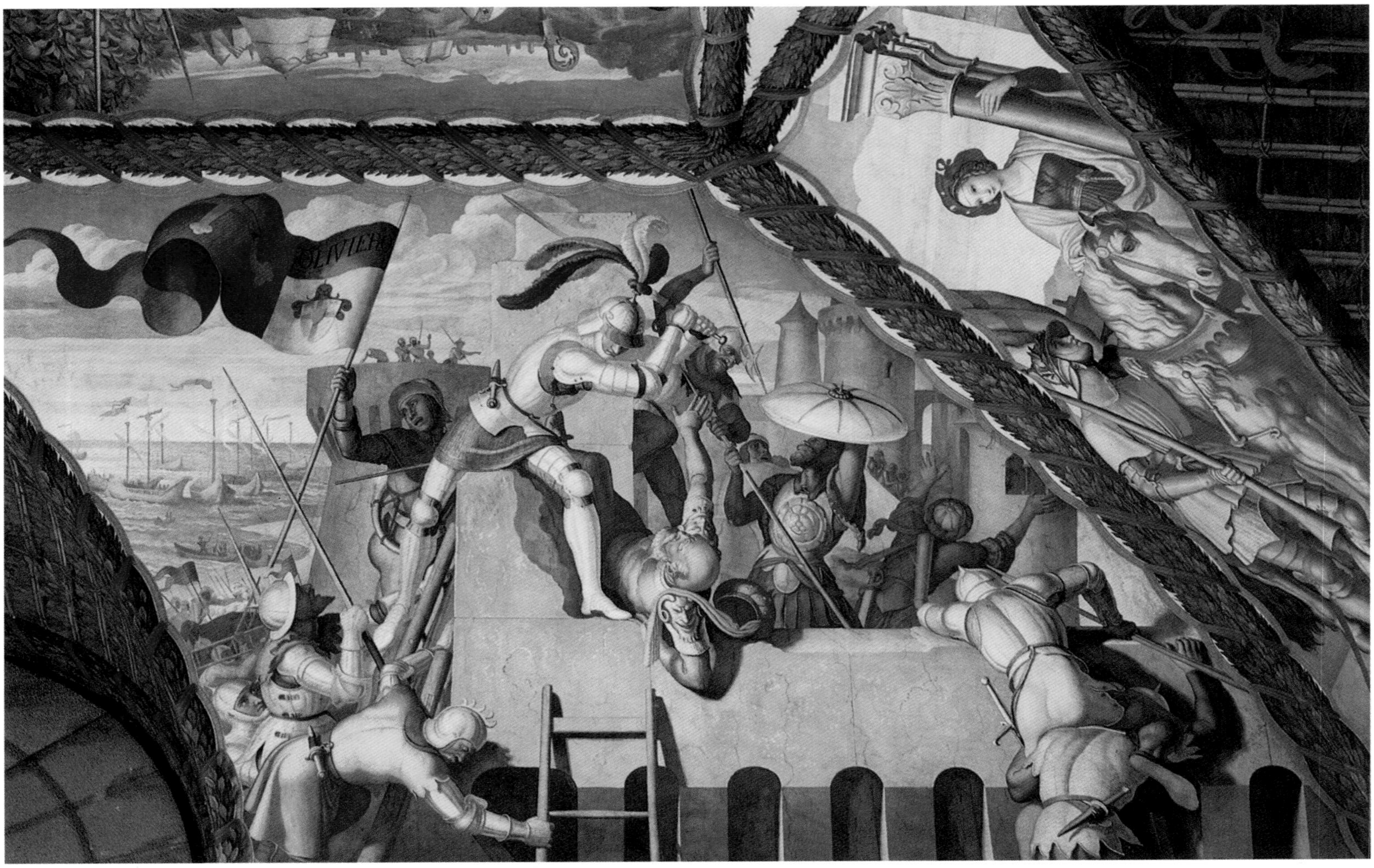

Philipp Veit

THE EMPYREAN AND SPHERES OF THE PLANETS

1818–1824
fresco
Sala di Dante, Casino Massimo

The Casino Massimo contains the last collective labour of the Nazarenes. The first chamber was decorated with scenes from Dante's *Divina Commedia*, painted by Philippe Veit and Joseph Anton Kock. The next was decorated by Julius Schnorr von Carolsfeld with subjects from Ariosto's epic *Orlando Furioso*. Overbeck frescoed the last of the rooms with scenes from Tasso's *Gerusalemme Liberata*. They imitated the stylistic purity of Tuscan Quattrocento painting, with its rather harsh colouring and hard outlines. These frescoes enabled the Nazarenes to overcame the hostility of art circles in Rome.

Architecture between the Late Nineteenth and the Early Twentieth Century

Rome became the capital of a united Italy in 1870. The reorganisation of the city involved conflicts caused by the new relationships between the old families and the newly rich, between the nobility and the business classes, between supporters of the papacy and those of the new monarchy. One architect who profited from the opportunities offered by Rome's urban development was Gaetano Koch, who designed Piazza Esedra. However, it was the "stile umbertino" that left its mark on Roman architecture at the turn of the century. Examples of it are Guglielmo Calderini's Palazzo di Giustizia and, above all, the grandiose monument to Victor Emanuel II.

Gaetano Koch

PIAZZA DELLA REPUBBLICA, FORMERLY PIAZZA ESEDRA

1887–1898

This square is an important point of entry to the city because of its proximity to the Termini mainline station. The middle of the square is dominated by the monumental Fountain of the Naiads. Two imposing semicircular buildings by Koch mark the ancient perimeter of the great terraced exedra that provided seating for spectators of the athletic events held in the adjoining Baths of Diocletian.

Gaetano Koch and Mario Rutelli

FOUNTAIN OF THE NAIADS

1888–1912
marble and bronze

In the middle of the piazza is the monumental fountain designed by Gaetano Koch and subsequently decorated by Mario Rutelli with four groups of bronze figures and the central figure of Glaucus.

Guglielmo Calderini

PALAZZO DI GIUSTIZIA

1889–1910

Of colossal dimensions and richly decorated, the law courts were one of the biggest projects built in Rome when it became the capital. The façade, covered with travertine, is surmounted with a bronze, four-horse-drawn chariot. Statues of eminent jurists line the lower order.

Emilio Gallori

EQUESTRIAN MONUMENT TO GIUSEPPE GARIBALDI

1895
marble and bronze

The promenade on the Janiculum, a splendid panoramic avenue laid out in 1880–1884, is lined with statues: an equestrian monument to Anita Garibaldi by Mario Rutelli and a series of marble busts of the "Hero of the Two Worlds." This leads to the central square, dedicated to Garibaldi himself. It is dominated by his statue, notable for its shrewd realism.

Giuseppe Sacconi

IL VITTORIANO (ALTARE DELLA PATRIA)

1885–1925
marble and bronze

Though the design is based on the elegant volume of the altar of Pergamum, this outsize "altar of the fatherland," dedicated to Victor Emanuel II, is a piece of clumsy rhetoric and completely out of place. Designed by Giuseppe Sacconi after the king's death in 1885, it was only inaugurated in 1925. It is made of white Brescian marble with a tall Corinthian colonnade running along the top, above broad flights of steps. The rich bronze decorations include winged lions flanking the central steps to the equestrian statue of Victor Emanuel II above and the chariots poised on the propylaea.

Carlo Fontana

CHARIOT OF UNITY

1927
bronze
Il Vittoriano

Art Nouveau in Rome

In Rome, Art Nouveau (called *stile Liberty* in Italy) was strongly hybridised with earlier styles. Its decorative forms were superimposed on the dominant neo-Cinquecento style to create a local vocabulary clearly exemplified in Ernesto Basile's extension to the seventeenth-century Palazzo Montecitorio. Its turreted façade faces onto Piazza del Parlamento, a square laid out for the new building by demolishing an interesting urban area.

Ernesto Basile

PALAZZO DI MONTECITORIO

Façade on Piazza del Parlamento
c. 1905

The rear façade has restrained floral decorations. The design shuns the striking asymmetries and capricious lines of international Art Nouveau.

Ernesto Basile
and Giulio Aristide Sartorio

CHAMBER OF MONTECITORIO

View of the gallery with the frieze
1908–1912

The present chamber of Parliament, built over the earlier courtyard by Carlo Fontana, replaced a temporary timber structure erected in 1871 by Paolo Comotto. The chamber forms a hemicycle; it is panelled in oak and richly decorated in Art Nouveau style. Under the great skylight an allegorical frieze on canvas by Giulio Aristide Sartorio runs all round its perimeter. It depicts notable episodes of Italian history.

Galleria Nazionale d'Arte Moderna

An exhibition was organised in 1911 to mark the half-century of Italian unity. For the occasion, Cesare Bazzani built the Palazzo delle Belle Arti. It soon became the premises of the Galleria Nazionale d'Arte Moderna, which now contains the collections previously housed in the Palazzo delle Esposizioni. The architecture combines classical, Renaissance and Art Nouveau elements. It has a large portico borne on paired columns, with access by a broad staircase, flanked by flower beds and sculptures by artists such as Consagra and Lipchitz. The nineteenth- and twentieth-century collections are housed in the wings, while the central block is used for temporary exhibitions.

GALLERIA NAZIONALE D'ARTE MODERNA

detail of the principal façade
1911

below
Giovanni Boldini

PORTRAIT OF THE MARCHESA LUISA CASATI

1914
oil on canvas
Galleria Nazionale d'Arte Moderna

Giuseppe De Nittis
RACES AT THE BOIS DE BOULOGNE

detail
1881
pastel
Galleria Nazionale d'Arte Moderna

The side panel of a triptych, this painting represents a scene from bourgeois life. The Impressionist influence is evident in the choice of subject and photographic angle.

Umberto Boccioni

PORTRAIT OF FERRUCCIO BUSONI

1916
oil on canvas
Galleria Nazionale d'Arte Moderna

This is a work of the artist's maturity. It was painted in 1916, when Boccioni was a guest of the musician Ferruccio Bosoni at Pallanza. He died a few months later, aged only thirty-four. These later works, with their careful study of expressive technique, have clear affinities with Cézanne.

Paul Cézanne

LE CABANON DE JOURDAN

1906
oil on canvas
Galleria Nazionale d'Arte Moderna

An example of Cézanne's mature style, this painting displays his characteristic breakdown of the pictorial structure into geometrical forms and the constructive use of colour. This approach enabled Cézanne to go beyond the Impressionists, who focused on the surface of things, by probing appearances for their inner reality.

Carlo Carrà

OVAL OF THE APPARITIONS

1918
oil on canvas
Galleria Nazionale d'Arte Moderna

In the same year as de Chirico's *Disquieting Muses*, Carrà transcribed this imaginary vision, in many ways reminiscent of de Chirico's work: the Castle of Ferrara is replaced by a commonplace skyscraper, while on the stage a tailor's dummy, the emblem of metaphysical painting, dominates the scene flanked by an enormous fish and a statue.

Giacomo Balla

MADWOMAN

1905
oil on canvas
Galleria Nazionale d'Arte Moderna

Mario Sironi

LONELINESS

1925
oil on canvas
Galleria Nazionale d'Arte Moderna

Renato Guttuso

CRUCIFIXION

1941
oil on canvas
Galleria Nazionale d'Arte Moderna

The leading interpreter of neocubist realism, Guttuso combined themes from popular Sicilian art with the language of the international avantgardes. Here the influence of Picasso's *Guernica* and the German Expressionists is not merely formal but ideological, used to create a free and expressive art with a firm political commitment that presents an incisive social criticism.

Città Universitaria

In Fascist Rome, cut off from the international trends in architecture, rationalism (allied to functionalism) was stifled by a pompous academic monumentality. A rare exception is the Città Universitaria, one of the few important architectural complexes from this period.
It includes a number of works of great interest. The project was the fruit of close collaboration between academic and rationalist architects under the direction of Marcello Piacentini. The whole project has a rigorously symmetrical layout, yet the individual volumes are freely articulated.
The basilica plan envisaged a monumental entrance with a pillared portico set between two propylaea, with fountains designed by Arnaldo Foschini. A path on the main axis leads through the portico to the spacious Piazza Minerva. This is dominated by Piacentini's administrative block and flanked by the twin faculties of Jurisprudence and Humanities, designed by Gaetano Rapisardi.
Less conspicuous in the general plan are interesting buildings by Pagano, Aschieri, Ponti and Michelucci, which are still considered important examples of the rationalist current in Italian architecture.

Marcello Piacentini

ADMINISTRATIVE BUILDING

1932–1935
Città Universitaria

At the centre of the main square, Piazza della Minerva, Arturo Martini's impressive statue of the goddess stands in front of the massive administrative block. The façade, clad with travertine, has a pillared portico with access provided by a broad flight of steps. The building contains the main hall decorated with Mario Sironi's striking fresco of *Italy between the Arts and Sciences.*

Arnaldo Foschini

ENTRANCE TO THE CITTÀ UNIVERSITARIA

1932–1935
Città Universitaria

The entrance is marked by a monumental portico flanked by two propylaea linked to the Institutes of Orthopaedic Surgery and Hygiene, also designed by Foschini.

Giuseppe Pagano

INSTITUTE OF PHYSICS

1932–1935
Città Universitaria

Its restrained scale and sober brick facing distinguish Pagano's work from the general monumentality of the complex. It is less showy and more subdued than the other buildings. Pagano was less interested in giving his buildings an individual identity than in adapting them to their urban context.

The Foro Italico

One of the principal urban projects of the Fascist regime was this huge complex located in the green belt on the slopes of Monte Mario. Called the Foro Italico, it combined sports facilities with a centre for ideological training. The initial plan was the work of Enrico del Debbio in 1928 and was distinguished by its concern for the environment. The entrance to the complex was marked by a monumental obelisk of Carrara marble dedicated to Mussolini. Behind it rose the twin buildings of the Academy of Physical Education and the Academy of Music, between which ran the main avenue leading to the stadium, the Stadio dei Cipressi (converted in 1952 into the Stadio Olimpico). Its harmonious volumes and architectural unity were badly altered by additions by Costantino Costantini and above all Luigi Moretti, who in 1936 finally managed to oust Enrico del Debbio from the project. Moretti's Casa delle Armi, with its refined massiveness, distorted del Debbio's master plan. Moretti's work was greatly admired by the Italian officialdom and he took over the whole project. In 1938–1940 Moretti drafted numerous schemes but they remained on paper. Further damage was later inflicted on the harmony of the complex, but one can still understand the undeniable artistic quality of some of the buildings, such as the Casa delle Armi, rashly converted into a courthouse in 1981.
The main buildings of the Academy of Physical Education and the Academy of Music now house the Isef, the state television auditorium and the Coni (Italian Olympic Committee).

Enrico del Debbio

STADIO DEI MARMI

1928–1932
Foro Italico

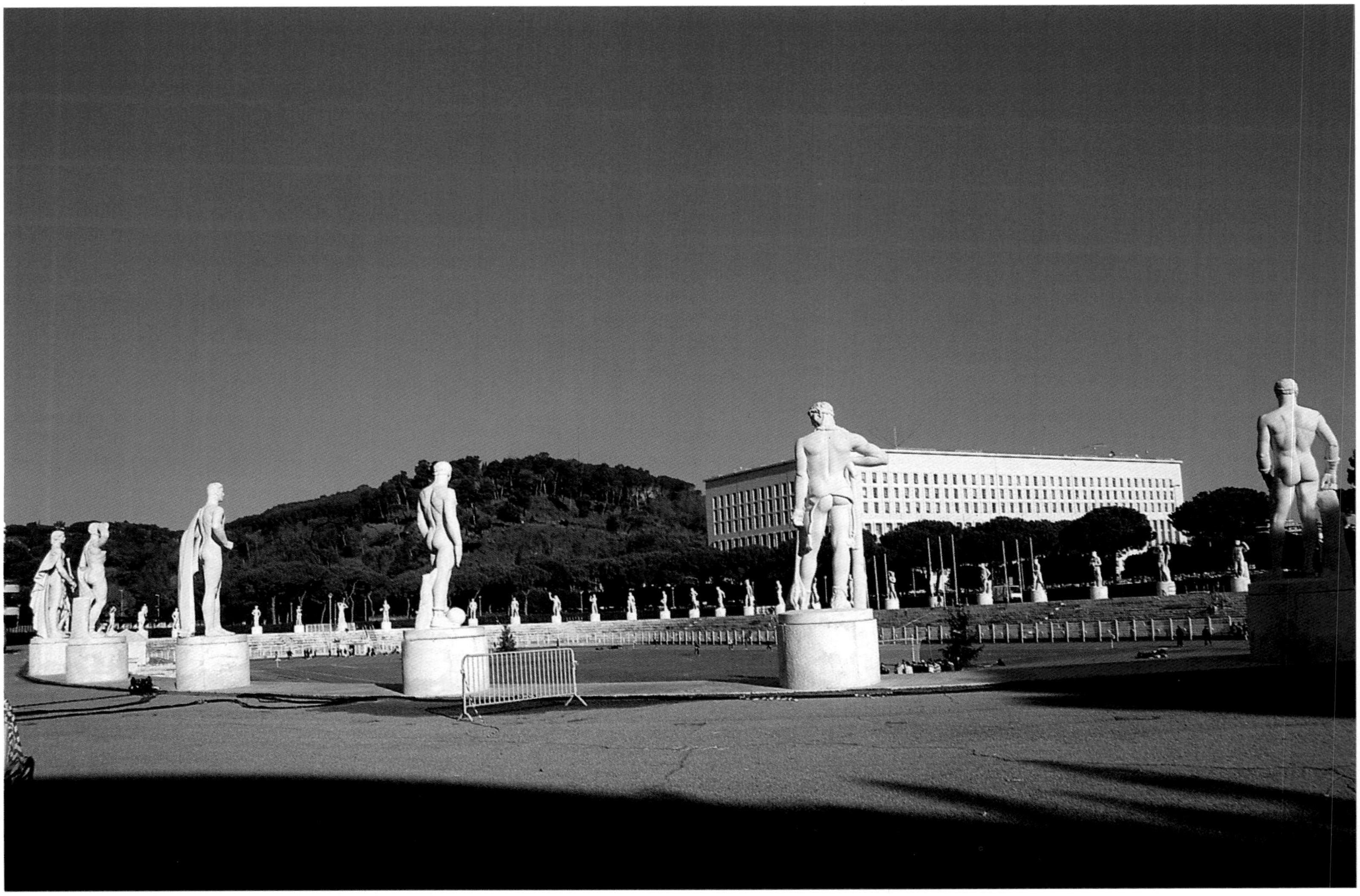

Enrico del Debbio

ACADEMY OF PHYSICAL EDUCATION (CONI)

1932–1933
Foro Italico

Luigi Moretti

CASA DELLE ARMI

1933–1936
Foro Italico

The outstanding architectural achievement in the whole complex, distinguished by the elegance of its plan and the originality and functionality of the interior. It is articulated as two orthogonal blocks linked by a suspended passage. Originally it housed a gymnasium, a salon for receptions and a library. The exterior is wholly faced with veined Carrara marble. Following its conversion into a courthouse the building suffered extensive alterations that greatly affected the design of the interior.

The Eur

The Universal Exposition of Rome (Eur) was supposed to celebrate the twentieth anniversary of the Fascist revolution in 1942. It was meant to embody the new, strategic imperial policy and illustrate the new Fascist character of Rome, while also stimulating the city's expansion toward the sea. The general plan was drafted in 1936 by a team of architects that included Marcello Piacentini and Giuseppe Pagano. In addition to the exhibition pavilions, it envisaged permanent buildings and facilities and extensive green areas. The definitive plan of 1938, produced by Piacentini himself, retained the general layout but overplayed the celebratory purpose of the complex. The result was a monumental complex in classical style, laid our on a grid of streets that created long vistas and guided the eye to screens of buildings. A new grandiose road axis—Via Cristoforo Colombo, formerly Via Imperiale—ran from Piazza Venezia to the new exhibition site. The main entrance was flanked by a piazza with a double porticoed exedra and the Ina and Inps buildings. The exedra led into the great Piazza Imperiale, chosen as the site of the exposition buildings. The first transverse axis intersected with the piazza and extended as far as the Palazzo della Civiltà Italiana by Giovanni Guerrini, Ernesto Bruno La Padula and Mario Romano, and the Palazzo dei Congressi by Adalberto Libera, the most important and representative buildings of the complex. Work was suspended in 1942. It only began again in the fifties with the development of a new plan that converted the Eur into a functional business centre.

Ludovico Quaroni

POSTER FOR THE ROME UNIVERSAL EXPOSITION

1942
drawing

Fortunato Depero

ARTS, CRAFTS AND PROFESSIONS

1941–1942
mosaic in polychrome stone
with parts in glass and enamels
Museo delle Scienze, Eur

Giovanni Guerrini, Ernesto Bruno La Padula and Mario Romano

PALAZZO DELLA CIVILTÀ ITALIANA

1938–1942
Eur

Enshrining the monumental aspirations of the general project, this building—a reinforced concrete cube faced with travertine—obsessively repeats the arch motive, which reflects the regime's celebratory aims. The arch is repeated 216 times on the four identical faces of the building, a banal evocation of the imagery of de Chirico's metaphysical paintings.

View of the Janiculum

Indexes

Index of Names

Index of Places and Works

Photographic References
Archivio Electa, Milan
Archivio fotografico Monumenti
e Gallerie Pontificie, Vatican
Archivio Scala, Florence
Nicolò Marchetti, Rome
Luca Mozzati, Milan
Soprintendenza Archeologica, Rome

Cover illustration
© Francesco Vignali/Grazia Neri

This volume was printed for Mondadori Electa S.p.A.
at Martellago Mondadori Printing S.p.A.,
Via Castellana 98, Martellago (Venice) in 2005